D0981141

"IT'S BEING DONE"

ACADEMIC SUCCESS IN UNEXPECTED SCHOOLS

"IT'S BEING DONE"

ACADEMIC SUCCESS
IN UNEXPECTED SCHOOLS

KARIN CHENOWETH

HARVARD EDUCATION PRESS
CAMBRIDGE, MASSACHUSETTS

Second Printing, 2007

Copyright © 2007 by the President and Fellows of Harvard College

All rights reserved. No part of this publication may be reproduced or transmitted in any form or by any means, electronic or mechanical, including photocopy, recording, or any information storage and retrieval systems, without permission in writing from the publisher.

Library of Congress Control Number 2006939814

Paperback ISBN 978-1-891792-39-7
Library Edition ISBN 978-1-891792-40-3

Published by Harvard Education Press,
an imprint of the Harvard Education Publishing Group

Harvard Education Press
8 Story Street
Cambridge, MA 02138

Cover Design: Alyssa Morris
Cover Photo: Molly Roberts

Pictured on the cover are Tony Levato (left) and Amairany Santos of Frankford Elementary School in Frankford, Delaware.

The typefaces used in this book are Adobe Minion Pro for text and Castle for display.

CONTENTS

ACKNOWLEDGMENTS

First and foremost, I would like to acknowledge the teachers, principals, and other educators whom I met in the course of researching this book. I am filled with admiration at their thoughtfulness, dedication, and good humor.

The research for this book was made possible by a group of organizations that came together to form The Achievement Alliance and then hired me to find schools that demonstrate that all children can learn. Those organizations are Business Roundtable, Citizens' Commission on Civil Rights, National Center for Educational Accountability, National Council of La Raza, and The Education Trust. I would like to acknowledge the help and support they have given to this work. In particular, The Education Trust's director, Kati Haycock, has helped lead the nation through a major conversation about student achievement and the kinds of schools we have provided to poor children and children of color. Without her vision and work, this book wouldn't have been possible. In addition, staff members at The Education Trust cheered me on and listened to my stories. Daria Hall in particular, but also Shana Kennedy and Nicholas Alexiou, spent many hours helping identify schools and making sure all the data included in this book are accurate. Any mistakes that remain (I hope none) are present despite their work, not because of it. Heather Peske helped me sort out the salient features of the Benwood Initiative, and she, Ross Wiener, and Candace Crawford made valuable suggestions to improve the manuscript. Ellen Garshick helped make the book more coherent and readable.

Finally, I'd like to thank my family—David, Emily, and Rachel—for putting up with all my talk about schools and education. This can't have been easy, especially for Emily and Rachel, who were simultaneously having their own encounters with schools and education.

FOREWORD

I recently spent a couple of days with groups of principals in Chicago and Detroit. Over and over again, I was struck by their sense of energy and optimism. These are principals in tough schools in tough cities with *really* tough problems. Most of them aren't yet getting very good results. But instead of being defeated by the conditions around them, they seem to be infused with both a sense of possibility and a belief that the job they have taken on is worth doing.

That they see their jobs as worthwhile is probably no surprise. Educating the next generation of Americans—the young people whose contributions and problems will shape the very future of our country—is the most important job anyone in a democracy can do.

Their spirit, energy, and sense of possibility, however, may be a little harder to believe. After all, aren't these the same principals "under the gun" of No Child Left Behind? Haven't they heard that it is "unfair" and "unrealistic" to expect them to teach their children to high standards? Educators, after all, are continually told that poor children and African American, Latino, and American Indian children cannot achieve at high levels because poverty and discrimination create too many hurdles to learning. Far too many have swallowed that argument—hook, line, and sinker.

But these principals in Chicago and Detroit haven't swallowed it, and neither have many other educators like them in cities and small towns all across America. When people tell them that it is unfair to expect the poorest children to reach high standards, they reply, "Unfair to whom? Surely, in this era when anything less than a quality education sentences a young person to a life on the margins, you're not suggesting that aiming high is unfair to the children?"

As a nation we've made a policy decision to no longer tolerate widespread failure in schools serving poor and minority children. We have decided that all children should be taught to state standards, no matter what neighborhoods they live in or how poor their parents are. Certainly, we don't yet know all the things we need to do to reach our goal. But the drive has started, and it is long overdue.

We have to remind ourselves of the facts: By the time African American and Latino children reach the age of 17, they typically have been taught only to the same level as 13-year-old white children. Compared to their low-income white counterparts, African American and Latino children are much less likely to graduate from high school or enter college, and once there they are less likely to graduate. Indeed, young people from families earning more than $80,000 per year are now more than eight times as likely to complete college by age 24 as young people from families earning below $30,000 per year. That's unacceptable.

It is also unnecessary. The proof is in the fact that there have always been educators who have beaten the odds and achieved high levels of success with kids who had been written off by others. Out of the limelight, such educators have been shaping a new vision of what is possible. I cannot emphasize enough how alone many of those educators have felt. Surrounded by people who told them that poor children could never achieve at high levels, they got little support and few resources for their efforts. Even when they succeeded, their results were dismissed as flukes, and nobody ever visited their classrooms or said thanks.

But now that all schools are expected to help all their students achieve high standards, there is a new-found hunger for information about what successful schools have done.

That's exactly what those principals in Chicago and Detroit want. They aren't interested in hearing how difficult their jobs are. They know very well the challenges that poverty and discrimination pose for their students; many have themselves battled poverty and discrimination in order to get to the positions they now hold.

Instead of dwelling on the difficulties, these principals are looking for images of success, for concrete strategies and ways they can move their schools forward. For them—and for many other educators around the country—this little book you hold in your hands provides just those images.

The educators interviewed in this book don't make excuses. They provide clear goals with high expectations and ongoing assessments. They make sure that in every classroom there is a strong teacher who knows the subject and knows how to teach it. They insist on a rigorous curriculum and on giving extra help and extra time to students who are behind.

The schools profiled in this book provide evidence for a truth that should be obvious and yet has been obscured in recent decades: If you teach poor children and children of color at high levels, they will achieve at high levels. If you expect great things from children, they will produce great things.

With this book, teachers, principals, parents, and students have the ammunition they need to prove that low achievement among poor children and children of color is not inevitable, as well as some very clear ideas about how to make high achievement a reality in their own schools.

Kati Haycock
President, The Education Trust
January 2007

INTRODUCTION

One of the big questions facing American education is "Can it be done?" Can schools help all children learn to high levels, even poor children and children of color? Is it even possible for schools to help children who face the substantial obstacles of poverty and discrimination to learn to read, write, compute, and generally become educated citizens?

As a longtime reporter and columnist writing about schools and education, I knew the answer was "yes," but I knew it as an article of faith rather than as actual knowledge. I had never actually seen such a school. I had seen glimmers of hope in the fifth-grade classroom of Linda Eberhart, where African American boys and girls from a very poor area of Baltimore met state math standards at higher rates than in any other school in the state. I had seen hope in the extraordinary kindergarten class of Lorraine Gandy, who could boast without fear of contradiction that in thirty years she had taught just about every one of her students to read. I had also seen hope in a couple of schools that were committed to educating every child. But a whole school where the average poor child or child of color could walk in from the neighborhood and be pretty sure he or she would learn to read and do math and otherwise succeed academically? That I had never seen.

Instead, I had seen standard suburban schools where middle-class and wealthy white children—particularly the girls—seem to do well, but where the poor, African American, and Latino children—particularly the boys—do terribly. My husband and I sent our own children to such schools, in fact. (The principal of our middle school used to say, publicly, "Thank goodness for our white girls—they really carry us.")

I had also seen schools where just about all the kids were white and middle- or upper-middle-class. Those schools flew past all the markers that schools have been judged by in the past. The elementary schools had high average state test scores, and the high schools had high average SAT scores and boasted dozens of kids accepted to Ivy League colleges. But even in those schools I had seen tedious classes and heard many horror stories of bad instruction from disillusioned parents and alienated students.

I had also seen what I call "crummy poor-kid schools"—that is, the inadequate schools that too many poor children must attend—which gave me the same edgy feeling that I've felt in jails, as if something terrible could happen at any time. In one such school I encountered dull and dulling classrooms, filled with worksheets and entertainment movies shown on televisions, and I saw a young, unsure administrator holding off a crowd of unruly teenagers in a lunchroom with a yardstick.

I had talked with teachers in crummy schools who told me, with great condescension, "These kids aren't like *your* children," meaning that most of the children they taught couldn't be expected to learn as much as white, middle-class children of college graduates. They would often add that advising their students to go to college was a waste of time.

Instead of dedicating themselves to making sure that all children learned to high standards, it seemed that the schools I saw simply sorted their children into different categories, each with their own educational opportunities. The "high" kids were offered what passed for a real education, although with reliance on the parents to provide a lot of the teaching; the "middle" kids were given some aspects of a real education; and the "low" kids were babysat until they were old enough to leave school. In crummy poor-kid schools, just about all the children were considered "low." The lucky few were skimmed off into magnet schools or other special programs.

I knew that I hadn't seen the full spectrum of what American education offered, but my optimism was based more on a hope than on actual knowledge. I had difficulty letting go of the notion that our public schools are places that offer all children the chance to become educated, places where, if children work hard, they can gain access to all the opportunities our country has to offer.

The folks at The Education Trust have not given up on that notion, either. The Education Trust is a national education organization that for years has identified schools where poor children and children of color do better than their peers in other schools. But The Education Trust had only identified those schools through their data; they had never explained how what they call "Dispelling the Myth" schools have such dramatically different results from other schools. In late 2004, The Education Trust joined with four other organizations—Business Roundtable, Citizens' Commission on Civil Rights, National Center for Educational Accountability, and National Council of La Raza—to form "The Achievement Alliance," and they hired me to visit such schools and describe the kinds of things they do.

Since then, with money donated from Bristol-Myers Squibb, Caterpillar, Contran Corp., EMC, Intel, Prudential, State Farm, and Texas Instruments, The Achievement Alliance has given me the opportunity to visit schools that share the American idea that schools exist to ensure that all children learn. At these schools, just about all children meet or exceed state standards or are rapidly moving toward that goal. At these schools many, if not most, of the children are poor, and many, if not most, are children of color. Some of these schools are in neighborhoods that many middle-class parents would never consider allowing their children to set foot in. Some would say these schools could never be expected to teach their students to high standards. And yet the teachers and principals in these schools are demonstrating that, by carefully organizing their time and resources, they can make sure that their students learn to "read, write, and cipher," as one old-fashioned educator said to me— and much, much more.

These schools are not just good schools for poor children and children of color—they are good schools for any child. Most of them are far enough along in their improvement process that I fervently wish my children could have attended them. Some still have a way to go to get to that level, but they are headed in that direction.

The two years I spent visiting schools were a revelation in a lot of ways. I began this project not knowing at all what I would find. I was identifying schools solely on the basis of their student achievement test scores, and for all I knew (and feared), I would find the soul-deadening test-prep factories that we are told characterize high-poverty and high-minority schools that do well on state assessments. Perhaps, I worried, I would find schools where the teachers and principals are worn to a frazzle, burnt-out and bitter with all the expectations that have been placed on their shoulders. Or even worse, maybe I would find schools where the teachers were robotic automatons robbed of all their creativity.

I found none of that. Instead I found dedicated, energetic, skilled professionals who talk about the needs of children and who care deeply about whether all their students have access to the kinds of knowledge and opportunities that most middle-class white children take for granted. That means they care about and include in their teaching art and music and physical fitness and field trips and science and history and all the things that some people say must be cut out of schools in order to focus on the reading and math skills tested in state assessments. That doesn't mean that the people in the schools I have visited don't care deeply about reading and math and about doing well on state assessments, but they know that it is a mistake to "narrow the curriculum" and "teach to the test"—two of the epithets that are floating around the education world.

And, happily, I found teachers and principals who love their jobs. They work hard, and some work long hours. They may occasionally be tempted to move to schools where it might be easier to teach. But they stay on the job because, as one teacher said to me, "We're successful. And we're like family." Many are bolstered by the idea that they are engaged in important work—work that, if enough people paid attention, could improve the teaching profession and to some extent the nation itself. But stunningly, their work has gone almost unnoticed. Here are schools that are doing what some people insist cannot be done, and yet they are pretty much unknown to the public.

Early on in this project I was talking with a very thoughtful principal, Mary Russo, who has led great improvement in her school, Richard J. Murphy K–8 School in Boston. I said that many people think that schools cannot help children who are damaged by poverty and discrimination catch up to their more privileged peers. "They say it can't be done," I said. She replied simply, "It's being done." I spent the next two years proving her point and then stole her words as the title of this book.

I would like to invite readers to join me on a journey through the schools I have visited. I begin in chapter 1 by explaining how and why it is possible to find schools that are successful and how schools were selected for visits. Then, in chapters 2–16, I present the stories of the schools in the order I visited and wrote about them (many of the stories originally appeared on the website of The Achievement Alliance, http://www.achievementalliance.org). Wherever new data have been published since I first wrote about the schools, I include that information in the charts and the Postscript section, along with any other changes that may have occurred in the school. Finally, I conclude with a chapter in which I describe the characteristics that I found to be common among all the schools.

The schools described in this book are among the most exciting ones in the country, but I make no claims that I have done more than just scrape the surface. There are many more great and rapidly improving schools in the United States. There is also much more to learn and write about these schools than is in this book. All I have done is try to put a little flesh on the bare bones of quantitative data, to give readers some idea of what it is the people in these schools are doing and how they are doing it. I hope this brief glimpse is enough to demonstrate that the important work of educating all children is within our grasp.

SPELUNKING THROUGH THE DATA

Before I get to the actual stories about the schools, I need to explain how I found them. But even before that, I have to give a little context for how it was possible to find them.

Most people outside the education world don't realize how difficult it is to know what goes on in schools. Kids stream into schools in the morning and out in the afternoon, and what goes on inside those buildings is a bit of a mystery to all but those inside—and sometimes to them as well. Harvard University's Richard Elmore calls schools the "black box," and that's about right. Even parents find themselves mystified, particularly when their children respond to questions about what they did that day with the all-purpose phrases, "Nothing" and "I don't know."

If you are curious and the principal permits it, you can wander around a school and get a sense of atmosphere and general purpose. For example, you can usually tell whether people have a sense of pride in what they do and whether students are active and engaged. You can look at bulletin boards to see if they display student work that increases in complexity and sophistication through the grade levels. If you have more time, you can sit in on one or more classrooms and get a sense of how much instruction goes on and how much time is wasted. If you are somehow able to make yourself invisible, you can sit through lunchtime in the teachers' lounge and gauge whether the teachers are dispirited and bitter or energetic and excited.

But these are just partial glimpses—they don't really get at whether a school is teaching children what they need to know and be able to do. Even in a school where everyone seems happy and engaged, teachers and students might be engaged in random and purposeless activities. And even if you see what you know in your gut is fabulous instruction in one classroom, it might be completely unconnected to what happens in any other classroom in the school. To know whether schools are genuinely teaching their students at high levels—or even at low levels—you need data about student achievement.

This is part of what is being missed in the debate about whether as a nation we are testing our children too much. If we don't test them, we have no way of knowing whether children are learning the baseline knowledge and skills that they should have before they leave school. That doesn't mean that there isn't much more to know about a child than how he or she performs on a state test. It also doesn't mean that children should be taking tests all the time. But if we think it is important to be able to read, write, apply mathematical formulas, and understand political and scientific issues enough to vote sensibly, serve on a jury honorably, and in general be a productive citizen, then we need to make sure children can do those things before they leave school. And, further, we need to make sure that schools are doing the job we pay them to do—to teach our children. Tests are the only way we can do both of these things. To paraphrase Winston Churchill's famous line about democracy, tests are the worst way to assess student and school performance—except for all the others.

HOW WE GOT HERE

For the most part, schools have not been organized for the purpose stated above—that is, to make sure that all students learn enough to become productive citizens. This isn't the place to give a full history of American education—many have done that already. Suffice it to say that throughout most of the twentieth century, most schools were organized in a way that sorted children and then offered them very different kinds of education. Baby boomers will remember the "tracks" that their high schools offered—college preparatory, business, and vocational. Most school systems stopped calling the different pathways "tracks" sometime in the 1970s and 1980s, but have continued the sorting practices all the same.

The ideological justification for sorting was that some children were considered able to learn to high levels and others weren't, so there was no sense in wasting educational resources on the latter group. For the most part, this was considered a self-evident proposition, particularly for African American, Latino, and American Indian children, who for most of the last century were physically separated from white children. One occasion when the issue of sorting was publicly battled out by educators was in the early part of the twentieth century, when floods of immigrants from Southern and Eastern Europe and Asia overwhelmed the schools. The winning side of the battle argued that the vast majority of these new Americans were obviously "uneducable," and all they required was some basic instruction in reading and writing and some training in hygiene and low-level vocational skills. High schools were refashioned so that instead of simply having one high school curriculum, as they had had previously, they offered differentiated tracks based on student "ability" or "potential," which was assessed by teachers and by what were then the newfangled IQ tests and norm-referenced tests, which array students on a bell curve.

Although many of the Jewish, Hungarian, Italian, and Chinese children who sparked the sorting debate eventually proved themselves not only "educable" but capable of enormous achievement, there was never a dearth of children to take their place on the low end of the education ladder, and the sorting processes continued, extending into younger and younger grades. Many parents found themselves puzzled by the casual way their children's lack of academic achievement was dismissed by teachers and principals, and savvy parents knew that they had to get their children into the right classes and the right schools or their children were likely not to learn enough to go to college or hold a job that required high-level skills and knowledge.

In the latter part of the twentieth century, the open and unapologetic racism that fueled the practice of sorting students was replaced by a new analysis that began with the work of a highly respected sociologist, James Coleman. Coleman had been commissioned by the then U.S. Department of Health, Education and Welfare to assess whether educational opportunity was equal in the nation, and he did a massive survey of students, teachers, and principals. One of Coleman's 1966 findings was considered quite surprising by many: that family background played a large role in academic achievement. Coleman's report never said that school quality was unimportant; in fact, he specifically cited the verbal skills of children's teachers as being an important factor in students' academic achievement. But his finding that family background has a strong predictive role in academic achievement began a long train of reasoning that has ended with the idea that most students of poverty and students of color cannot be expected to reach high academic standards. The corollary to this is that schools serving large numbers of children of poverty or children of color cannot be expected to be high achieving. Teachers and future teachers have been told repeatedly in the past few decades that they could have little effect on this demographic reality. In other words, instead of reacting to the Coleman Report by thinking deeply about what schools need to do in order to offset the ill effects of poverty and discrimination on academic achievement, the education profession as a whole used it as what could be called the "demographic excuse"—poor children don't do well because they are poor, and schools can't do anything to change that.

This is not to say that all teachers and principals agreed with this analysis. Many have found themselves frustrated by it and have successfully challenged it in their classrooms and schools. But their individual efforts, as meaningful as they were to their students, did not change the overall ways that most schools were structured. As a result of this organizational structure, some children graduate from high school with relatively high levels of skill and knowledge, while others—many of them children of poverty and children of color—can barely negotiate their way through a simple newspaper article.

The American public as a whole never totally bought into the demographic rationale for failure. For the most part, they assumed that the job of schools was to teach children, and they eventually tired of hearing stories of children who spent twelve or thirteen years in school without ever learning to read. The public began demanding that schools demonstrate that they educate children rather than simply house them. One manifestation of that national demand was the 1994 reauthorization of the federal Elementary and Secondary Education Act (ESEA), in which Congress told states that if they wanted to continue receiving federal Title I money, they had to demonstrate that poor children actually benefited from the money. ESEA, first passed in 1965, was one of the Great Society programs proposed by President Lyndon B. Johnson with the purpose of making sure poor children had access to the same kind of schooling that nonpoor children had. Title I was the main funding program of ESEA, and for forty years it has poured money into schools of poverty.

Whether because of Title I money, desegregation, or some other factor, achievement gaps between poor and nonpoor children and between African American and white children narrowed throughout the 1970s and through most of the 1980s, but right around 1988 that progress halted and achievement gaps began growing again. From 1988 on, it was difficult to make any claims that Title I was helping poor children catch up with their middle-class peers, and there was considerable evidence that Title I money was often used in ways that actually made the achievement gap worse. Many schools, for example, used Title I funds to hire untrained and poorly educated teaching aides who were assigned to take "Title I kids"—that is, poor children—away from classroom instruction to do basic remedial work. Not only did those students miss classroom instruction, but they often weren't provided with high-level instruction to compensate. That is why, in 1994, Congress told the states that they needed to show results with their Title I money—that is, if they got money to support poor children, poor children should show academic gains.

Before deciding what academic gains should look like, states first had to decide what children should learn. For the most part, until then this question had been left to textbook publishers and individual teachers, which had led to chaos. Children who were sick in fourth grade could forever more say they "missed long division," because that is when most math textbooks covered the topic; and children whose teachers loved dinosaurs and the Egyptian pharaohs never learned much about electricity and the American Revolution. In the 1990s, the nation's governors, working through the National Governors Association, agreed that their states should develop standards to codify what they would expect children to learn in school. Some states set ambitious goals for their children, some set low goals, and some set incoherent goals. Although a few states began testing against those newly written-down standards, most states received waivers from the 1994 ESEA's testing requirements, which is why the full effect of the testing requirement was not felt until the 2001 reauthorization of ESEA, known as the No Child Left Behind Act, or NCLB.

No Child Left Behind was the first time the nation ever declared that schools have a responsibility to teach every single child to meet their state's standards of learning. To those accustomed to the idea that the job of schools is to sort all children rather than to educate them, NCLB has come as a shock, and some teachers, principals, and superintendents around the country have spent the past few years saying that No Child Left Behind's goals are patently ridiculous given all the different kinds of kids there are, with all the different kinds of family backgrounds and issues they bring to school. To demonstrate its seriousness about the goal of all children meeting state standards, the U.S. Department of Education has given no waivers for the requirement that in order to receive Title I money, states must test all children in the third through eighth grades and once during high school to see if they are being taught to state standards. Reflecting the same kind of differences as in the standards, some states have drawn up tests that are thoughtful measures of what students need to know and be able to do and that allow students to feel a sense of accomplishment if they meet or exceed standards. Other states have adopted fairly low-level tests that only measure basic reading and math skills and don't allow students to feel much of a sense of accomplishment, no matter how well they do. But even those low-level tests give us some information about whether children are learning the very minimum they should be learning.

No Child Left Behind also requires all states to report the results of those tests publicly as part of state report cards. Finally, parents, teachers, and community members have a little window on the "black box" of schools. Anyone can go to his or her state education department's website and pull up information on an individual school to see what proportion of the students meet state standards in at least reading and math and, depending on the state, in other subjects as well. In states that have had the same standards and tests for a few years, an interested person can compare student results over time to see whether there is improvement or falling off. Because No Child Left Behind also requires that schools not only report overall scores but break out those scores by different kinds of students—that is, "disaggregate" the results—it is possible to see how well those schools serve different groups of students.

Although all that information is available, some states provide the information only in clunky and cumbersome formats that succeed better in confusing the public than in educating them. To short-circuit the state websites, Standard and Poor's posts a quick summary of the available data on its website, http://www.schoolmatters.com, which many educators, parents, and community members might find useful.

One of the really exciting by-products of the student achievement data is that for the first time, members of the public can find schools that do a better job than other schools in educating the same kinds of students. Anyone with a little data analysis capacity can, for example, create "peer groups" of schools where most of the children are poor, or most of the children are African American or Latino, and see which schools in the same state are doing a better job with the same kinds of kids. It isn't possible to compare across state lines meaningfully, because state standards and tests vary so widely, but results can be compared within states. The National Center for Educational Accountability has done just that, and anyone can see the information at http://www.nc4ea.org.

The Education Trust has built a different Web tool, available on the Internet at http://www2.edtrust.org/edtrust/dtm/, that allows users to generate a list of schools that meet a variety of criteria. For example, users can ask to see a list of schools where more than 50 percent of the students are poor and that perform in the top 25 percent of the schools in the state. That Web tool, called "Dispelling the Myth," is where I and Education Trust analysts began the search for the schools described in this book, but that was just the beginning of the process I call "spelunking through the data." We pored over state report card data and applied many criteria before we identified a school as being what we considered "visit worthy." Such criteria included the following:

1. **A significant population of children living in poverty and/or a significant population of children of color.** We used the usual proxy for poverty, which is the percentage of students who qualify for the federal free or reduced-price meal program. By "children of color" we meant African American, Latino, and American Indian children. Although some people include Asian children in that description, for the purposes of these comparisons we did not, because Asian American children in general do not perform at rates lower than white children, and in some cases they perform at higher rates. This is a generalization, however, that applies mostly to second- and third-generation Chinese and Japanese immigrants, not to many other people who have been lumped into the "Asian" category. For example, the Hmong refugees from the mountainous regions of Laos and Cambodia have been plagued with low academic achievement since moving to the United States. For that reason, we were happy to find Dayton's Bluff Achievement Plus Elementary School, where not only substantial percentages of African American children, but also Hmong children, meet state standards. The criteria for what we meant by "significant population" varied somewhat depending on the states, which have widely varying demographics. The absolute minimum requirement was about 25 percent of the population of a school, but most of the schools described here have much higher percentages of students of color or of poverty.

2. **Either very high rates of achievement or a very rapid improvement trajectory.** This criterion varied somewhat by state, but in general we wanted to see proficiency rates in the 80 or 90 percents. In addition to an absolute high rate of achievement, we also looked for sustained and rapid improvement, on the theory that improvement is never an accident and deserves to be studied.

3. **Relatively small gaps in student achievement in comparison with achievement gaps statewide.** In every state, poor children and children of color post lower rates of proficiency than do nonpoor children and white and Asian children. This is known as the *achievement gap*, and although some states have made significant progress in closing those gaps (Delaware and Massachusetts, for example), others have seen no progress or have even experienced some widening of gaps in recent years. We were looking for schools that had closed gaps or narrowed them sufficiently that one could imagine them closing within a few years.

4. **At least two years' worth of data.** This criterion alone eliminated schools in a number of states that had changed their tests or their scoring system within

the previous two years, for without at least two years' worth of data it is impossible to see whether a school is making progress.

5. **In the case of high schools, high graduation rates and higher-than-state-average promoting power index (PPI).** Graduation rates are notoriously unreliable and rely on sometimes quirky definitions. The nation's governors have all agreed to work toward getting better graduation rate data, but in the meantime we looked for graduation rates that were higher than the state average. As a corrective for the overly rosy view that graduation rate data provide, we used PPI, which is a measure developed by Johns Hopkins University researchers Robert Balfanz and Nettie Legters. PPI compares the number of seniors to the number of freshmen four years earlier, and thus gives a sense of whether the high school holds on to its students across the years and advances them through the grades, or whether it either pushes them out or keeps them at a grade level for two or more years. PPI is a crude measure because it doesn't follow the students through to graduation and can't take into account major demographic shifts, such as the closing of a housing project or some other legitimate reason for a drop in population between freshman and senior classes. But it does provide additional information that we considered.

6. **Adequate Yearly Progress (AYP).** AYP, an artifact of No Child Left Behind, is a measure of whether a school has met state standards for improvement. All of the schools with individual profiles in this book met AYP requirements before I visited them, except for Granger High School in Washington's Yakima Valley. The reason for this exception is explained in the chapter that describes Granger, and the fact that Granger has since met AYP confirms that I was right to make that exception.

7. **Open enrollment for neighborhood children—that is, no magnet schools, no exam schools, no charter schools.** This criterion was adopted not because magnets, exam schools, or charters are unworthy of study, but because any gains they make are often dismissed as being the result of "creaming." Even when all of their children are poor, they are said to enroll only the "ambitious poor," with parents who are more supportive or in some other way different from the parents in the local neighborhood schools. I wanted to eliminate that factor as one that might have contributed to a school's success. In a few cases, such as Centennial Place Elementary School in Atlanta, the school has extra room and so also enrolls a few children from outside the neighborhood. And in one instance (University Park Campus School), the school is too small to take all the children in the neighborhood and must hold a lottery for admis-

sion, but there is no entrance requirement other than filling out a form. Other than those very minor exceptions, all of the schools profiled in this book are regular neighborhood schools.

A NOTE ABOUT THE DATA

Whenever possible, the data used are from the state report cards, which report the percentages of children who meet state standards, not from the data the state used to calculate AYP, which is used to determine whether a school has met its targets in reading and math. In an attempt to be fair to schools, all kinds of mathematical manipulations are performed on student achievement data to calculate AYP. For example, students who weren't present the entire school year aren't counted for purposes of AYP. Similarly, students who are learning English are not counted for accountability purposes the first year they are in the country and are permitted to take reading and math tests in their native language for three years after arriving in the United States (though few states provide those native-language tests). For these and other reasons, AYP numbers are usually somewhat rosier than state report card data. In all cases, the source of the data used will be cited so that readers can do their own data spelunking. Wherever possible, data from 2006 were included as part of the charts that accompany each chapter. It should be noted that under No Child Left Behind, states are obligated to publish school report cards by the beginning of the school year, but many states fail to do so, which means that in some cases the last data shown are from 2005. Sometimes the demographic information in the charts is slightly different from the information in the text. I apologize if this is confusing, but I wanted to give the latest information and the changes underscore the point that schools are constantly in flux.

Because different states have different standards, a school that looks really good on paper might not be as good as another that seems a little worse on paper but is in a state with higher standards. Still, the kids and the staff in the first school are meeting the standards they are expected to meet, and usually at much higher rates than students across town. That is worth celebrating, and it is worth studying how they were able to improve, even while the folks in that state should be working to improve the standards.

One final point: Some of the schools in this book had a lot of support and help from their districts in terms of professional development and expertise, but others did not. In fact, some have had to contend with the anger and jealousy that sometimes emerges when a school outperforms its expectations.

People in typical crummy schools are used to being able to say, "Well, we're not very good but look what we're working with—no school that has to deal with our kinds of students is any good." Or, as teachers at Frankford Elementary School used to say rather pungently, "You can't make chicken salad out of chicken shit." When a nearby school does much better with the same kinds of kids, it stands as a rebuke to the other schools. Ideally, the success of a neighbor would come as a wake-up call to the people in the crummy schools, and they would study the success and try to emulate it. Too often, however, they retreat into other excuses, such as "That school is cheating" or "That school gets a lot more resources than we do." Sometimes, they even come up with a new characterization of the kinds of kids the successful school has. One principal told me with great amusement that other principals in her district had decided that her town had always had a "strain of brilliant children," as though academic achievement were something of a genetic disease.

The principals in the schools that have difficult relations with their districts have asked me not to highlight this issue because they don't want to make a difficult situation worse, and I have acceded to their wishes. I hope readers won't be able to tell which of the schools described in this book are in that situation, but I did want to say that district support for success cannot be assumed in all cases. Some schools have had to achieve their level of success all on their own, with virtually no outside support whatsoever, which makes their accomplishments all the more admirable.

Make no mistake—every school described in this book has accomplished something admirable. They are taking in children who are considered "hard to teach" by many in the education world, and with thoughtful hard work they are producing academic success. They could have saved themselves a lot of trouble by falling back on the tired old excuses that many other schools use—that "these kids" can't be expected to do much academically because they are poor, because their parents don't support their education, because their home lives are chaotic, because they don't speak English at home, because they didn't get the proper foundation at earlier ages, because they don't eat breakfast, because they don't have a culture of academic achievement, or any of a number of other excuses. At none of the schools included in this book did I hear any of that kind of language. The teachers and administrators know that the children in their schools can learn, and they know that it is up to them to figure out how to teach their students.

FRANKFORD ELEMENTARY SCHOOL
FRANKFORD, DELAWARE

INTRODUCTION

I remember seeing the numbers for Frankford Elementary for the first time. An intern had come across its data as he was sifting through state report cards and he made a chart with the results. I literally stopped in my tracks when I saw the bar graphs reaching up to 100 percent. Some people say that it is foolish to expect that all children will meet state standards, yet here was a school where they had. Within days I had driven out from my home in Maryland to see the kind of school it was. There I found an almost breathless enthusiasm conveyed by teachers and the principal, who were thrilled someone had noticed the work they had been doing. Later they were to win the National Blue Ribbon award from the U.S. Department of Education and garner many other accolades, but back then their accomplishments still had not been widely recognized.

One thing that I learned when I got to Frankford was that long before No Child Left Behind imposed federal accountability on all schools, Frankford's school district had been under the supervision of the federal government. It had been found guilty of violating civil rights laws by identifying too many African American children—particularly boys—as requiring special education services and then segregating students in special education from the rest of the school. Because the school and district were under the scrutiny of the Department of Education's Office of Civil Rights, Frankford became used to gathering and reporting data years before No Child Left Behind required other schools and districts to do so. I was fascinated that Frankford's principal gave credit to the federal scrutiny for jump-starting reform. It had forced her to learn to read the data carefully and use them to drive instruction.

I started to see the value that federal accountability could have for individual children. For example, when the teachers at Frankford saw that the data

FRANKFORD ELEMENTARY SCHOOL
FRANKFORD, DELAWARE

2006 Enrollment: 447 students in prekindergarten through fifth grade
2006 Demographics: 27% African American
                          38% Latino
                          34% White
                          76% meet qualifications for free and reduced-price lunch
Locale: Rural

Grade 5 Reading
Delaware Student Testing Program (DSTP)

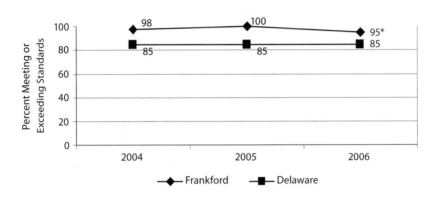

*The 2006 report-card data says > 95 percent. The exact percentage could not be determined.

showed that not all children were learning to read, they researched the issue and started using an additional reading program, one that included systematic, explicit phonics instruction—and saw their reading scores go up.

Frankford took a very pragmatic, cutting-the-Gordian-knot approach to what has often been referred to as the "reading wars," a debate over the best way to teach young children to read. On one side are those who say that learning to read is a natural process that will emerge if children are sufficiently surrounded by interesting, compelling written material. On the other are those who say that on the contrary, reading is not learned intuitively and that most children need to be systematically taught what is essentially the code of the alphabet, meaning that they need to systematically learn which sounds are represented by which letters and combinations of letters—in other words, "pho-

Grade 5 Math
Delaware Student Testing Program (DSTP)

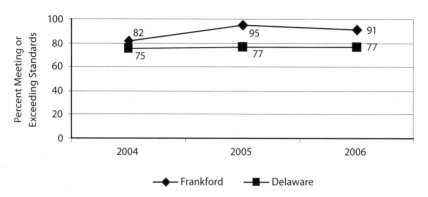

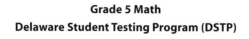

In addition, in 2006, 98 percent of Frankford's fourth graders met state science standards (compared to 92 percent in the state) and 90 percent met state social studies standards (compared to 64 percent in the state).

Source: Delaware School Profiles, profiles.doe.k12.de.us

Note: These graphs use the latest information that was available at the time of publication, which is more recent than was available when the school was visited.

nics." In 2000, the National Reading Panel, which had been asked by Congress to review all of the relevant research on the question of why some children have trouble learning to read, declared what it hoped would be the end of the reading wars by saying that children needed both to be surrounded by interesting, compelling written material and to learn to systematically and explicitly "decode." The National Reading Panel said further that although all children should be exposed to systematic and explicit phonics for 15 or 20 minutes a day in kindergarten and first grade, some children needed more intensive instruction in phonics to become fluent readers. This report did not end the reading wars as the panel had hoped, since educators in what used to be called the "whole language" camp continue to say that systematic, explicit phonics instruction is boring and even harmful to children.

By pragmatically looking at achievement data, Frankford had essentially confirmed what the National Reading Panel had found—that although many children don't require intensive phonics instruction, some do. And by allowing their data to drive instruction, Frankford continues to demonstrate that just about all children are able to learn to read.

· · · · ·

Frankford Elementary in Frankford, Delaware, is demographically tough by any standard. When I visited in 2005, 76 percent of its children met the standard for free or reduced-price meals, and most of the rest hovered near the standard. It is fair to say that almost all of the kids were poor. Thirty-six percent of the students were white, 36 percent black, and 28 percent Latino. Many of the Latino children were very recent immigrants from Mexico, the children of agricultural workers who themselves had little education. Twenty-two percent of the students were considered to be special education students.

The area is rural, one of the communities that beachgoers in the Washington, D.C., area drive through on their way to the ocean resort town of Bethany Beach. As the historically black school in a rural area, Frankford has never been attractive to most of the area whites. The affluent white families in the catchment area of the school tend to send their children to magnet programs or other schools, since the district permits school choice. When asked about her children's backgrounds, the principal, Sharon Brittingham, could think of only four children who could be said to come from professional families, and their parents were teachers. This is in part because African American graduates tend not to return to the area if they leave for college and professional training. Most of the parents work either in the nearby poultry plant or as service workers in the beach communities.

When Brittingham arrived in 1997, the school was very low-achieving, with scores tracking the demographics, as they do at many schools: African American boys did the worst, then African American girls, and white boys and girls posted the highest scores.

But after steady improvement, by 2003 an impressive 97.5 percent of the fifth graders met Delaware's state reading standards, including 100 percent of the boys, 100 percent of the African American students, and 100 percent of the low-income students. Half of the fifth graders with disabilities met state math standards, and a third of them met the writing standards.

"It is a hard process, but it's achievable," said Brittingham. "But first you have to believe it's achievable." In a later conversation she added, "And teachers have to believe they [themselves] are capable of achieving it."

When she first came, the entire district was under legal review by the Office of Civil Rights because of a class action suit against ten Delaware school districts charged with racial discrimination. Special education students were kept completely segregated, and African American boys were suspended at disproportionate rates. According to Brittingham, that was the beginning of the intense focus on data by the district in general, and by her in particular. At the time, she said, the attitude of the teaching staff was that African American children could not reach high academic standards and that teachers couldn't be expected to produce academic achievement with so little to work with, demographically speaking. The most commonly heard assessment by teachers was, "You can't make chicken salad out of chicken shit," a particularly redolent phrase, since many of Frankford's parents work in the chicken industry.

"We had some battles," Brittingham said. She told the teachers, "If you don't believe all kids can learn, what are you here for?" Brittingham was supported throughout those battles by a new superintendent, Lois Hobbs, who brought a similar tough-mindedness to questions of whether children can learn. "If you take all these excuses that kids come from poor homes or speak Spanish, then you don't get anywhere," Hobbs said. "You raise the bar for the adults, and then you raise the bar for the children."

All the battles over whether children can learn are now over at Frankford. Almost all conversation at Frankford is about how to make sure they do learn.

The reading specialist, Tracy Hudson, meets with each teacher two weeks into the year, once they have gotten to know their kids a little bit. She sits down with a teacher and goes over all the available data on each child—state test data, Stanford Achievement Test data, and the school's homegrown assessments—using them to get a sense of where the child is and to diagnose any problems. The two then develop an individual plan for each child. A child who needs extra work on phonemic awareness gets it. Another who is reading well gets additional enrichment in the form of more challenging chapter books.

Houghton Mifflin's Invitations to Literacy textbook series provides the core of the reading instruction, but when the teachers found that the series did not have enough emphasis on phonics instruction, the school bought the Open Court series of books, correlating its lessons with Houghton Mifflin to make sure each phoneme was introduced in the right order. For the most part, Open Court is used only in kindergarten and first and second grades unless a particular child—usually one who transfers in from another school—needs additional phonics instruction. In addition, teachers have Horizon, Accelerated Reader, and other commercial reading programs at their disposal for any other interventions they think necessary.

Reading and writing instruction is geared toward learning to read not only fiction but also nonfiction. Science and social studies lessons are times to read and write, and Hudson spends a good deal of time working with teachers on figuring out which children need "preteaching" of vocabulary and background knowledge before they are taught science and social studies lessons. "Rather than remediation, we work to make sure the children know what they need to ahead of time," Hudson said. The science curriculum is provided by Smithsonian Science, a series of hands-on science kits, complete with dirt and earthworms and other materials. A Houghton Mifflin social studies textbook series is "used as a resource," said Hudson, but is heavily supplemented by trade books and reading books. Teachers have received a lot of training in both the science and social studies curricula, and the kids' test scores reflect that. Almost all the children meet state standards in both subjects.

Each class of children has a data sheet on which the teachers have recorded the achievement levels of each child. Reading down the chart of one class's data, you might easily think that the 90th percentile was the baseline score on the Stanford 9, a nationally normed test in which 50 percent is the average national performance.

In 2004, only 82 percent of the school's fifth graders met Delaware's standards in math, so the school instituted a major push to improve math instruction in 2005. That push began with intensified training for the teachers. New teachers went to district-sponsored "math clubs" where they learned both the math and how to teach the math, and where they discussed lesson plans, viewed model lessons, and received support. More experienced teachers who no longer needed the math clubs received training in assessment and in how to support their fellow teachers, including by providing model lessons.

Individual students at the school were identified as needing extra support with math and were brought in for their own math clubs occasionally during recess, but not regularly, because Brittingham didn't want any one child to miss recess too often. Other support for children was offered before school and in the afterschool "homework club." Such support was offered not only to struggling children. If teachers observed that a student was easily mastering material and needed extra enrichment, the student could get that instead during those after-hours sessions. Most of the time, the children played math games to make the sessions fun.

This kind of individual diagnosis, support, and thoughtful instruction is the strategy that had worked to get almost every student meeting state reading standards, and Brittingham expected it to bring up the math scores as well. When the 2005 scores came in, she was proven correct: 94 percent of the third graders met state math standards, and 95 percent of the fifth graders, including 81 percent of the students with disabilities.

Discussion in the school is focused on instruction and the kinds of academic interventions children need to be successful, but this is not because the teachers and principal are unmindful of the outside lives of their students. Brittingham said she herself grew up poor. After she had become a teacher, she visited her mother, who was living in a trailer park. She looked out the window and saw a family shivering around a small charcoal brazier that could be bought at a convenience store for less than $2. "What are they doing?" she remembers asking her mother. "They're cooking," was the reply. "They don't have electricity." Brittingham remembers that a light went on in her head when she thought, "And their teachers will be wondering why they didn't get their homework in."

That is why she has a homework club after school to help kids with their homework, and why she works to make sure that all the instruction the children need is offered at school. Most of the children's families cannot support instruction, so she makes sure the school does. This effort goes far beyond simply making sure they can read and do math. For example, in afterschool sessions, her music teacher and an instructional assistant offer small-group lessons in instrumental music. "I want them to be successful in the world, and they need a lot of experiences to make that happen," Brittingham said. She is even working with a research group to see if helping children develop gross motor skills is helpful to them academically, so she has a classroom equipped with trampolines, tumbling mats, and hula hoops.

Brittingham expects all her students to achieve, and she expects her teachers to have the same expectations. "Now," she said, "they'll tell you that they *can* make chicken salad out of chicken shit."

POSTSCRIPT

At the end of 2005, Sharon Brittingham retired, and her place was taken by Duncan Smith.

My first reaction to the news that Brittingham had retired was one of dismay. I had fallen in love with Frankford and feared that all that Brittingham had built up could be destroyed with a new principal. Certainly that has been known to happen at other schools. However, Brittingham assured me that Smith was well trained and very competent and that the structures in place at Frankford and in the district would carry Frankford forward.

The 2006 data—the first that Smith could take full credit for—bear Brittingham out. On most of the tests, in most of the grade levels, more than 90 percent of the students met or exceeded state standards, even though "cut scores" had increased for some of the tests—that is, children needed to answer more questions correctly in order to be considered as meeting or exceeding standards. At the same time, the percentage of students meeting the standards for free or reduced-price meals at Frankford increased to 82 percent, and the percentage of Latino students increased to 38 percent. "Even though we have a lot of kids with a lot of needs, we do very well," Smith said.

Smith gave some credit for Frankford's continued progress to a program begun under Brittingham that brings in more than 150 volunteers from the community to work with students. Coordinated by a paid staff member, volunteers—who are mostly retirees attracted by the nearby beaches—are given particular lessons and topics to cover when they work with their students. The students go for three 30-minute sessions a week, mostly for help in reading. "I was a mentor and saw how important it can be," Smith said. The student he worked with had only been in the country for a year and a half, Smith said, but he passed all his state tests. In addition to the volunteer corps, English-speaking students studying Spanish at the local high school come weekly to work with the younger students, helping the younger students with their reading and English language while themselves benefiting from the extra practice in Spanish.

Many of the teachers have applied for grants from local businesses and have purchased SMART Boards, which are interactive boards that combine the functions of blackboards, laptops, and more. And training provided through the district by Carol Gardiner, Max Thompson, and Rick DeFour, all nationally known education consultants, has helped Frankford teachers develop professional learning communities where they "talk about essential learning, come up with common assessments, go over results together, and come up with additional supports students need," Smith said. "The professional learning communities," he added, "have given the teachers a real voice. They're not working in isolation anymore. And you see it when you go class to class. They are all talking about the same things."

UNIVERSITY PARK CAMPUS SCHOOL

WORCESTER, MASSACHUSETTS

INTRODUCTION

Organizations around the country are working to help schools and school systems improve. MassInsight, based in Massachusetts, is one such organization. I explained what I was doing to the folks there and told them that I was looking for schools to visit, and they said that I absolutely had to visit University Park Campus School, a school that goes from seventh through twelfth grade. All of its tenth graders had passed one of the most rigorous high school graduation tests in the country, the Massachusetts Comprehensive Assessment System (MCAS).

University Park is a very unusual school, founded by a partnership between Clark University and the city of Worcester, pointing to the important role universities could have in school reform if they took on the issue in a serious way. University Park is very small—just a few more than 200 students—but deserves special attention because it has worked out many of the problems faced by schools where most of the students are poor. I was entranced by the dedication of the teaching staff and the way the students themselves had absorbed the idea that high standards were not just for students but for teachers as well. They told me the story of a new teacher who wasn't teaching them as much as they thought they should be taught, and they complained not only to him but to the principal, eventually causing him to leave. That speaks to the culture of the school, where great things are expected of everyone.

Students know that at University Park, all tenth graders passed the high school graduation test from 2002 until 2005, and they are determined that their class not only match that rate but increase the number of students who exceed graduation standards. It has become a bit of a competition, and students boast, as one did to me, "It's not that hard a test." This is the test that has caused great

UNIVERSITY PARK CAMPUS SCHOOL
WORCESTER, MASSACHUSETTS

2006 Enrollment: 230 students in seventh through twelfth grade
2006 Demographics: 12% African American
                         35% Latino
                         19% Asian
                         34% White
                         70% meet qualifications for free and reduced-price lunch
Locale: Urban

Grade 10 English Language Arts
Massachusetts Comprehensive Assessment System (MCAS)

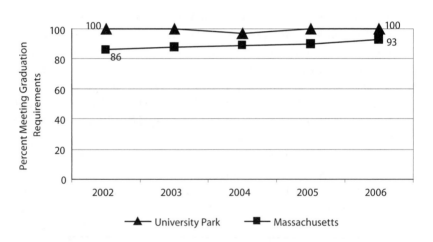

Source: Massachusetts Department of Education, http://profiles.doe.mass.edu/

heartache among those who claim that it is an insuperable barrier to students, particularly to poor students and students of color.

Many years ago I heard Albert Shanker, then president of the American Federation of Teachers, talk about the effect a standards-based test has on the relationship between students and teachers. Teachers with high standards, Shanker said, were often seen by students as enemies imposing arbitrary standards that were often indecipherable—particularly if students had had teachers with lower standards in previous years.

Grade 10 Math
Massachusetts Comprehensive Assessment System (MCAS)

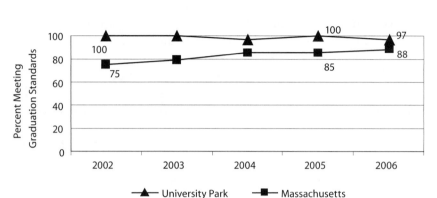

But, Shanker said, the effect of an external exam, such as the national exams taken by students in many countries, is to produce a partnership between the teachers and the students, where teachers are the resources students need in order to master a difficult objective. In preparing for an external exam, students see teachers with high standards not as cruel and arbitrary taskmasters but as people who can really help them—something like hard-driving coaches who help their players win in a big game.

At University Park Campus School, I saw exactly what Shanker had described. Faced with a difficult and challenging graduation test, the students and teachers worked together as partners to master the knowledge and skills tested by MCAS.

• • • • •

Worcester, Massachusetts, has seen better days. Despite new downtown development undertaken to rejuvenate the city, it still houses more than its share of empty, trash-strewn lots bound by chain-link fences, blank storefronts, and people scuttling to leave before dark. Clark University sits in one of the poorer sections of Worcester, apart from the downtown area and surrounded by densely packed housing, most of which consists of wooden "triple-deckers"—three-floor, three-family houses—and low-rise apartment buildings. More than a decade ago, Clark University officials realized that fewer families would be willing to send their children to the well-regarded university if the neighborhood got any poorer or more dangerous, so it began working with the neighborhood on housing issues. This is part of the reason why much of the housing surrounding the campus looks in reasonable repair.

"It was a matter of enlightened self-interest," said Thomas Del Prete, director of the Jacob Hiatt Center for Urban Education at Clark University. "Clark realized that its own future was at stake." Enough work was done to improve the neighborhood that the president of the university moved into an old Victorian house adjoining the university. Lured by financial incentives, a handful of faculty have followed suit. Clark officials realized, however, that the quality of schools in a neighborhood affects whether families are willing to live there. "We knew . . . that if we helped create outstanding public schools for neighbors, people would want to live here and stay here," said Jack Foley, executive assistant to the president of Clark University, and one of the key people behind Clark University's engagement with the community.

So Clark did a number of things, including pledging that any student who lived within approximately eight blocks of the university and could meet the admissions criteria for the school could attend Clark for free. Also, its Center for Urban Education formed a partnership with the local high school as a "professional development school," meaning, among other things, that it offers professional development and mentoring to high school faculty members, allows them to take university courses for free, and provides student teachers for the school.

It also worked with the district, Worcester Public Schools, to start a new school just for neighborhood children. A steering committee composed of four representatives of Clark University and four from the Worcester schools selected a principal (Donna Rodrigues, a longtime teacher from Worcester) and set the basic direction. The school began in 1997 with just a seventh grade and grew one grade a year, until it outgrew its original space on the Clark University campus and moved to an old elementary school one block away. Built in 1885, the building is one of the oldest schools now in use, and its creaky wooden floors, big windows, and sizable classrooms make it a distinctive place to go to school.

Since its founding, University Park has demonstrated the power of a coherent instructional program taught by knowledgeable, skilled teachers to transform the academic lives of children. The school's students—who typically arrive two or more grade levels behind in reading—all pass the state high school exit exams, most of them at high levels, and they all go to college. Most of them go to four-year colleges, some of which have difficult entrance standards, such as Clark, Brown, Georgetown, and Tufts universities and Trinity and Holy Cross colleges.

This is in direct contrast to most secondary schools. For the most part, middle and high schools are engines of inertia: Students who enter at high levels tend to stay at high levels; students who enter at low levels tend to stay at low levels. But at University Park, students enter at low levels and accelerate up to high levels. There is no magic to how this is done. The school offers excellent instruction in a focused college preparatory curriculum taught by teachers who know their fields, are convinced their students can and must learn at high levels, and are willing to support them. That's all, but it is rare enough to be worthy of study.

Part of the excellent instruction involves a very tightly focused curriculum. Only a small number of courses are taught, and students are expected to take English, math, science, and history each year. All students take Spanish for three years; no other language is offered. All high school classes are honors or college-level. Usually the college-level classes are Advanced Placement courses, but occasionally a Clark professor will come to the school to teach a course. Students with a strong desire for other courses are permitted to take classes at Clark University, and as a result, by graduation, two-thirds of all students have taken at least one college class, either at the school or at the university.

Another part of the instruction is a strong teaching staff, which includes a mixture of veteran and new teachers. Most of the new teachers have been trained by Clark University's Center for Urban Education and complete their student teaching at University Park.

Finally, the school's instruction includes strong personal support of students. "The principal knows everyone," is how one student put it. It is a small school, with just over 200 students total, 44 or fewer per grade. That means that all the students know all the teachers, and all the teachers know the students and where they live. In fact, the children who attend University Park must live within an approximately eight-block radius of the school, meaning that, by definition, they must come from a poor neighborhood. As a result, 70 percent of the children qualify for free or reduced-price meals. Some of the children's parents work at Clark University as building-service or food-service workers, but only one student is the child of a graduate student at Clark University, a visiting student from Iran. None is the child of a faculty member. About 78 percent of the children speak English as a second language, and many show up knowing little or no English. The most common languages are Spanish and Vietnamese, but Eastern Europeans are the largest group, and the school has quite a few Albanian children. Because there are too few slots to admit all the children from the neighborhood, families fill out an application and are selected by lottery. There are no grade requirements for admission, however, which means that University Park has a big challenge—a challenge it takes very seriously.

A free, academically oriented, Clark-sponsored summer camp, staffed by teachers and older students, may be the first experience a child has with University Park. Or he or she may have an older brother or sister there. (Because siblings are automatically admitted, half of the students in the current seventh grade have siblings in the school.) But most students first enter University Park in the summer before seventh grade, when they attend a three-week before-school session. "I always teach English, to get a baseline on their reading," said the principal, June Eressy. Eressy is the second principal at University Park, and she was the school's first English teacher.

"I do a mini running record on each student," Eressy said, referring to a technique reading teachers use to note how fluently and accurately children can read. "I can gauge fluency, I can tell if they decode." Because so many of the students are English-language learners, she said, "it's even more complex."

Those students who need help with the basics, such as decoding, get help after school from an elementary-level reading teacher. In previous years, University Park had the funding to stay open an extra 90 minutes past the regular school day, so it was able to incorporate that kind of instruction into the school day. Cuts in district funds have now returned the school to regular hours, but a federal 21st Century Community Learning Center grant allows it to provide an afterschool homework center and some additional tutoring.

In any case, Eressy said, "the most critical thing is to get kids to practice reading." The English teachers at University Park do a fair amount of reading to their students, partly to model good reading, partly to build students' appreciation and understanding of complicated syntax, and partly to get students hooked on great stories. They may even begin with picture books to jump-start discussions of personification, metaphor, and genres, and then move to somewhat higher-level reading. "I pick highly motivating reading selections on a fifth- or sixth-grade reading level so they can access it, but it's not insulting," said Peter Weyler, the middle school English teacher, who said he assumes most of the kids will come in reading at the third- to fifth-grade level. "I've had [students] say that the first book they ever read was in my class," Weyler said. He also tries to expose them to language and literature in other ways, such as by arranging trips to local poetry slams and encouraging students to organize their own poetry slams and performance art events.

Students are expected to read a lot and write a lot at University Park. They write extensive analyses of literature that are graded according to rigorous standards and are allowed to be rewritten. But they are also expected to do a great deal of what is called "low-stakes writing," meaning writing that isn't criticized but merely checked to make sure students are practicing writing and thinking about literature. Such low-stakes writing includes reader journals, first drafts, and poetry. History teachers assign not only textbook reading but also novels and historical fiction tied to the period being studied. Math and science teachers require students to write extensively as well.

English class is certainly the epicenter of reading and writing instruction, though. James E. McDermott is one of the high school English teachers. A veteran teacher, McDermott was one of the teacher consultants who worked to develop the MCAS. McDermott is scathing about the current state of urban education. "Wherever you go in urban public education, you will hear excuses—'you do not know our kids' or 'we haven't enough money or computers or facilities.' Here we figure if you allow excuses, you take yourself out of the equation as a possible solution. So we have a no-excuses policy."

McDermott teaches high school English as if he were teaching in an exclusive college preparatory school, with an emphasis on creativity and what he calls "intellectual play." His reading list for the first semester of tenth-grade English, with the theme of "the individual and society," includes *Antigone, One Flew Over the Cuckoo's Nest, Catcher in the Rye, Lord of the Flies, Julius Caesar*, and *Their Eyes Were Watching God*. In a paper on teaching, McDermott wrote, "We will read the classics from Sophocles to Shakespeare to Faulkner, Conrad, Joyce, Eliot, Tennyson. . . . I am determined to expose my students to the greatest of literary works."

To introduce a unit on poetry, McDermott began with the Paul Simon song "I Am a Rock." On the first day of the unit, students were told simply to write an essay analyzing the song. "It was a setup," McDermott said. "I knew they couldn't do it." And, in fact, their first attempts consisted mostly of short, simple paragraphs with little detail and few sophisticated concepts. So the next day McDermott began scaffolding the task for them, explaining how to look for alliteration and metaphor, how to notice diction, and how to talk and write about all three in the context of an author's meaning. He showed them how to go back to the text to find support for their statements.

The next attempts by the students were longer, more sophisticated, and much more detailed and thoughtful. They took turns reading their efforts in small groups, and students nominated those classmates whose pieces were exceptional to read to the class. Each composition read aloud was followed by a supportive round of applause by fellow students and some kind of critique by McDermott. For example, McDermott pointed out that one student's opening line ("'I Am a Rock' is an interesting poem") was flat, but then explained that it was fine in a first draft as a way to get the writing juices flowing.

"People are going to screw up," he said later, "but that's part of the process." He wants his students to take risks in their writing. "I don't want the kids looking for a walk—it's more fun to swing and miss."

As one of the statewide panel of teachers who helped develop MCAS, McDermott is well aware of the structure of the test and the grading standards. He grades his students' work by the same standards and permits students to rewrite a badly written essay until it meets high standards. In that way, test preparation is built into all the instruction at University Park, but additional instruction in test strategies is offered after school and just before the MCAS is administered. Students are well aware of the MCAS and know how well previous classes have done. "It's kind of a challenge," is the way junior Jacqui Carey describes it. Juniors are proud that their class passed with higher scores than the previous class.

"It's not a hard test," junior Reed Powell said. But other students around the state have not found it so easy. In Massachusetts as a whole, 11 percent of the tenth graders failed the English language arts portion in 2004; 15 percent failed the math part. In the rest of the Worcester school district, 24 percent failed the English part of the exam and 36 percent failed the math section. Also in Worcester, only 37 percent were advanced or proficient in English, and 30 percent in math.

Official figures show that 3 percent of University Park's students failed in 2004, but that represented a student who no longer attended but was carried on the school's books. Other than that student, all of University Park's tenth graders passed. But more impressive was that very few were in the just-passed, or "needs improvement," category; 83 percent scored advanced or proficient in the English language arts test, and 86 percent did so in math.

University Park, in other words, is demonstrating that schools have the power to help all kids learn to high levels, even students who enter already behind. English teacher McDermott is unsurprised. "We know what works in education. The research is prolific. Amazingly, then, the question today is not about what works, but about why we do not implement what we know works in all schools for all kids."

The students have another perspective. When asked what contributes to the school's success, junior Katie Brown said, "the passion." Teachers at University Park have high expectations of the students and keep on them all the time, she and other students said. When one of his teachers gave him an 88, "That was a wake-up call," said junior Benny Vega. "He said I wasn't pushing myself." The teacher gave Vega and his friends very challenging math problems to solve. "He'd seen that we would . . . slide by with a low A or a high B, and he didn't let us," Vega said.

Another junior, Josh Kozaczka, said that the smallness of the school helps. "All the schools I went to I didn't do well. I got into trouble. I read fine and I could always get the grades, but none of the teachers cared—I didn't do well because no one was pushing. My mother was always working." One of the things that turned him around, he said, was that at University Park, "Dr. Mac [McDermott] said I was smart and could get good grades. Having someone [who is] that intelligent and that smart say that really meant a lot." Said Stephanie Ryan of the teachers, "They respect you, and letting them down is like letting your parents down." Echoing that thought, junior Dan Sargent said, "It goes straight to your head and to your heart."

A great deal of attention is paid at University Park to the culture of the school. It is a culture of support and respect, and upperclassmen—that is, juniors and seniors—are explicitly expected to be role models for the younger students. In fact, math teacher Dan Restuccia said that when the eighth graders were having some behavior problems, "We put them in a room with five twelfth graders, and the adults left the room." The students, said principal Eressy, "don't want this to be just another urban school where kids swear and write on the walls." And, in fact, there is no graffiti, and many students don't even bother to lock their lockers.

"Early on, a student coined the phrase 'It's cool to be smart,'" said Clark University's Del Prete. "The culture that fosters that is very strong." Students at University Park are expected to do two to three hours of homework a night, and teachers have high expectations for students. "The students have standards for the teachers as well," junior Katie Brown said.

The fact that University Park is so small gives it enormous strength in building a culture and community. But the smallness also has drawbacks. For one, each department (math, history, and so forth) consists of only three teachers— the middle school teacher and two high school teachers. That means there are few colleagues to collaborate with, plan lessons with, and look at student work with, at least from the perspective of an academic discipline. (Faculty members do look at student work during regular Wednesday meetings while students are in "specials" such as art, music, and physical education.) The smallness also means that students have few choices of classes to take, and if they play football or some other sport, they must play at the regular city high school.

"Our greatest strength is our smallness," is how Ricci Hall, a high school history teacher, puts it. "And our greatest weakness is our smallness." He teaches four separate courses, each requiring its own preparation time, although his situation is unusual (most teachers teach two sections of each class). Despite that, he said, "Teaching here is like teaching in heaven." Discipline problems that plague badly run schools are nonexistent at University Park, meaning that his time is spent thinking about instruction and how best to get his students learning more, rather than how to deal with recalcitrant students.

That isn't because the students at University Park are angels. One student was sent to University Park after assaulting a teacher. The school system lost a battle to expel him, but didn't want him back at his old school. "We took him," said Eressy. "He hasn't been a discipline problem here." Because siblings have automatic admittance, his sister came as well. "She had been in a behavior management class all her life. I haven't had a single behavior problem with her. But she had major gaps in her learning. She told me once that her teachers 'played the radio and we danced'—in her English class, no less." That girl is known in the school as being an eager learner. "The passion in her eyes for doing something new" is what most strikes math teacher Restuccia.

Students who were discipline problems in schools where they may have gotten lost in the crowd and were not expected to learn become responsible students in University Park's atmosphere of respect and learning. "We have the power to change things" is the way Eressy put it.

But the key to that power is the belief that it exists. Eressy asks all prospective teachers, "Do you really believe all kids can learn and that they can meet rigorous standards?" That belief is the core of University Park's success and is reflected in a statement made by Rodrigues, the founding principal, at a forum at Harvard's Graduate School of Education in the winter of 2004. She was addressing the idea that it is foolish to think that schools can close the achievement gaps between poor and nonpoor kids. "Kids go to school to learn," she said. "Educators need to be prepared to take the gap on."

POSTSCRIPT

Massachusetts moved its test from May to March in 2006, which, as Dan Restuccia pointed out, makes it "two months" harder. This made the school nervous that for the first time it might have students not pass the exam, especially because two of the tenth-grade teachers were new. Those fears turned out to be justified. One student failed the math portion of the MCAS and a smaller proportion of students were proficient and advanced than in past years. Restuccia said that the student who failed should easily pass on the retest because "her skills are strong." The school is hopeful that scores will improve next year as the teachers become more familiar with the standards and the assessment.

James McDermott has retired and is teaching in the Clark University education program. As of September 2006, June Eressy assumed not only the principalship of University Park Campus School but also of a small K–12 school around the corner, Accelerated Learning Laboratory, which also has a partnership with Clark University. Teacher Ricci Hall became "coordinator" of University Park, which in effect means assistant principal.

OAKLAND HEIGHTS ELEMENTARY SCHOOL
RUSSELLVILLE, ARKANSAS

INTRODUCTION

The Education Trust had identified Crawford Elementary School in Russell-ville, Arkansas, as showing some really nice improvement, so I went to look at its data. In comparing the school's and its district's data, I could see that another school in the small district must be outperforming Crawford. A little more data spelunking, and I found that the school outperforming Crawford was Oakland Heights. "Maybe it's a rich-kid school," I thought. But, no, more than two-thirds of the kids were poor, and it was racially mixed among white, African American, and Latino students. Its African American students met state standards at rates two and three times those of the state of Arkansas as a whole, and the school had improved rapidly in the past three years. It didn't have the same kind of success rate as Frankford (chapter 2) or University Park (chapter 3), but on the theory that improvement is never an accident, I decided to go to the school, which is located about an hour west of Little Rock.

Before driving out to Russellville, I drove around Little Rock, looking for the famous high school where in 1957 the "Little Rock Nine" had demonstrated the resolve of African American children to have access to the same educational opportunities that white children had. I stopped the car in front of the impos-ing Central High School and thought about how high the hopes had run back then that gaining access to the same buildings would mean access to the same instruction. Recent research has made it crystal clear that poor children and children of color consistently have less-experienced, less-qualified teachers than their more privileged peers, and are often sorted into completely different edu-cational pathways. This is not solely a racial and class issue—plenty of middle-class white children have been sorted out of high expectations—but it has af-fected children of color and of poverty most of all.

OAKLAND HEIGHTS ELEMENTARY SCHOOL
RUSSELLVILLE, ARKANSAS

2004 Enrollment: 370 students in kindergarten through fourth grade
2004 Demographics: 15% African American
                                          17% Latino
                                          66% White
                                          72% meet qualifications for free and reduced-price lunch
Locale: Town

Grade 4 Literacy
Arkansas Benchmark Exams

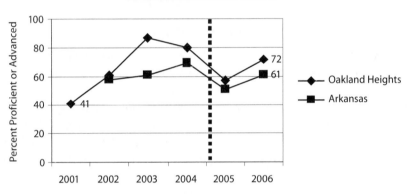

Grade 4 Math
Arkansas Benchmark Exams

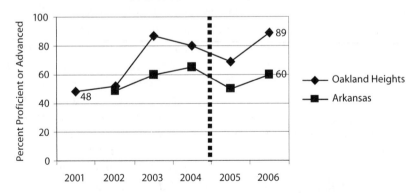

Note: Arkansas raised its standards in 2005, causing proficiency rates to fall in both the state and Oakland Heights Elementary School. Results in 2005 and 2006 are not comparable to results before. They are shown here only as a way of seeing Oakland Height's performance in relation to the state.

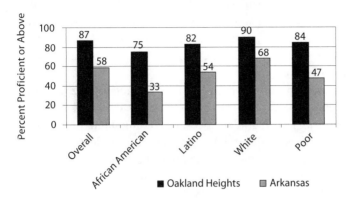

Grade 3 Math, 2005
Arkansas Benchmark Exams

■ Oakland Heights ▨ Arkansas

Source: Arkansas Department of Education, http://arkansased.org/performance_report/performance_report_2005.html

Enrollment and demographic information from Standard & Poor's, www.schoolmatters.org.

Note: These graphs use the latest information that was available at the time of publication, which is more recent than was available when the school was visited. Previous report cards can be found at the state department of education website.

Sorting often begins in elementary school, but at Oakland Heights, I found a principal who was leading a staff dedicated to making sure all their students learned a great deal. That's not all I found, however. I also found lists and charts and data sheets that tracked every student and every teacher. Data were the bedrock of how the school had made its dramatic improvements. This was a school that was still working out how they were going to make sure all children met state standards, and they were still in the process of inventing wheels. But they had come a long way.

• • • • •

In most of Arkansas—as in most of the country—the kind of demographics that Oakland Heights Elementary School has would spell low achievement levels and large gaps in achievement. Parents of Oakland Heights students—except for the few who are self-employed in fields such as car repair and carpentry—generally process chickens at the nearby Tyson plant or make frozen dinners at the ConAgra plant. "They're mostly working poor," said the principal, Sheri Shirley, about Oakland Heights families. The main exceptions are teachers who send their children to Oakland Heights. About 70 percent of the children in the school are eligible for free or reduced-price meals. Most of the school's 380 or so K–4 students are white, but about 15 percent are African American, and another 15 percent are Latino, part of a rapidly growing population of Mexican and Central American families who began arriving in Russellville only a few years ago.

In Arkansas, 76 percent of the white fourth graders, 59 percent of the poor fourth graders, 64 percent of the Latino fourth graders, and 49 percent of the African American fourth graders met state reading standards in 2004. That's a 27-point gap between white and African American students.

At Oakland Heights, however, gaps have been narrowing as all children have begun to achieve at higher levels. For example, 80 percent of all students met or exceeded state reading standards in 2004—81 percent of the white, 82 percent of the Latino, 74 percent of the African American, and 78 percent of the poor students. Although the 2004 data represent a slight dip from 2003, Oakland Heights has a higher percentage of students in some subgroups meeting or exceeding state standards than the rest of the state. For example, 78.4 percent of Oakland Heights's economically disadvantaged fourth-grade students met state literacy standards—a higher performance rate than the overall population of the state had, at 69 percent.

Not that the grown-ups in the school are satisfied. "The goal is 100 percent," said principal Shirley. "We still have a ways to go." But she added, "It's not a matter of *can* we—it's a matter of *how* can we." The fact that so many of the children live in poverty is not used as an excuse. "Just because you're poor doesn't mean you can't learn," said third-grade teacher Sherry Wilson. "I grew up very poor," the Russellville native added, giving an insight into the commitment teachers at Oakland Heights have to making sure that poverty is not a barrier to an education.

The staff at Oakland Heights is in the middle of a difficult task—transforming a low-performing school into a high-performing one. When Shirley arrived in 2001, 59 percent of the fourth graders had met state reading standards the previous year, and 52 percent met state math standards; both of these figures were significant improvements over the previous year, but they were still the lowest in the district. So the staff began at what Shirley called "square one": She and the teachers sat down with the state's standards and their test scores, looking for where their students fell short.

One thing that was obvious once they looked at the data was that, in math, their students did poorly on measurement and patterning questions. In reading, the students did poorly on questions requiring that they compare and contrast, recognize symbols, use idioms, and make inferences.

The teachers then organized in "vertical teams," meaning across the grade levels, and they went through the curriculum, the standards, and the classroom data piece by piece. In general, they found they were not teaching in enough depth. They were teaching two-dimensional measurement, such as how to find a perimeter, but not three-dimensional, such as how to determine volume. They were teaching patterns such as ABAB, but not the more complex pattern recognition required by state standards. Teachers in the earlier grades found themselves stunned at how much sophisticated reading and writing would be expected of their students once they reached fourth grade. In 2004, Arkansas tested elementary students in fourth grade; as of spring 2005, third graders also took state tests.

All the teachers found they had to ramp up their instruction considerably. After a year of analyzing the test data, several teachers left for other positions. That left a group of teachers—a mixture of veterans and new teachers—who were ready and eager to begin a new approach to classroom instruction. Many of the veterans had been working hard for years and had not been happy with the results. Now they had a road map to improvement.

As Shirley summed up, "We took that first year of disappointing scores and analyzed them and visited schools, studied best practices, got retrained." Shirley, who is herself a National Board Certified teacher, put several structures in place to make sure that instruction at the school became "systematic, explicit, and intentional."

One important step taken by the school was to make all the data transparent. Every classroom teacher knows not only his or her own data, but also the data of other teachers. This permits teachers to compare and be able to say that, although they may have taught one standard really well, another teacher has done better in teaching another of the standards. The teachers can then consult and learn from each other.

In each classroom, children are taught in an hour-and-a-half "literacy block" —sometimes in large groups, sometimes in small groups, and sometimes one on one, depending on what skill the children need to work on. As their beginning instruction, the kindergarten teachers have chosen to use a reading program ("Animated Literacy") that systematically introduces sounds and their letters (day 1 begins with *p*, day 2 with *u*, and on day 3 the kids put those sounds together to make a word—*pup*). The students sing songs with hand gestures, thus working on gross motor skills, and draw and color animals identified with a letter, working on their fine motor skills.

Beginning in first grade, the teachers work on letter blends (*st*, *bl*) and other reading skills as part of what Arkansas calls "balanced literacy," but explicit phonics instruction currently takes a back seat to what is called "embedded phonics instruction." However, dissatisfied that not all children have reached reading proficiency, the first-grade teachers are considering whether to add more systematic, explicit phonics instruction.

Throughout their elementary years, students read books chosen for their reading level, so they can read most of the words without trouble. But once students are beyond the picture book stage, they read "chapter" books—longer books organized into chapters—from the library as part of the commercial Accelerated Reader program, which allows teachers to keep track of what books the children are reading and whether they have some understanding of what they are reading.

"Accelerated Reader gives us a little more accountability than DEAR time," Shirley said, referring to a popular program adopted by many elementary schools, "Drop Everything and Read," in which all children and teachers are expected to read silently for 15 or 20 minutes, but with no monitoring of what the children read or of whether they understand it. Oakland Heights children are given time to read during the day, and the library and all classrooms have comfortable spots for reading. Some of the third-grade classrooms even have teacher-built "reading lofts," platforms lined with cushions that hover a few feet from the tall ceilings.

In one attempt to ensure that instruction is consistent throughout the school, all teachers agreed to teach expository writing using the same program, Step-Up-To-Writing, which uses, among other things, a method of color-coding particular kinds of sentences (green for topic sentences and conclusions; yellow for reasons, details, and facts; red for "stop and explain," which are sentences that give background for whatever is being discussed). All expository essays are expected to have all kinds of sentences. All narratives are expected to have a beginning, a middle, and an end. Teachers are sensitive to the idea that such writing can become formulaic, but argue that a formal structure gives students a way to begin to learn how to write sophisticated prose. Fourth-grade teacher Julie Ann Hilton said, "We start with this format and then extend. Kids need some background."

Students are assessed formally at the beginning and end of each year, and intermittently throughout the year if needed. But they are also assessed frequently by a teacher who listens to them read and keeps "running records," a way of recording accurate word calling and fluency. Those running records are used to guide student instruction in small groups on a daily basis. Diagnostic information, together with all the data pertinent to how that child is doing, is kept in his or her folder, where the teacher and Shirley can go over it and analyze how the student is doing. Those children who are not proficient in meeting state standards have an individual program designed for them, which the state calls an AIP (Academic Improvement Plan), designed by the teachers and approved by Shirley and the parents, who are given packets of information about how they can help their children improve. Those packets have been well received, said Shirley, who added, "So many of our parents failed in their school experience" that they welcome specific assistance in helping their children succeed.

Although children who are behind know they need to catch up, Shirley said that they don't feel discouraged or stigmatized because "everybody knows what direction they're going in." Lead teacher Liz Mullins said that the teachers tell the children, "It's our job to get you all to the train station."

Teachers are very cognizant of the "benchmarks," as they call the Arkansas state assessments. Fourth-grade teachers use released items from previous tests to assess their students starting in November. This allows them to see who needs extra instruction in literacy and math to be ready for the official administration in the spring. Released-item tests are given several times throughout the year to monitor student growth and to target nonproficient students with additional remediation. (Because in 2005 the third-grade test had never been given before, third-grade teachers could not do that.)

But teachers do not speak of the benchmarks as intrusions or interruptions in their teaching. Rather, they say the benchmarks give their teaching direction. "The reason our standardized tests are so good," said fourth-grade teacher Hilton, "is that they are matched with our standards," which she also said are good. And that seems to be a common outlook. Brad Beatty, who has looped between third and fourth grades, said, "The new standards are really good." Nor do teachers consider teaching to the standards a check on their creativity. "Not if we are innovative in *how* we teach," Hilton said.

Despite some direct instruction in how to take a test and in the kinds of questions found on Arkansas's benchmarks, for the most part instruction in the school is focused on the standards, not the test. Students read books and write about those books. Students write and publish essays on their heroes. They graph data gathered by observing the rainbows made by sunlight going through prisms. They are not, in other words, doing endless test prep.

The first year Shirley was principal, the school was so focused on reading and math instruction that, she said, science and social studies were given short shrift. Now that reading and math are under control, science and social studies are being incorporated more fully. And Shirley said she has found that "integration of the subject areas is much more effective."

Teachers are constantly looking to improve their instruction. At the beginning of each school day, while the instructional aides are getting the day started with the children, lead teacher Mullins meets with the teachers from one grade level. Mullins, who has her National Board Certification and has taught at Oakland Heights for many years after teaching in several other districts, goes over new ways to teach specific topics and brings things she has learned at conferences and from journals, such as the journal of the National Staff Development Council, *JSD*.

One day, she worked with the third-grade teachers on how to teach about metaphors and similes, as part of a series of discussions on how to teach children to compare and contrast. The method she taught that day was simple, derived from training she had received at a state conference. She told the teachers to choose two apparently random words from a word list, put one on the top left and one on the top right of a large sheet of paper, and then list attributes of each in turn underneath the word. Once the lists were complete, she told them to draw lines between connected thoughts. Mullins told the teachers she had done this activity earlier in the week with a group of first graders. "I pretended to pick the words randomly, but of course I didn't. First graders are already random; you can't be." The words she had selected for the first grade were *idea* and *lightbulb*.

For *idea*, Mullins said, the children listed things like "shows your thinking" and "you change them if they don't work," and for *lightbulb*, "makes things light up" and "change when they don't work." It was then easy for the first graders to make the connection that "ideas are like lightbulbs," thus gaining insight into a simile that is so common it could be considered a cliché. But then they were off and running, comparing *snow* and *paint*, and other pairs of words. Mullins told the third-grade teachers that one of her first graders had randomly chosen *friends* and *fishing*, and was able to say that making friends is like fishing because you have to use the right kind of bait and you can be happy if you catch lots or just one really good one. "Can you believe he thought that up?" Mullins said to the teachers, delighted with the performance of a first-grade student about whom, she said, "I never would have thought he had ever gone fishing."

Then the three third-grade teachers themselves chose words randomly and generated their own lists. Some of the words were seemingly too disparate to compare, such as *The Beatles* and *Etch-a-Sketch*, but third-grade teacher Brad Beatty managed just that—"They're both becoming popular again," he said.

After going through the lesson, the third-grade teachers were all expected to try the activity with their students and then to report back how it went.

The vertical, cross-grade-level meetings also provide an important forum for teachers to discuss instructional issues. Shirley and Mullins trained teachers in how to make the meetings productive and successful. Teachers then set expectations for the meetings, including the requirements that teachers will express any concerns at the meeting rather than in the parking lot and will provide the principal with minutes and finished products, such as lessons with grading rubrics.

Third-grade teacher Sherry Wilson said of the vertical teams, "That has helped us improve as a school more than anything else," in part because teachers are able to make sure that no instructional gaps occur between any of the grades and that all the standards are taught. Also, Mullins said, the vertical teams make sure that all the teachers feel that they "own all these kids."

The teams are part of what Mullins called "intentional" teaching. A sign in her room said, "An effective teacher instinctively uses high-yield strategies," meaning instructional practices that produce gains in achievement. Another sign said, "High-yield strategies have the greatest impact on student achievement when effective teachers use them intentionally." It is the intentional part that Mullins works on every morning—making sure that academic goals and instructional strategies are clear and that important things are not left to chance. "We're working on making sure all our instruction is explicit and systematic," said principal Shirley.

To allow teachers to observe other teachers' instruction, Shirley or Mullins will fill in for teachers during the day. In addition, all teachers proctor the state assessments when they are given, which gives the teachers of the younger grades an idea of what their children will experience by the time they finish fourth grade. "They had no idea what those children had to show," Shirley said. This is another way of making the school and what goes on transparent—not just for outsiders but for the teachers themselves.

Shirley also uses her instructional aides—paid for by federal Title I money, which is aimed at schools with large numbers of poor children—very strategically. For example, she teams her most experienced and expert instructional aides with her newest teachers, and new aides with her more experienced teachers. Although the decision is not popular, she doesn't allow an aide to work in a single classroom for more than one year. Shirley said rotating aides is important in order to "spread good practices." "I don't want greatness closed up in one room," she said.

In another attempt to build a larger community of achievement, Oakland Heights holds a yearly retreat with another high-poverty school in Russellville that includes all staff members, not just teachers. Team-building activities, reflective discussions about instruction, and karaoke singing help build a sense of community among the grown-ups in the school, but also expand the sense of transparency.

Shirley spends a great deal of time in classrooms herself, watching for effective teaching methods that can be shared. In one instance, she knew that the children in one classroom were mastering many more "sight" words (words read automatically without having to laboriously spell them out) than in others, even though all the teachers were doing the same activity—using flashcards to go through words. By sitting and watching, she noticed that in the less-successful classrooms, if the children missed a flashcard word, the teachers would simply read the words to the children. In the more-successful classroom, any time the children missed a word the teacher would teach them a "trick" to read the word more quickly. She might point out, for example, that there was a "word within the word" that the children already knew (stAND). That simple practice on the part of the teacher was helping kids read better, and by noticing it, Shirley was then able to initiate conversations among teachers about effective teaching practices.

In addition to focusing time and attention on reading, writing, and math, Shirley also spent a good deal of time during her first year focused on discipline. "The year before I came, discipline was the primary conversation in the school," she said. In her first year, teachers were sending many children who caused an interruption to the principal's office because they didn't know how to effectively deal with them in the classroom. Shirley began a book club, in which she and the teachers discuss a book she has chosen. One book was *Framework for Understanding Poverty*, by Ruby K. Payne, and another was *Cooperative Discipline*, by Linda Albert, which gave the entire instructional staff a common language and set of practices to use regarding discipline questions. Now, after a year spent discussing discipline methods and issues, the teachers are much clearer about the kinds of things they can handle, and Shirley is only receiving those problems that "teachers shouldn't have to handle themselves," as she said.

In addition, the school's counselor has worked closely with teachers to recognize children for displaying the character trait of the month in the school's character education program. As a result, Shirley said, "Kids who aren't necessarily recognized as kids who behave well can be recognized for a specific character trait," such as honesty or kindness. The physical education teacher also takes part in the discipline policy by working with the counselor to resolve issues of sportsmanship and help the children resolve conflicts that arise in their games. Lead teacher Mullins is convinced that the diversity of the school also helps in building a good disciplinary environment. "I've heard other teachers say that the Oakland kids know how to behave."

A district policy that Shirley cites as being helpful with discipline, as well as helping keep children on track academically, is that the district will bus children who move within the district back to their original school. This means that, although Oakland Heights still has a lot of children flowing in and out— typical of many high-poverty schools—it is able to hold on to its children who move within the district.

Shirley said that "there is no one single thing that works." She has instituted many changes in Oakland Heights, beginning with a focus on achievement data, a lot of attention to discipline and school climate issues, and a requirement that teachers and instructional aides work closely together and make sure they understand everything they are supposed to be teaching. ("Small misunderstandings among teachers can make for big misunderstandings among kids," she said.)

No one at Oakland Heights thinks the job is done. The school still has some distance to go before all students (including students with disabilities or with limited English proficiency) meet state standards. But it has made huge strides toward that goal, strides that took a lot of work, a lot of thought, and a willingness to change and look at difficult facts without flinching. The slight dip in scores in 2004 caused the staff to look closely at their practices and intensify their instruction. If the scores dip again, Shirley said, she knows exactly what she will do. "We'll start back at square one and pull out the state standards again."

Shirley said she has embraced those feelings of discomfort that change represents, and she expects her teachers to, as well. One mark of how willing they are to take on that challenge is that, in addition to the three National Board Certified teachers already on staff (including Shirley), three other teachers are candidates, meaning that they have undertaken a grueling evaluation process relatively few teachers in the country are willing to go through. (Arkansas provides an additional $5,000 per year to any teacher who is board certified. Some Arkansas districts match that; Russellville does not.)

Shirley was careful to credit the teachers at the school with being willing to take on such a big challenge as getting all students to meet state standards.

"There have been many innovative leaders who were unsuccessful because the staff was not willing to follow their leadership. Most other schools could not have handled so many expectations at once." She said that it is important for a principal "to acknowledge that change is hard. Change is feeling uncomfortable. However, only by changing can we assure students are successful in the future."

POSTSCRIPT

In 2005, Arkansas raised its standards. This is why Oakland Heights's scores appear to have dropped a bit that year. Unfortunately, Arkansas doesn't appear to have done a good job of explaining its changes, which meant that the folks at Oakland Heights were very disappointed with their 2005 results. "It was a rough year," Shirley said. Happily, the scores—at least at the fourth-grade level—bounced back up in 2006, once the teachers became more familiar with the higher standards. The third-grade teachers, Shirley said, were still becoming familiar with the test. "They have already begun to evaluate what they were doing, and I fully expect that they will bring up their scores," she said.

As of the 2006–07 school year, the Russellville school district had available to them state-written assessments that can be given after every four-week curriculum module. These assessments look like the Arkansas Benchmarks and can be scored within minutes. The results will let teachers know much more accurately whether their students have mastered the material, Shirley said. "We were producing our own benchmarks," Shirley said, "but there were real problems when we realized that the questions weren't worded exactly correctly to get good reliability."

In addition, the district provided Oakland Heights with a large modular building to house art, a counseling area, and a staff room where data could be posted all the time. "That will make a big difference," Shirley said. She added that despite all the difficulties inherent in being the principal of a high-poverty school, "I wouldn't trade this job for anything."

ELMONT MEMORIAL JUNIOR-SENIOR HIGH SCHOOL

ELMONT, NEW YORK

INTRODUCTION

It had been so easy to find University Park Campus School (chapter 3) that I got spoiled. I thought it would be easy to find more high schools. But I was wrong. All the resources of The Education Trust—and they are considerable— had been spent trying to find high schools that were successful in educating poor kids and kids of color, and they were coming up empty. That doesn't mean there are no such schools out there; many states just don't organize their data systems in ways that make it possible to find them.

For a while I worried that we would never find another secondary school. Every time we thought we had found one, we would look a little deeper and find that the school somehow "lost" half its students between the freshman and senior years, or that it didn't bother administering the state tests to half of its students, or that it required students to pass an exam to enter, or in some other way was disqualified from being considered. After an exhaustive search involving many long days, Education Trust senior policy analyst Daria Hall thought she might have found something—Elmont Memorial Junior-Senior High School in Nassau County, Long Island, New York.

The day I visited Elmont, I arrived a few minutes late because I had been stuck behind a garbage truck on the narrow streets surrounding the school. The principal, Al Harper, gently chastised me, saying he had a full day planned. And did he ever. It was the most organized visit I have ever had to a school, which was indicative of the kind of school it is. Harper was anxious for me to see classroom instruction, speak with teachers, and meet with his "cabinet" of school leadership, and the schedule he had arranged allowed for it all.

That evening I called the office and said, "I have found the Holy Grail." I didn't say that because the visit was well organized, but because every lesson I

ELMONT MEMORIAL JUNIOR-SENIOR HIGH SCHOOL
ELMONT, NEW YORK

2005 Enrollment: 2,039 students in seventh through twelfth grade
2005 Demographics: 74% African American
13% Latino
11% Asian
2% White
23% meet qualifications for free and reduced-price lunch
Locale: Urban-Suburban

Regents English Exam, Class of 2004

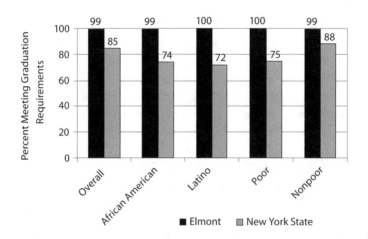

■ Elmont   ▨ New York State

saw was engaging and instructive—I learned things about Macbeth *and ideal gases that I had never before known—and because everyone seemed to want to be at the school. They liked it—students and staff alike. Outwardly similar schools—big, sprawling buildings with upward of 2,000 students—had made me nervous to walk around; so many people were unhappy and angry. Here, the main security guard was an older gentleman who walked with a limp, and students and teachers greeted each other with genuine pleasure and interest.*

The moment I knew that this was an extraordinary school was when I asked administrators about how many students were "ineligible." In the context of high school, an ineligible student is one who is doing so poorly academically that he or she is not allowed to play sports or participate in other extracurricular activities. At Elmont, and at many schools, students must maintain at least

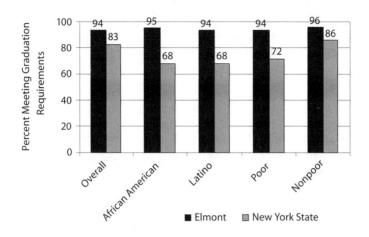

Regents Math Exam, Class of 2004

Note: The class of 2005 data looked very similar for Elmont, except with higher rates of math proficiency, but state results had not yet been published by the publication deadline. Class of 2006 data for Elmont had not been published by the publication deadline.

Source: New York State Education Department. New York State Report Card, http://www.emsc. nysed.gov/repcrd2005/schools/280252070002.shtml

a 2.0 grade point average and may not fail more than one class in order to stay eligible. But the assistant principals revealed that not many students were ineligible. They explained that students who had a legitimate reason for being ineligible could appeal, and most are "put on contracts" and allowed to continue with their activities as long as they meet their obligations to get extra help. They might be having a really hard time, explained one of the assistant principals, such as experiencing a death or serious illness in the family, and they might really need the support of other students at that time. "We wouldn't want to take that away," she said.

This was such a humane approach to the question that it struck me that not only did the school have high academic standards, but it was populated with really nice people who cared about kids and could thus make kids care about them. They used the ineligibility policy the way it should be used—as a swift kick in the rear to students who needed it, not as a kick in the head to someone who had been knocked down by the tragedies of life. As a result, only about 3 percent of students are ineligible to participate in afterschool activities. I contrasted that with figures such as more than one-third of students ineligible in *many schools where I live—almost half of the African American and Latino students—a status that simply serves to isolate them further from school.*

I look back on my visit to Elmont as a turning point in my school visits. The folks there approached their complicated task with such sophistication and expertise that I found my own perspective had deepened. From Elmont on, I was looking at schools with an even more critical eye.

• • • • •

Elmont Memorial Junior-Senior High School in Elmont, New York, is a big, intimidating brick building housing about 2,000 students in seventh through twelfth grades. It draws from surrounding neighborhoods of small, tidy, working-class homes on the narrow, densely packed streets of Nassau County, Long Island—just over the border from Queens and blocks from the Belmont racetrack. About three-quarters of the students are black, most of them African Americans, but with a sizable minority of recent immigrants from the Caribbean and Africa. Another 11 percent are Hispanic, and 11 percent are Asian, Pacific Islander, or American Indian. About 16 percent of the students qualify for free lunch, and another 8 percent qualify for reduced-price lunch. Between 11 and 20 percent of the students qualify for public assistance.

Unlike many other schools that the New York State Education Department identifies as "similar," Elmont posts very high achievement, with very small achievement gaps among groups of students. It also holds on to its students at much higher rates than schools with similar demographics (its senior class is 83 percent the size of its freshman class), and 100 percent of its seniors graduate, 97 percent then going on to college.

"But we're not aiming our students to go to college," said Elmont's principal, Al Harper. "We're aiming higher than that—we're aiming them at graduating from college." Partly for that reason, Elmont encourages students to take Advanced Placement classes and tests. In fact, The College Board recently recognized Elmont as the high school that gets more African American students taking and passing AP World History (a score of 3 or higher) than any other school in the country (23 students in 2003).

Harper has been principal for three years, but before that he was assistant principal for nine years, and he both has been shaped by and has helped shape the culture of the school—a culture of high expectations where every student is expected to behave well and perform well, and where every teacher is expected to teach well.

At a lunchtime gathering of the school's "cabinet"—the principal, the three assistant principals, and the chairs of the departments—Peter Gaffney, the chair of the athletic department, described the culture of Elmont as follows, to the approbation of his colleagues: "Mr. Harper sets the bar very high for the cabinet; the cabinet sets the bar high for the teachers; and the teachers set the bar high for the kids." Throughout the school, the emphasis is on instruction— instruction by teachers of students and by administrators of teachers.

"I taught in the City for four years and thought I was a pretty good teacher," said eighth-grade English teacher Wendy Tague, who came from teaching in New York City. "But until I came here I had never taught a lesson." She credits the intense system of observations by administrators with helping her become a better teacher. "We're observed seven times a year until tenure, and, once tenured, we observe each other," she said. The observation process is "designed to help the teacher," she said.

That observation process is at the core of what Elmont is about, according not only to Tague, but also to Harper and his cabinet members. Department chairs and assistant principals are responsible for observing lessons and making detailed suggestions for improvement in presentation, questioning techniques, ways to engage students in the lesson, and more. A lesson that has very little to improve is often identified as needing to be taught to another teacher.

Assistant principal John Capozzi called observation the "tool" for instructional growth. "Instruction drives the building," he said. "We talk about it all day." Before observing a teacher, for example, the observer is supposed to look at the previous observation to see what the recommendation for improvement was. "Next time, you want to see an improvement in that area." A common "action plan" for new teachers is to observe other teachers teach a lesson in order to learn new techniques or strategies.

The administrators themselves are also expected to improve their observation techniques—periodically, lessons are videotaped, and administrators all watch the lesson together, then write up their observations at home overnight. They then meet the next day to discuss these observations. This way, the administrators develop insight into other ways to observe and other things to recommend.

Tague said that when she first arrived, she thought that a lesson might consist of introducing a poetic term to a class and giving a few examples from some poems. Now, she said, she knows that she needs to "scaffold learning" by linking back to previous lessons, making sure that each student understands the concept, and giving students multiple opportunities to learn the term and incorporate it in their own writing.

The systematic observation of teachers that Tague credits with helping her improve is one sign that teachers at Elmont are considered to be part of a larger enterprise. They receive a lot of support and encouragement, not punishment. For example, a teacher whose class did less well on the Regents Exams or the Advanced Placement exams than was hoped is not assumed to have done something wrong, according to Harper. "How can you ask someone who has worked her heart out and tried so hard, 'What went wrong?' No, you sit down and say, 'You did really well. Is there something more we can do?'"

"We are all responsible for training our teachers," is the way Eileen Kramer, chair of the music department, put it. George Holub, an eighth-grade science teacher, put it another way: "This school almost has a family atmosphere. A new teacher is taken under somebody's wing."

The school's schedule is built around opportunities for teachers to work together. In the seventh and eighth grades, teachers are teamed in traditional middle school fashion (core subject teachers all share a group of students), and the teams meet every day with a guidance counselor, who is an integral part of the team. Most of the discussion surrounds instruction, but the presence of the guidance counselor means that discussions of individual students can be followed up directly by the counseling department. In addition, the seventh- and eighth-grade teachers "loop" with their students, meaning that the teachers who teach incoming seventh graders move with them to eighth grade the following year and then drop back to seventh grade the following year. This way, the students and teachers develop strong personal and academic bonds that last through the high school years through hallway and after-school encounters.

In the high school grades, teachers meet by department and work on lessons, pacing, and assessments. They do not necessarily teach the same thing at the same time, but they are all aiming at the same goals.

New York has the well-known Regents exams as the marker of whether students achieve academic success. The state established 55 as a sufficient grade to receive a "local" diploma without a Regents endorsement. (For students entering ninth grade after 2000, there is no longer a local diploma.) In 2003, nine students earned a local diploma at Elmont. No students at Elmont received a local diploma in 2004, and 69 percent of them earned a Regents diploma, which means that they passed at least five Regents exams with a score of 65 or above. (Beginning in 2005, all diplomas were required to be Regents diplomas, and the number to watch was "Regents Diplomas with Advanced Designation.")

Even this figure of 69 percent Regents diplomas doesn't tell the full story. On the math exam, 28 percent of the students earned above an 85 in Math A, the math that is required of students. And Elmont has steadily increased the number of students taking Math B, the higher math sequence that leads to pre-calculus or calculus. Of the 86 students who took Math B in 2004, 94 percent scored above a 65, and a full third of the students scored above an 85. In English, 96 percent of the students (including 78 percent of the students with disabilities) scored above 65, and 65 percent scored above 85.

Contrast this with the 2003 performance at the Humanities and the Arts Magnet School (the former Andrew Jackson High School) just down the street in Queens, where only about half of the freshman class graduated within four years, only 23 percent graduated with Regents diplomas, and fewer than a dozen kids scored above 85 in math and English.

The Regents exams provide a focus around which instruction is organized, but teachers at Elmont bristle at the thought that they care only about the Regents scores. "Many classes culminate in Regents exams," said the chair of the English department, Alicia Calabrese. "But many don't. We push our kids to excel in all their classes. If I hear that a student is arriving at gym unprepared or isn't doing well in art, I'll ask him about that."

Teachers can be carefully selected because each opening has an average of 350 applicants. "Teachers have heard about Elmont and want to work here," said Harper. Department chairs sort through the applications and forward perhaps eight to the appropriate assistant principal, who will ask the applicants to teach sample lessons. Two applicants will then be forwarded to the principal, who interviews the finalists to see if they have an "Elmont heart."

"I know they have the content knowledge and the skills," he said, because of the vetting they have already undergone. "I'm looking for intangibles—can they teach with their heart, not their head?" Questions he asks include, for example, what teachers would do if one of their students were struggling, and how the teacher would reach out to the student's parents. Prospective teachers are also forewarned about the intense system of observations and the expectation that everyone is expected to improve. Assistant principal Capozzi said, "Before they ever begin here, we explain this is an ongoing learning experience and it should never stop."

By taking such care with hiring, Elmont is sure to begin with a teaching staff committed to working together, improving instruction, and having high expectations for the students. Even so, teachers new to Elmont are not necessarily ready for all the challenges of teaching in a large, urban high school. Harper told of a second-year teacher who came into his office crying, saying she couldn't stand it anymore and was quitting. "I had the department chair cover her class and we talked for an hour," Harper remembered. "We buddied her up with another teacher, we had the chairperson work with her, we worked on lesson plans with her, we had a number of intensive interventions." Several years later, Harper said, "She is the most improved teacher I have ever seen. Her assessment results this year are through the roof."

That intense kind of commitment produces the kind of social atmosphere where staff members regularly have barbecues and Christmas parties together. During one winter break, toward the end of February 2005, the principal and several staff members with their families—a total of 35 people—traveled together to spend a week at the beach in the Dominican Republic. "People who work together and like each other and have a common goal get together," Harper said. The science department started out having a bagel day once a month, and now they have an elaborate monthly "fete."

When some students at the school wanted to do something to help the victims of the Indian Ocean tsunami, Harper worked with them to put on a Saturday morning pancake breakfast to raise money. One man ladling out the batter was unfamiliar to him. "He was the boyfriend of one of our new teachers. That's the kind of school this is," Harper said.

Teachers chuckled when Harper said, with tongue slightly in cheek, "We have no discipline problems." But they agreed that discipline problems are not a constant plague, as they are in many nearby schools. For the most part, students show up for class and do the work asked of them. Not only that, but many of them are in the school building long after classes end, as part of clubs, playing sports, or getting help from teachers. "We keep our kids very active," said Harper. As an example, any student who wants to play basketball makes the team—the athletic department simply hires more coaches to accommodate the numbers. "We don't cut anyone," the head of the athletic department said. Assistant principal Mary Hannon said, "The child who is involved in music or sports is more successful. It is part and parcel of a full education." Other teachers refer to the full set of afterschool activities as Elmont's "hidden curriculum" and one place where Elmont students develop their intense relationships with the school and their strong sense of belonging and sportsmanship. Harper bragged that other principals often praise his students for their excellent behavior at sporting events.

Capozzi, who handles many of the school's discipline problems, said he is on the constant alert for problems. Some of the kids at Elmont, he said, are "tough" kids. But if a student doesn't respond well to a greeting in the hallway—for example, if he doesn't smile back, or doesn't quickly take off a hat when reminded—Capozzi will invite that child into his office, where he tries to see if there is a problem bothering him or her. Often he will find there is a problem at home or elsewhere, and he is able to deploy a counselor or social worker to help. When one student's family was about to become homeless, the school social worker hooked the family up to county resources to help them stay housed. This kind of intervention could be viewed as the school discipline version of the "broken window" theory of policing, where very small signs of unhappiness or unrest are taken seriously.

New students who are unused to the atmosphere at Elmont, Capozzi said, sometimes "have to be Elmontized" before their behavior is acceptable. "The goal of discipline is to change the behavior," Capozzi said. Elmont has its share of suspensions—257 in 2004. But, Harper said, "I've seen [Capozzi] suspend a student when the student thanks him." Harper attributed that to the respect and concern that Capozzi has, even for students he is suspending. This goes along with what Harper said is his philosophy of discipline: "If you treat that child the way you want your child to be treated, you'll always be right."

Harper and Capozzi gave another example of how this philosophy has worked. A football player who had graduated from Elmont several years ago and was about to graduate from Lehigh University with a degree in engineering at one time almost had to give up football at Elmont because he needed to watch his younger sister during the afternoons. "All we did was let him leave and get his sister, who sat and did her homework in the end zone," Capozzi said. "After a while, we had a day care in the end zone," because other players had the same issue, and volunteer high school tutors helped the younger children with their assignments.

"You've got to do everything to help every single student," said Capozzi. "We don't have discipline issues because [students] are focused on achievement," said Harper. Harper, Capozzi, and the others at Elmont know that the stakes are high for today's high school students. They need a good education, and Elmont is where they need to get it. Thus, expectations are extremely high for students.

"We push our kids to excel," said English department chair Calabrese. "When you believe they can do that, they rise to the challenge." It is the culture of high expectations that makes a difference, according to the head of the math department, Anthony Murray, who taught for years in the New York City system. "The kids are the same wherever you go," he said. "But the expectations are different."

Those expectations are clear in the classrooms. But it isn't just about expectations—it is about careful instruction to meet those expectations. In a twelfth-grade Advanced Placement English composition class, for example, Pat O'Leary told her students about a reading passage from Cormac McCarthy's *The Crossing* that had been used in a previous Advanced Placement exam. "This is a challenging piece," she told the class. "You're up to the challenge." She then gave the students time to read and discuss the piece in small groups, as she traveled among the groups gathering comments and insights that she shared with the class, leading the students to deeper understandings of the text.

In an eleventh-grade "core" class (Elmont has two levels of classes—core, or Regents, and advanced, which includes the Advanced Placement classes), teacher Kevin Sullivan led students through a reading of *Macbeth*. Sullivan asked different students to read different parts, and he took on the part of the Third Witch. It was the scene in which the witches first see Macbeth and Macduff and make their acid observations and predictions. Every few sentences, Sullivan stopped to scaffold the learning for students. "Let's break that down," he said, or "I want to paraphrase that," or "Let's tap into social studies—what's treason?"

About the line "Lesser than Macbeth and greater," Sullivan asked, "How can someone be lesser than Macbeth and greater?" One student, slouching and mumbling slightly, said, "He might have a lesser title or position, but might be a better man." "That's brilliant," Sullivan said, applauding the concision and precision of thought the student had displayed. This particular class had taken the Regents exam earlier in the year, and 92 percent passed, 52 percent at the "mastery" level—that is, with a score of 85 or above.

Most classrooms at Elmont are equipped with projectors, which permit teachers to show short video clips, documents, or artwork, resources often found by the school librarian, who helps teachers find interesting materials that illustrate their lessons. To enliven his presentation, Sullivan used a projector that projects images loaded onto the computer to show students paintings of the three witches by different artists with different ideas of what they looked like. The students gasped at the hideous bearded images.

In a tenth-grade chemistry class, Michelle Seeley taught a lesson about the behavior of ideal gases by comparing them to "ideal boyfriends," ensuring that students understood that under some circumstances (low pressure in the case of gases, being in the presence of parents in the case of boyfriends), gases and boyfriends are more likely to behave in an ideal fashion. Although seemingly frivolous, the comparison made for a vivid mnemonic device.

In Michael Indovino's Advanced Placement World History class (the class that during the previous year had achieved College Board notoriety), Indovino linked a discussion of the kitchen debate between Richard Nixon and Nikita

Khrushchev back to previous lessons about Stalin, the USSR, Castro, and the Spanish-American War before he read aloud part of the debate, explaining any word that he thought might cause problems in understanding.

Walking through the halls and glancing into classrooms revealed lively instruction going on all through the school. When asked what makes the difference at Elmont, Harper credited school system unity, including a supportive school board and superintendent. He also credited the teachers and his administrative staff, and the students themselves. "It's not magic," he said. "It's hard work."

A product of the New York City school system (Andrew Jackson High School, just blocks away from Elmont) with degrees from Howard University, Adelphi University, the Graduate Center of the City University of New York, and St. John's University, Harper is passionate about the need to make sure all kids get a good education and the need to make changes in the way children are now educated.

"You can change it, you must change it," Harper said, dismissing all talk of the difficulties of getting poor children to meet high standards. "Because a child is poor doesn't mean he can't learn. Because a child lives in the projects doesn't mean he can't learn. If there are gaps, we as a society must fill those gaps."

He knows that many teachers around the country have become discouraged and will often blame kids for low performance. "If you say 'the kids, the kids, the kids,' you'll be there forever. We know that kids who are failing are not doing their work. We know they're not coming for extra help. We know that. That's a given. But what are we doing instructionally in the classroom, what are we doing to make sure the kids are learning? If you have good teachers doing good, exciting instruction, kids will learn."

And, he added, if a teacher doesn't believe all children can learn, "He should be in a different business. He should work for IBM or another big company. He shouldn't be a teacher."

Although he thinks that the federal No Child Left Behind Act should have been backed up with more funding and better training, he does not dismiss it as unrealistic. And he has little patience for those who argue that schools cannot be expected to make up for the deficits that poverty and discrimination cause. By accepting that argument, he said, "As a country we [would be] condemning a whole group of people to not getting an education. We [would be] condemning our black and Hispanic youth to menial jobs—at best—and to never attaining the American dream."

POSTSCRIPT

At the end of 2004, Al Harper became superintendent of the elementary school district that feeds into Elmont Memorial Junior-Senior High School (Elmont is one of the few places left that have separate school districts for elementary and secondary schools). Just as when I heard that the principal of Frankford Elementary had retired, my heart sank when I heard that Harper had left. I felt much better when I learned that former assistant principal John Capozzi had replaced him as principal. That fall, Capozzi led a team of teachers and administrators at The Education Trust's national conference, and he argued forcibly that Elmont's improvement isn't just about a single person, but about all the systems that are in place to keep Elmont moving forward. The close collaborations among teachers, the careful attention to classroom instruction, and the setting of incremental goals, year by year, are what make the difference at Elmont, he said. He was the third principal since Elmont had begun its improvement process, and he said improvement would continue. The 2005 test scores bore him out. Unfortunately, New York is rather dilatory in publishing test results, and the 2006 scores were not officially published at the time of writing. However, Capozzi said that, when published, the 2006 data would show that 99 percent of the senior class graduated and 96 percent went to college. More than 90 percent of the students earned a Regents diploma, and the percentage of students earning an advanced Regents diploma increased from 31 percent in 2005 to 41 percent in 2006. "That's huge," Capozzi said. His goal for the 2006–07 school year was for 50 percent of students to earn an advanced Regents diploma. One of the requirements for the advanced diploma is passing Math B. "That's where we are really closing the achievement gap," Capozzi said. "If you look at other minority schools, they're not close to it. But I don't want to be compared to minority schools, but all schools."

In the fall of 2006, Capozzi was still waiting for the test scores from the seventh- and eighth-grade assessments in English language arts and math, but he said that in science, 86 percent of students had met or exceeded standards, which he was very pleased with, and that in social studies, 70 percent had done so. "We have to look at that. We have to break down the data and see where our weaknesses are." He went on to say, "Our first goal is to improve academic achievement. Our second goal is to create an atmosphere of civility and respect. Our third goal is to get the good word out. I'm tired of having people keep saying we can't succeed."

LINCOLN ELEMENTARY SCHOOL
MOUNT VERNON, NEW YORK

INTRODUCTION

I had been hearing about Lincoln Elementary School for a couple of years—it had been identified by The Education Trust as a "Dispelling the Myth" school in 2003, and television journalist John Merrow had visited it and broadcast a story about it. Its principal, George Albano, almost cannot stop talking about Lincoln and how wonderful it is, and frankly, I just didn't think it could be that good.

I was wrong. It is a wonderful place for children. Its building is odd—it looks like a huge brick box on stilts, so that its play area is underneath the school— but what goes on in there is astounding, from the music instruction, to the reading and writing instruction, to the amazing emphasis on chess, music, and art. I sat through a second-grade class where it became clear to me that the students knew more about writing than I did when I was a graduate student in journalism school.

Albano argues that by allowing urban schools to deteriorate, the nation has allowed its cities to deteriorate, thereby exacerbating suburban and exurban sprawl and the attendant environmental problems they have brought. If urban schools were reliably good, he says, more middle-class families would stay in cities, and our schools would be much more integrated—economically as well as ethnically.

He further argues that one of the most important contributors to urban educational decline is the fact that most principals are terribly trained and often don't even know how to organize supplies and schedules, much less how to support high-level instruction that incorporates the arts. Because principals do not properly support teachers, he says, the nation loses good teachers every day. Certainly statistics back him up. Many idealistic young people who want

LINCOLN ELEMENTARY SCHOOL
MOUNT VERNON, NEW YORK

2005 Enrollment: 744 students in kindergarten through sixth grade
2005 Demographics: 47% African American
                          26% Latino
                          25% White
                          58% meet qualifications for free and reduced-price lunch
Locale: Urban-Suburban

Grade 4 English Language Arts, 2005
New York State Testing Program

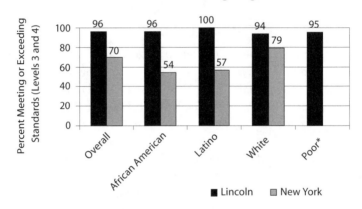

Grade 4 Math, 2005
New York State Testing Program

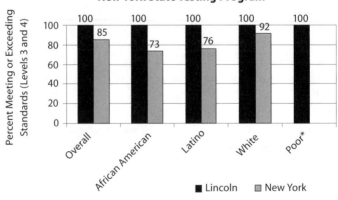

* Could not determine New York State results for poor students.

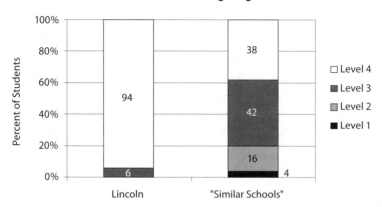

Grade 4 Science, 2005
New York State Testing Program

Source: New York State Report Card, http://www.emsc.nysed.gov/irts/reportcard/

Note: New York State Education Department defines the levels as follows:
Level 1: Serious academic deficiencies
Level 2: Needs extra help to meet standards
Level 3: Meets standards
Level 4: Exceeds standards

"Similar schools" are schools with similar demographics to Lincoln as defined by the New York State Education Department.

to teach poor children and children of color spend one or two years in one of the country's dysfunctional poor-kid schools and then leave, sometimes saying things like, "You couldn't pay me enough to work here one more year."

Lincoln is a powerful example of how schools organized to make sure all students learn could help turn around our cities and make them once again places where middle-class families would want to raise their children.

· · · · ·

L incoln Elementary School in Mount Vernon, New York, has become so used to performing toward the top of the state that its performance hardly seems remarkable anymore. When the preliminary results from the 2005 state English language arts test showed that all but one of the fourth-grade students scored at or above state standards, the staff was pleased, but their only surprise was about the student who did not score well. "I know he can do the work; I guess he just had a bad day," said his teacher, Mary Anderson. Some years—such as 2004—no one has a bad day, and Lincoln posts 100 percent of students meeting or exceeding state standards.

Few people expect schools like Lincoln to perform at such a high level. A large school, it has 800 or so students; when I visited, 43 percent were African American and 21 percent Latino. In 2005, 41 percent of the children received free lunch, and another 11 percent received reduced-price lunch. Twenty-seven percent of the children—more than 200—have limited English proficiency. The most common language among non-English speakers is Brazilian Portuguese, but students also speak Spanish, Korean, Russian, French, Haitian Creole, and Chinese.

And yet, Lincoln performs comparably to much wealthier schools in Westchester County. It has a much higher percentage of students meeting and exceeding state standards than do schools identified by New York State as demographically similar. At those schools, only 57 percent of students meet or exceed state standards, in comparison with students at Lincoln, whose passage rates fluctuate from 95 to 100 percent. In science, 82 percent of Lincoln students don't just meet state standards but exceed them (in comparison with 32 percent of the students in similar schools).

Lincoln's performance on state tests is just the beginning. Performance in chess matches is just as valued—chess trophies stack up at the entrance to the school, a mark of the many competitions students win. Art fills the first-floor hallways, and so does the sound of classical music. Students love to show off their reading and writing, which is posted throughout the school, and they enjoy playing a version of stump-the-guest with difficult vocabulary words. At the school's science fair, projects range from the usual elementary school plant-growing projects to much more sophisticated engineering projects demonstrating the feasibility of magnetic transportation and molecular separation.

Ask the teachers what makes Lincoln special, and they say the principal. Ask the principal, George Albano, and he says that he manages the school in such a way that teachers can do their best. "I didn't think I was doing anything out of the ordinary," Albano said. "I thought most American schools operated this way." But when test scores began to be published in 1999 and Lincoln began outperforming many other schools (even including much wealthier ones), Albano realized that his school was, in fact, out of the ordinary. And he is convinced that the reason other schools do not match the performance of Lincoln is simply poor management, a problem that could be solved with better training of school leaders. "The teaching force is there," he said. And, he added, today's teachers are often better trained than he was at the beginning of his career. He boasted that he has no trouble finding excellent teachers, though he acknowledged that the school's being an easy train ride from New York City has helped. But, he said, poor management drives so many teachers out of the profession that it appears the nation has a teaching shortage, when in fact the real shortage is in skilled principals.

As Exhibit A, he produced fifth-grade teacher Hilary Harness. Harness began teaching after college as part of the New York City Teaching Fellow program, which recruits new teachers. Her assignment was to teach special education in a school in the South Bronx.

"It was a terrible experience," she said. The school, she added, was badly managed, meaning that among other things, discipline was a serious issue. "It wasn't a healthy environment. I was called all kinds of names that I wouldn't repeat in this school—and it was accepted." Disruptive students knew they wouldn't be called to account for their behavior. "When I got to teach, I loved it. But I didn't get the opportunity to teach much." She was on her own, with little support from other teachers or administrators. "I asked my principal for a reading program," she said, because her students needed phonics instruction. She said that he said no "because it didn't matter—they're special ed." She also kept asking for books and materials, which were never provided. "The principal would literally hide from me when I brought my class into the hallway."

She was ready to quit her dream of teaching and go to law school, but she thought she would give it one more try. She had heard that Lincoln was different, and she visited, interviewed, and was hired. "After the first three days I felt that there's no way I'd leave here." She now plans to teach long enough to retire from the profession. "The kids are basically the same," she said, comparing Lincoln with her old school. "But it's the administration. One of my [former] principal's favorite things was to tell us what bad teachers we were. Mr. Albano tells us what a great job we're doing, and he has an incredible mentoring program that tells us the direction to go in." For his part, Albano pointed to Harness as an example of an excellent teacher who was almost "lost to the profession" because of poor managerial practices.

When Albano first arrived at Lincoln, 26 years ago, it was to clean up a mess. A desegregation order had quickly changed the demographics of the school. The new building had been open for only three weeks when African American students were bused to the previously all-white school, and white families began fleeing to the private school next door. The private school "went from having 13 in their classes to having 43 students in their classes—practically overnight," said Albano. "The black families didn't feel welcome. But [the white families] weren't fleeing from integration. They were fleeing chaos." Discipline was a serious problem, and very little teaching was going on, Albano said.

Albano, who had taught U.S. and world history in high school for seven years, was already an experienced principal. He had served as a principal in a middle-class black school and then in an inner-city black school. He wasn't eager to take on such a chaotic situation as Lincoln, but the school is only two blocks from the house where he was born and continues to live, and he agreed to accept the challenge.

Built in the 1970s, the school has a design that contributed to the chaos. Except for the kindergarten, almost all of the classrooms are open classrooms—with small alcoves opening onto common areas. "Teachers were always shouting to be heard, and the noise was terrible," Albano said. He began playing quiet classical music throughout the building and told teachers and the students that if they couldn't hear the music, they were speaking too loudly. He spent the first year dealing with discipline. "We developed a zero tolerance for disrespect," Albano said. And that works both ways—teacher-to-student as well as student-to-teacher disrespect. Early on, nine teachers transferred. "They left," Albano said. "I've never fired a teacher." Now the atmosphere is one of courtesy and respect. Students say please, thank you, and excuse me, and are eager to show teachers and administrators their latest project or paper; teachers greet children by name and with affection and interest.

Although graffiti appears on the school building perhaps once a week, it doesn't last a day—building maintenance takes care of it immediately, so that from the outside the school looks orderly. Inside, the walls are unscuffed, and the hallways and classrooms are free of debris. Albano said there haven't been any thefts in years. The biggest discipline problem he has faced recently came when an elderly neighbor came in to complain that he had almost been hit by an industrial-sized roll of toilet paper that had been thrown from a bathroom window a couple of stories up. After investigating, Albano found the culprit and, when he talked with him, found that the boy had the night before learned that his parents were getting divorced. "I gave him community service, and so forth," Albano said, but more importantly, he was able to refer the child to a counselor for help.

When he arrived, Albano immediately established a policy that report cards must be picked up by a parent or guardian, in order to establish a home-school connection. The first year, he said, only 40 percent of the report cards were picked up. Teachers called home, and Spanish-speaking parents and staff called the Spanish-speaking families to remind them. After a while, it became part of the school's culture, and now just about all report cards are picked up. Some parents were unhappy initially, but Albano eventually convinced them that it was not difficult to stop by the school. "I'm here at seven in the morning, and I'll meet a parent as late as ten o'clock if they need it," he said.

Parents and guardians are deliberately incorporated into the life of the school whenever possible, but in such a way that all can participate. For example, writing projects are completed in school, but they are often illustrated at home, where parents can help. Students and parents work on changing the extensive hallway displays every week—and parents who can't come in to help cut out letters at home. "We have wonderful parents who don't have a lot of means . . . but they want to give back," said Albano.

Many schools with demographics similar to Lincoln's are not calm, well-ordered, and high-achieving places where parents participate regularly. Albano said bad management is often to blame—sometimes monumentally bad management. He told the story of a school in which he was assistant principal. He walked in to complaints that there was vastly insufficient money for supplies. His first step was to inventory what was in the building. "There were 900 gallons of ditto fluid sitting next to the furnace room. The place was a time bomb." The previous principal, he found, had simply submitted the same supply request year after year without ever reviewing or changing it. After donating ditto fluid to every school in the area, Albano quickly got control of the supply issue. At the same school, he found that textbook distribution was a job given to the building maintenance people. "You had first graders with fourth-grade books and fourth graders with second-grade books, et cetera." He immediately straightened that out. At Lincoln, schoolwide curriculum committees work together to select materials, and then each teacher puts in an order for books and supplies before the end of the year; when they arrive back before school starts, the books and supplies are waiting for them in their classrooms.

But managing a school isn't just about books and supplies. Albano's key management strategy is hiring good teachers and then keeping them. "We select the best in the profession and then retain them," Albano said. He was able to bring a few teachers with him, including Diana Messisco, who is now the reading specialist, and fourth-grade teacher Mary Anderson, who is now 75. "My accountant tells me it costs me $8,000 a year to keep working," she said. For a few years, Albano had opera singer Dana Bhatnagar teach music, until she moved to Colorado to continue her music career and get married. Now the music teacher is Fred Motley, who among other things leads the jazz band at St. John's University and the pep band at Hofstra University. "I've taught for 31 years," Motley said. "[Albano] cares about every aspect of the school from graffiti to the arts. . . . He creates an environment where I can teach—I've been in schools where I'm a policeman for 95 percent of the time."

Teachers in the Mount Vernon district make less than teachers elsewhere in Westchester—sometimes as much as 20 percent less. But, Albano said, he is able to retain them because they "know they're appreciated and part of something special." The way Anderson put it is that Albano gets 50 teachers to feel that "the best time of their life is spent here."

Albano looks for skill and potential everywhere. For example, one day office manager Veronica Schaeffer (who was lured from a corporate administrative job) told Albano that an unemployed father who brought his children to school every day had been, until he was laid off, a NASA contractor. Albano hired him as a lunchroom aide and arranged for him to enroll in Fordham University's two-year master's program. Under that program, he received master of education courses for free and a stipend of $300 a month. When he was done, he got a job at Lincoln, where he leads the science education program. His influence can be seen in the heavy emphasis on engineering projects in the science fair.

Although Albano is bound by district hiring rules, he has few applicants from within the district. Instead, he solicits resumes from all over. Coming from a family of educators (18 members of his extended family teach in the New York area), he has connections throughout the region. But he is not the only one involved in hiring decisions. Teaching applicants meet with a committee of teachers and parents and teach a model lesson in front of a classroom of children and five adults from the school before they're hired.

"Then we have to give them support," Albano said. "New, insecure teachers" need a lot of support, he adds. For example, a new teacher just out of school was paired with reading specialist Messisco. "I mentored [her] two hours a day, every day," said Messisco. "She's very bright and capable, but she didn't know the curriculum."

Teachers feel supported in lots of different ways. Although teachers work hard, veteran fifth-grade teacher Jim LeRay said, "the burnout issue doesn't arise" because of the good management of the school. "The reason you don't burn out is the frustrations aren't there. When you have a discipline problem, a supply issue, a furnace issue—that burns you out." In addition, Lincoln provides a family atmosphere for its staff. "I was in the hospital for gall bladder," said teacher Esther Ehrman. "The first person who called was Mr. Albano." Albano encourages monthly staff breakfasts in the auditorium. Each grade level takes a turn arranging the room and ordering the food.

Albano, in other words, has created a school in which teachers feel comfortable both in teaching and in learning to be better teachers. Seventy-five-year-old Anderson said, "I was not as good a teacher with four other principals." Part of that is the fact that Albano encourages teachers to take risks. For example, Anderson felt strongly that there should be a chess program in the school, to give the children some intellectual excitement and a new field to conquer. Her husband volunteered to be the sponsor of a chess club. The club proved popular, and chess is now a cornerstone experience of the school. When a wealthy businessman wanted to make a donation to the school, Albano told him instead to donate to the National Scholastic Chess Federation with direction that the money be used to send chess masters to teach chess. Now, twice a week, Lincoln students receive classroom instruction in chess by chess masters using felt boards and pieces hanging in front of the classrooms. All students learn the fundamental principles and learn how to notate games. If they want to pursue the subject further, they join the chess club. Anderson bragged about the kindergartner who beat a wealthy Westchester County child who had "two personal chess coaches."

That story also illustrates how Albano pulls in resources in addition to the $13,807 per student the school receives from local, state, and federal sources. Although that amount sounds high in comparison to the money received by many schools in the country, it is considerably lower than the funds available to many other schools in Westchester County. Nearby Bronxville Elementary, for example, spends $19,711 per child per year. In any case, Albano is constantly looking for "ways to close the opportunity gap." He welcomes volunteers and has several working and retired professionals read to kids, play chess with kids, and have lunch with kids. When a local, exclusive private school was replacing its computers, someone from the school called to see if Lincoln wanted its old computers. The question was treated as an immediate call to action, with office manager Schaeffer and the building computer technician jumping in cars and renting a truck to move the computers. As a result, Lincoln now has an iMac computer lab. Albano writes to people out of the blue asking them to visit, and Lincoln has hosted actress Phylicia Rashad, author-illustrator Jerry Pinkney, and mystery writer Carol Higgins Clark.

But at the heart of what Lincoln does is classroom instruction, which is very carefully and thoughtfully built. It begins with reading. "We have a comprehensive, balanced reading program," said reading specialist Diana Messisco. In order to make sure no element of reading is left out, all the early reading teachers use a common curriculum supplemented by a wide selection of quality trade books. Great emphasis is placed on reading aloud, shared reading, and guided reading. "What makes us special is fostering a love of reading," Messisco said.

In addition to the daily emphasis on reading, the school sponsors all kinds of reading events, including a track-and-field day with contests that include children racing with books on their heads. "Hats Off to Reading Day" means that students wear hats of book characters. The Reading Is Fundamental organization provides books, and Lincoln holds regular book swaps for students. The PTA sponsors a picnic with blankets to sit on while children read. One year "VIP Reading Day" featured the custodian and the physical education teacher reading books to the children. "It didn't cost us a dime," said Albano. In addition, every classroom has a set of "books-in-a-bag," which consist of large sealed plastic bags, each containing a book and a worksheet with some kind of activity—a short character study, for example—to be taken home and completed every week. Teachers select books that are above, below, and on grade level; if the book is above the child's ability to read, the child is expected to find a grown-up to read it to him or her. Teachers are able to take quick stock of children's reading and comprehension from the activities, which are kept in a folder. Every time a child finishes a book, he or she is entitled to a sticker from the principal.

Reading is just the beginning, however. Writing is also carefully and systematically taught, and with just as much enthusiasm. Student writing is posted throughout the school, and the first thing a visitor notices is the handwriting. Papers are uniformly neat and legible, pointing to careful instruction in handwriting. "Everything is important," said Albano. "Spelling is important, handwriting is important, grammar, et cetera."

But it is also clear that great attention is paid to the content of writing. A few minutes in Lucille DiRuocco's second-grade classroom showed the level of instruction.

"When we write, we want our stories to be interesting. We say we want them to be 'juicy.' What makes a story juicy?" DiRuocco asked her class. The first student she called on, James, said, "We need a grabber. For example, dialogue, which is conversation between two people."

And then Jonathan: "Action—it's when you are doing something, like diving."

Camille: "You can use thoughts and feelings. For example, 'When I was outside I was thinking, What is that creature?'"

Sabrina: "Sound effects. For example, 'Splash! as I dove headfirst into the crystal-clear water.'"

Evan: "A question. For example, 'Where's Papa going with that ax?'" (This last is an example from *Charlotte's Web*, a favorite book at Lincoln, in part because its author, E. B. White, graduated from there.)

"What else do we have to put in our story to make it good, to make it juicy, to make it interesting?" asked DiRuocco, and a student answered, "A simile—a simile is when you put 'like' or 'as' in the middle of a sentence and compare two words. For example, 'My dad looks as brilliant as a diamond.'"

DiRuocco recognized that line from an essay the students had written about a special person. "When we wrote about a special person we used sense words," she reminded the students, asking for an example.

Yasmin: "My dad sounds calm like the sea."

DiRuocco: "Oh! Isn't that beautiful? That's a special person who sounds calm like the sea. You can get a real picture from that, can't you? That sounds better than 'My dad has a nice voice.'"

When students enter her second grade, DiRuocco said, "they don't know how to indent paragraphs." But toward the end of the year, they are entering into sophisticated discussions of how to write effectively. And student work posted all over the building shows the effects of such careful instruction.

Creativity is constantly encouraged and developed, but it is built on a solid base of knowledge. DiRuocco said, "Facts have to be memorized." Making flash cards—gluing paper onto both sides of a cut-up cereal box, for example—is a frequent homework assignment that can be done with family members. Time (analog and digital clock faces), addition facts, multiplication facts, and spelling words are all possible flash-card content. One student demonstrated the way students at Lincoln memorize facts. "We say the fact three times and then we close our eyes and we have to push it in three times" (with a hand gesture that shows him "pushing" the fact into his head).

Each student at Lincoln has a creative writing folder, a math folder, and a science folder (with a minimum of four experiments written up each quarter in the different areas of science—earth, physical, and life) that follow him or her through school and that are reviewed regularly by the teachers and by Albano. But students also monitor their own work using rubrics developed by the teachers, so they know before a teacher ever reviews it what standards the work is supposed to meet and whether it meets that standard.

Every aspect of the curriculum gets this kind of care. "Nothing is left to chance," said assistant principal Lyuba Sesay. Teachers meet regularly in grade levels and across grade levels to work on what will be taught when. Once a month, for example, they have a "science day" to plan the month's worth of science lessons. Classroom and teacher schedules are carefully choreographed to make sure that teachers get the time they need to meet to make sure children are getting the instruction *they* need. Instruction is not constantly interrupted. The teachers and administrators work hard to schedule all special services—counseling, occupational therapy, speech therapy, music lessons, and so forth—in such a way that teachers have their full classes at least 85 percent of the time.

Some of the instruction, certainly, is focused on preparing for the tests given by New York State. But the popular notion of a school doing mind-numbing "test prep" and "drill and kill" focused narrowly on the tested subjects doesn't describe Lincoln. "Test preparation doesn't have to be boring," Albano said. "What is chess? Critical thinking. What is music? Listening skills." Mock fossil digs teach students about geography, geology, and evolution. Spanish lessons once a week in kindergarten through sixth grade, provided by a special grant, give English speakers knowledge of a second language. Art and music lessons give students a sense of aesthetics and a way to be successful even before they learn English. "We had a student who spoke only Russian. We captured him with music and the arts," Albano said. "Then his academics flourished. Two years later he received a perfect score on the New York State English language arts assessment."

Instruction is provided by 34 classroom teachers supplemented by 5 teachers of English as a second language, 14 special education paraprofessionals, and 5 special education teachers, a resource specialist, and a reading teacher, all of whom work with classroom teachers to provide services as part of general instruction. Students are not pulled out of classrooms for these services. Instead, the services are "pushed in" to the classrooms. (The exception is that Lincoln has a special program of three classrooms for 24 students with autism.)

Toward the end of the year, Albano sits down with each teacher to discuss every child's progress. Out of 130 children in each grade level, two or three are usually held back each year—less than half the retention rate Albano started with. Albano doesn't take holding a child back lightly, but he also doesn't see it as a tragedy. "I was held back the year my father died," he said. "It was the best thing that happened to me." Sometimes, he argued, children simply need another year of intensive instruction and help before moving to the next grade.

Albano and all the members of his staff are passionate about their mission—to educate all their students and to demonstrate that well-run schools with enthusiastic, knowledgeable teachers are not only possible but necessary in order to give today's children a chance to succeed and thrive. "We can't give up on a generation of children," Albano said.

And the families of Mount Vernon seem to understand what Lincoln can do for their children; the private school next door that was booming in the late 1970s has since closed. Lincoln rents the space as its annex.

POSTSCRIPT

During the summer of 2006, Lincoln received its scores on the state science test, which is scored on a 1–4 scale, with 3 being *meets standards* and 4 *exceeds standards*. Principal Albano said, "We had 75 children who took the New York science exam, which includes hands-on experiments, not just answering [multiple choice] questions. All 75 scored at 3 or 4, with 73 scoring at a high 4. We're still waiting for ELA and math, but I know they will be between 95 and 100 percent." Late in 2006, Lincoln received a National Blue Ribbon School award.

DAYTON'S BLUFF ACHIEVEMENT PLUS
ELEMENTARY SCHOOL

ST. PAUL, MINNESOTA

INTRODUCTION

*A friend of mine is a teacher in St. Paul, Minnesota, and I told her about this
project to identify and describe schools succeeding against great challenges. She
told me I should look at the school at which she then taught dance. I politely
agreed but promptly forgot about it. She didn't understand the high standards
I had for schools, I thought. A couple of months later I finally got around to
checking her school's data, and they were startling. They showed a growth trajectory that looked almost exponential. The school had gone from being one of
the worst in the city to being just a regular school in the state, somewhat on the
high end of student achievement in math.*

*When I got to Dayton's Bluff, I found a very tired principal. He had been
there for five years and had taken the school from "the wild, wild West," in
his phrase, to a calm, ordered, purposeful school where most children were
learning to high standards. Most of the kids were either African American or
Hmong, refugees from the mountainous regions of Laos who had never had a
written language until coming to the United States. In general, both African
Americans and Hmong have very low achievement in Minnesota, which has
among the nation's biggest achievement gaps. And yet at Dayton's Bluff, they
were doing well.*

*Dayton's Bluff demonstrates the power that a comprehensive school reform
model can have in helping a school improve. America's Choice, which was developed by the National Center for Education and the Economy, is one of quite
a few programs that have been developed to provide coherent standards, curriculum, and teacher training. When a school is as disordered and chaotic as*

DAYTON'S BLUFF ACHIEVEMENT PLUS ELEMENTARY SCHOOL
ST. PAUL, MINNESOTA

2005 Enrollment: 312 students in kindergarten through sixth grade
2005 Demographics: 48% African American
                          21% Asian (mostly Hmong)
                          14% Latino
                          15% White
                          92% meet qualifications for free and reduced-price lunch
Locale: Urban

Grade 5 Math
Minnesota Comprehensive Assessments (MCA)

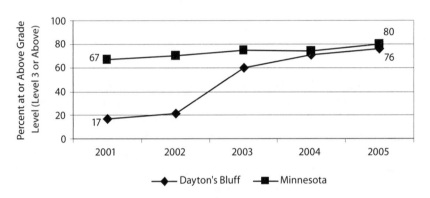

Dayton's Bluff was, a well-thought-through program like America's Choice can be extremely helpful.

My visit to Dayton's Bluff was the beginning of my changing view of principals. I had long been wary of what I called the "P.E. teacher with a flair for administration" who characterizes much of our nation's principal corps. But that is essentially what this principal, Von Sheppard, was, and he had achieved amazing results. I began to appreciate the way coaches approach issues by looking to improve potential by developing skill and motivating their team members—and by stealing any good idea they can from another team.

• • • • •

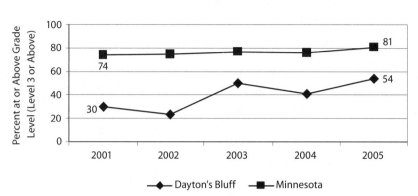

Grade 5 Reading
Minnesota Comprehensive Assessments (MCA)

Source: http://education.state.mn.us/ReportCard2005

n 2000, Dayton's Bluff was known as the worst school in St. Paul and one of the worst in Minnesota. Located on the eastern side of the city, surrounded by a neighborhood of wood-frame houses where the occasional crack house is easily spotted and two murders were reported in two weeks, nine out of ten children could not read on grade level.

"The school was in chaos" is the way Paul Wahmanholm put it. Wahmanholm, who then taught English to students who spoke other languages and later became the school's literacy coach, said that in the mornings little was taught or learned, but in the afternoons—after children came in from the melee of lunch and recess—nothing was taught or learned. Teacher turnover more than matched the high mobility of the children—most years, half the teachers left, and many never even finished a full year.

One of Wahmanholm's colleagues, Marilyn Wojtasiak, said that for the most part, teachers believed they couldn't teach much to the students. Most teachers would excuse students' low performance by saying that they came from families with little education or money. They would often say about the students, "They just need love," she remembered.

Today the school is very different. In 2004, more than eight of ten students at Dayton's Bluff met or exceeded the state reading standards, and the school was poised to post even higher gains for 2005. Classrooms are calm, students work hard, and, in 2005, no teacher left to teach at another St. Paul school. Perhaps most striking is that in math, Dayton's Bluff's third graders—who are mostly poor African American and Hmong children—met state standards at a slightly higher rate than white Minnesotan children did.

To understand the significance of Dayton's Bluff's success, it is helpful to know that white Minnesotan elementary school students outscore white children in the rest of the nation in math. But African American children in Minnesota lag behind not only white Minnesotans but also behind many African American children in the country. (For example, in 2003, 80.6 percent of white third graders in Minnesota met or exceeded state standards; only 44 percent of black third graders did.) It is also helpful to keep in mind that Hmong students—refugees from the mountain regions of Asia, mostly Laos—are among the lowest-performing groups in St. Paul.

Dayton's Bluff, in other words, is proving that students who do terribly elsewhere can achieve academic success. Not only that: It also demonstrates that a school's improvement can be both rapid and sustained; line charts of Dayton's Bluff's progress on test scores look almost exponential, with no significant change in the student demographic makeup.

"It is so important to dispel the myth that these children can't learn to high standards," said the principal, Von Sheppard. "There's a belief system out there that they're not as smart as white kids," he said about African American and Hmong students. "We're on a mission to conquer every myth and every test."

Dayton's Bluff's dramatic turnaround can be attributed to many factors, among them a new principal, an overhaul of the teaching staff, a new instructional design, a district program for high-poverty schools that provides community services, and an almost single-minded focus on instruction and data. But as important as all of those elements were, none made the top of the principal's list. "The first things I had to change," said Sheppard, "were the atmosphere and the expectations."

Sheppard was assigned as principal to Dayton's Bluff, a K–6 school with about 360 students, in 2001. With no elementary school experience—he had most recently been an assistant principal at a high school in St. Paul—he was a nontraditional choice by the relatively new (since 1999) superintendent, Patricia Harvey. Harvey, the former accountability director for the Chicago public schools, had come to St. Paul with the express intent of raising achievement levels of all students and closing achievement gaps. Early on she focused on Dayton's Bluff, along with a handful of other schools, as needing her close attention, and Sheppard credited her support, along with that of Chief Academic Officer Maria Lamb, as crucial to Dayton's Bluff's success.

Sheppard had been a star football player in high school and was recruited by more than 100 colleges. Considered one of the best football players ever to come out of Minnesota, he chose to play for the highly regarded University of Nebraska, where he played wingback—the pivotal running position in the Nebraska formation. Although he signed with the Minnesota Vikings, injuries prevented him from playing, and he ended his football career in Europe, followed by coaching some college ball and his son's football team.

Football provided Sheppard with an ethos of "no excuses," he said. You win or you lose. If you lose, you have to figure out why and fix the problem or face losing again. Complaining about a muddy field or an icy wind isn't acceptable. The game also helped him develop a sense of organizational structure—of separate, specialized teams all working toward the same goal—that he was able to put into practice at Dayton's Bluff, as well as a feeling for how coaches get the best performance from their players.

But he had never before worked with young children. "I was scared to death," he remembered. He was used to hardened older kids, not little kids who wanted to give him a hug. He was also coming in to a largely new staff. Because the school had been acknowledged by all parties to be in dire straits, school officials had negotiated with the teachers union to add ten days of professional development for teachers at Dayton's Bluff, which meant that the jobs could be reposted. Teachers who wanted to stay had to apply for their jobs. The rest were guaranteed jobs elsewhere in the system. Only about one-third of the teachers were rehired by the central office. The rest of the staff were a mixture of veterans from other schools and brand-new teachers straight out of college and ready to be trained. They had all agreed to work the extra days, which were devoted to professional development and shared planning, and to work with the instructional design chosen for the school, America's Choice school design.

The previous year, Harvey had given the school the choice of several comprehensive school reforms to adopt, and the teachers at Dayton's Bluff had chosen America's Choice, which was developed by the National Center for Education and the Economy. The way America's Choice works is that schools adopt the NCEE's "New Standards"—which are aligned with but more rigorous than Minnesota standards—and assign at least two coaches, a design coach and a literacy coach, to work with teachers on organizing their classrooms. America's Choice classrooms are built on a workshop model, in which teachers present ten-minute, very focused mini lessons and then lead students in independent and group work and a classroom-wide sharing of results, all geared to the standards.

The literacy coach is supposed to recruit one teacher and turn his or her classroom into a model, which—in theory—will then be emulated by other teachers. Marilyn Wojtasiak, who was the literacy coach and is now the design coach, and current literacy coach Wahmanholm said that although they tried to implement the model classroom as designed, they were unable to. Almost as soon as a teacher was trained, he or she would leave, meaning that at the end of one year's implementation, hardly any improvement could be discerned. They decided that for the following year they would implement the design schoolwide—all teachers would get trained at the same time in the same methods and practice in their classrooms, with support from the design and literacy coaches.

That was about the time the staff was changed and Sheppard was sent as principal. When he arrived, Sheppard said, the school was "the wild, wild West." Students danced and jumped on the tables, paying little attention to the teachers. The many doors to the outside meant the school was and remains very vulnerable to outsiders, so children would race their bikes inside, leaving skid marks in the hall, and parents would regularly march into classrooms and yell at teachers if they were angry about something. With a school in that much chaos, parents were often angry.

Sheppard felt he needed to establish a different atmosphere. "In my first speech to the staff, I said we would have an environment where teachers could teach and children could learn." So he locked the classroom doors and told parents that if they wanted to talk with teachers, they needed to first go through him. They could talk to teachers, "but not angry. I won't let that happen." He suspended students for poor behavior "left and right," Wahmanholm remembered. Suspending students was controversial because social workers and teachers argued that it simply meant students would spend less time in school, where they needed to be. "But I had to draw the line," Sheppard said. He no longer suspends many students but has no hesitation in doing so.

Wahmanholm said that the fact that Sheppard had not been steeped in the training many elementary school principals have undergone meant that he had no taboos against, for example, touching a child. Hugs are common at Dayton's Bluff. In fact, Sheppard instituted the practice of greeting each child in the morning. At the beginning of the day, someone—a counselor or teacher—is in the hallway, hugging or shaking hands with each child as he or she arrives and making sure that any problems from outside the school don't make their way inside. Sheppard is usually there as well, greeting children and asking how they are doing, alert to signs of unhappiness and doing some instant counseling. "If they're shown love, they'll meet any expectation you have," Sheppard said.

Sheppard eliminated the bullying atmosphere that had dominated recess by having "structured play," in which students would participate in teacher-directed activities such as four-square and double-Dutch rope jumping. That structure has since eased up a little, now that students know how to play with each other, but it is still in place.

Each day begins with a classroom "morning meeting," in which each child shares something about his or her life or experience and they all play a short game, which Sheppard has credited for the fact that students now mingle and play with each other. "All the races get along here," he said.

Dayton's Bluff is "site-managed," meaning that the leadership team of the school—the principal and the teacher leaders—has a lot of power to change the budget. For example, 13 para-educators were reassigned or laid off, and the money was then used to hire more teachers. New purchases of computers were postponed in order to hire teachers. As a result, the computers in the building are fairly old, but the 23 teachers have class sizes of about 15 or 16. "Highly qualified teachers are the best thing a child can have," said Sheppard, explaining the decision.

At the same time, major instructional changes were instituted. The old curriculum was based on basal readers and "a lot of worksheets," literacy coach Wahmanholm said. "There was not a lot of focus. There were all kinds of programs." America's Choice provided a narrow focus on instruction to standards with a lot of strategies to make it work. Teachers began by implementing the Writers Workshop, then Readers Workshop, and eventually Math Workshop using the Everyday Math curriculum.

Together, teachers learned about scientifically based research on learning, how the workshop method works, and the Responsive Classroom Behavior model. In addition, the schedule was built around teachers' having common planning time during which they are guided through looking at student work to see where the next lessons need to be concentrated.

The changes in instruction helped with the discipline issues. "Sitting in rows with work they couldn't negotiate," said Wahmanholm about the instruction before America's Choice was implemented, "kids would get frustrated and start playing with pencils, and then the situation would escalate." As teachers improved their instruction, discipline became much less of an issue, Wahmanholm said.

At the same time, the responsive classroom discipline methods that all teachers were trained in gave them a common language and a common set of classroom procedures, such as the morning meeting. It also provided a set of common measures they could use for a student whose behavior was disruptive. Students are first asked to "take a break." If that isn't sufficient, they are asked to develop a "fix-it plan," then to sit in a buddy class for a time-out, and then they are sent to the office; as a last resort, the parents are called. "Ninety-five percent of the time it works," Sheppard said. Kids are also "caught" being good and given praise and recognition if they act as good citizens by helping a fellow student or a teacher; whole classes are recognized for exemplary behavior in the hallways or elsewhere.

Discipline and instruction were improving, but Sheppard still wasn't completely happy with the teaching staff. "I had five toxic teachers," he said. "They didn't like kids. They talked about the kids and how they couldn't achieve and, being an African American male, I felt their comments." Sheppard said he never allowed the toxic remarks to pass unchallenged, and as the instruction in the school changed and more and more teachers became convinced of the possibility of improvement, those "toxic" teachers became isolated. At the end of the year, they left, but if they hadn't, he was prepared to take action. "A lot of principals use strong unions as an excuse for why their students don't perform," he said. But, he added, "when you get all the teachers on board, the toxic teachers stand out."

Wahmanholm said that there was a kind of tipping point. "When we got to about 50 percent of the teachers on board, that was the critical mass—then everyone jumped in when the achievement results came in." That first year, the test scores made a respectable jump—the percentage of students who performed at the lowest level of achievement declined to 57 percent, and slightly more than 20 percent met or achieved standards in reading. In math, 25 percent met or exceeded standards. It was nowhere near where the students should have been, but the improvement was noticeable and heartening. "We didn't expect to see the results so quickly," Wahmanholm said. With those tangible results, the teachers could see the benefits of looking at data together, looking at student work, fine-tuning their mini lessons, and making sure they were running their workshops well. All that work paid off in 2003, when about half the students performed at state levels, and again in 2004, when roughly 80 percent met state standards, almost matching the performance of white Minnesotans in reading and exceeding their performance in math.

Staff members at Dayton's Bluff are constantly looking at student achievement data, and the data drive instruction—not only on an annual basis, but also on a daily basis. Teachers don't have rigid lesson plans but, rather, look closely at student work in order to think about the next day's work. If, for example, students write stories that lack rich detail, the next day the teacher will talk about what kinds of details could be included and have the students work on that. If students are having trouble with commas, the next day's mini lesson will address how commas are used. "The plans for tomorrow are drawn from today's work," is how Wojtasiak put it.

The data are also transparent—test results are posted on the walls of the rooms where teachers gather and in the hallways for teachers, students, and parents to see. And each year the goals are posted. "We had that debate," Wojtasiak said. "Some teachers said we shouldn't tell the students where they should be because they are so far behind it would damage their self-esteem." Now that so many students are meeting the targets, those debates are over.

At the beginning of the year, for example, the goal for reading is posted and, four times a year, teachers sit individually with students to take a running record—a record of how fluent and accurate a child's reading is. As of March 2005, Dayton's Bluff students had met the targets set for June. Even the sixth graders—who were being watched particularly carefully because the year before they had not done as well on the reading assessment as the previous class of fifth graders—had met their targets.

"The teachers came to me and said there were a lot of low ELL [English-language learner] kids—I said there are no excuses," Sheppard said. "Excuses are dream killers," he said. When you make an excuse for poor academic performance on the part of a child by saying he is poor or doesn't have good family support, you are essentially saying that he will not be able to achieve, Sheppard added. Wojtasiak put it another way: "If the kids didn't do well, it's not their fault. The teachers need to work on their strategies."

Sheppard acknowledged that this is a hard-edged way to think. "I'm tough on the teachers," he said. "But I make sure they have every resource they need." For example, he sent four classroom teachers to a professional conference in San Antonio to make sure they have the most up-to-date knowledge and skills they could have. "It's expensive to send them," he said, "but they should go."

All ESL (English as a second language) services are provided in the classrooms. Because of the workshop method of instruction, very little whole-group instruction is done (that is mostly confined to the mini lessons); most instruction is one-on-one or small-group, with teachers moving from table to table, working with students.

No non-English-language instruction is provided in St. Paul, except for a few children whose parents ask that their children receive instruction in Spanish, the result of litigation in the 1970s that ended with the "Latino Consent Decree" that still binds the schools. Even though Hmong is now the most common language other than English spoken in St. Paul's schools, no Hmong instruction is provided. New immigrants with no English and no English support at home are provided ESL instruction for a short time in transitional language centers, but the idea is to quickly move them to their neighborhood schools, which provide ESL classes.

At Dayton's Bluff, ESL teachers co-teach with regular classroom teachers, a practice that has the additional benefit of putting the ESL teachers on the same footing with their colleagues. Sheppard said that he has noticed in other schools that ESL teachers are often accorded less respect from their fellow teachers, so the co-teaching "gives them the sense that they belong." At Dayton's Bluff in 2004, 54 percent of the limited-English students met or exceeded state standards in reading, and 57 percent did so in mathematics—not a level where the school wanted to be, but considerably higher than the district and state proficiency rates.

Inclusion is the rule for special education students as well. Special education teachers go into classes to provide the support and additional materials the children need. No children are pulled out of class for special instruction, and only a handful are in a self-contained special education classroom. Because few children identified as needing special education services are in each grade level, not all their achievement data are publicly available. But in fifth-grade math, for example, none of the ten students identified as needing special education were at the lowest achievement level, whereas in St. Paul and Minnesota as a whole, 42 and 36 percent, respectively, of children needing special education services fell into that category. Seventy percent of the students needing special education services at Dayton's Bluff were just below standards, and 30 percent met or exceeded standards. School staff members hope that this year those numbers will improve as a result of the close focus on instruction.

The school requires that students write a great deal. "When we first started," said Sheppard, "we could barely get a page worth of writing from most children." Now, student essays typically run four or five pages for each essay, and student work is posted all over the school. In one central hallway, each grade level has a section to respond to the school's "Book of the Month" selection, a book that everyone in the school reads and to which all students respond.

In addition, each grade level has a bulletin board to display writing samples that meet the New Standards, which are also posted. Although the New Standards are written in language much clearer than that of many state standards, Dayton's Bluff teachers have worked to put the standards into "kid-friendly" language. So, for example, the New Standard might say, "By the end of the year, we expect fourth-grade students to be able to produce a narrative account that engages the reader by establishing a context, creating a point of view, and otherwise developing reader interest." Below that is the school-developed, kid-friendly standard that says, "The beginning makes the reader want to keep reading your memoir." And then examples of student work are posted.

Early in the spring, teachers spend a day and a half studying testing data and released items from tests, thinking about where their students are and who might need what specific help in order to prepare for the state tests given later in the spring. They make sure their students know what kinds of questions are on the tests, and they even have pep rallies to pump the students up. But "test prep" is not what dominates the school year. Teaching to standards is what dominates instruction.

At the beginning of the 2004–05 school year, for example, the teachers as a group mapped out the math curriculum, making sure the Everyday Math program adopted by the school met all the standards required by Minnesota, and filling in the gaps that existed. This meeting was also an opportunity for the physical education, art, and dance teachers to think about where in the curriculum they could make sure they reinforced the concepts being taught in math class. "Diagonal is a big concept in dance," said Jane Kahan, the dance teacher, as an example. "You move on a diagonal, your arm is stretched in a diagonal, your leg is pointed on the diagonal." When math classes study diagonal lines in math, she is able to incorporate that into a dance class.

Kahan, a longtime dance teacher who has also worked as a classroom teacher, remembers how as a child she herself strengthened her understanding of math through dance. For example, she said, one day her dance instructor introduced a warm-up exercise that included movements to two sets of nine counts and three sets of six counts. "I knew 2×9 was 18 and 3×6 was 18, but that was the first time it occurred to me that they were the same amount."

Movement is very much part of the school day at Dayton's Bluff. In addition to the 20-minute-a-day recess and to regular gym, art, and dance instruction, all kids spend 10 minutes before lunch "walking and talking" in the gym to lively, movement-inducing music. This practice arose out of the need to fill a schedule hole, but it has become integral to the way the school works. "It gets their energy out a little," said Sheppard. "And they get to gossip—it's just kid stuff, but they need to do it and we don't permit it in the classroom." Walking and talking is a time for kids to socialize and for teachers to catch up with children, to commend them for their work or behavior, to enlist their aid for an upcoming class or project, or just to check in and make sure they are okay. If they find out that a student isn't feeling well or has a toothache, they are able to send the child to the fully equipped dentist's office or the nurse-practitioner's office. If a teacher thinks a child should be seen by a therapist or a family needs some kind of social service, such as housing assistance, that can be arranged as well, with little or no instruction time lost.

These resources are part of a constellation of services (called "Achievement Plus") provided to five schools in St. Paul in an attempt to boost achievement. Administered by the school system and funded largely by the local Amherst H. Wilder Foundation, Achievement Plus built additions to the five schools to house facilities such as a theater, dance studio, recreation facilities, and kitchen, which are used by both the school and the community. In addition, Achievement Plus funds afterschool programs and summer-school programs closely tied to the instruction provided during the school day and year. Most teachers teach summer school, and all children are invited to attend, which means that few students lose any learning during the summer. In all, the cost of the Achievement Plus services is estimated to work out to about $500 a child, according to a 2004 report issued by the St. Paul Public Schools and Achievement Plus. That Achievement Plus money was scheduled to run out in 2005 and the school was uncertain whether the program would continue, and if it did, what form it would take.

Moving from the worst school in St. Paul to one of the best in five years has required an enormous amount of work, and the staff have thought long and hard about how to institutionalize the changes. "I empower leaders," is how Sheppard put it. Many teachers lead committees or subcommittees. There is a school design committee, a leadership committee, a budget committee, a literacy committee, a discipline committee, and other committees that make major decisions for the school. In this way, although Sheppard has played an integral role as leader of the school, he has allowed leadership to be spread throughout the school in order to deepen the culture of focusing on instruction.

One of the ways he initially "empowered" teachers was by acknowledging early on that he had no experience as an instructor or in elementary education. "I didn't know anything about instruction when I first came," Sheppard said. "I took them on a journey. We all took the first steps together." That attitude endeared him to many of the teachers, who otherwise might have bristled at his no-excuses, no-nonsense leadership style peppered with football analogies. As part of his own professional development, Sheppard was enrolled, with several other principals from St. Paul, in the Institute for Learning led by Lauren Resnick at the University of Pittsburgh. He also interned with superintendent Harvey while he completed his own superintendence training.

By focusing narrowly on good instruction and the kind of atmosphere and environment that allows good instruction, Dayton's Bluff has become a school where children learn a great deal and teachers feel successful and look forward to going to work. One teacher said that one day she was driving on the highway—something she hates—and yet she felt happy. "All I could think was that it was because I was going to work."

Wahmanholm, literacy coach and teacher leader, gave the credit for that atmosphere to Sheppard. "He has made it fun to teach here."

"Relationships and collaboration make the difference," is how Wojtasiak, the design coach, put it. As Sheppard himself summed it up, "This is a place of respect and caring."

POSTSCRIPT

As it turned out, the school did post higher rates of proficiency in fifth grade in 2005, but it dropped somewhat in third grade, which the teachers and staff found very disappointing. Shortly after I visited Dayton's Bluff, Sheppard became an assistant superintendent in Minneapolis. Of all the people I met during this project, he was the only one who truly seemed burnt-out by the difficulties of the job. But he was succeeded by a seemingly very able administrator, Andrew Collins, who had been director of extended learning at Dayton's Bluff for years and who said he was determined to build on the past years' improvements.

"The progress that happened here was amazing," Collins said, adding that he spent his first year listening to staff and continuing good practices—"Why fix what isn't broken?"

During Collins's first year, 2005–06, he had to contend with the effects of serious state and local budget cuts—he lost 12 staff members, which is a big hit for any school. As it turned out, some of the Achievement Plus funding was continued, so Dayton's Bluff was able to keep many of the services that Achievement Plus represented, including a nurse-practitioner, dentist, and social worker. For the 2006–07 school year, a housing advocate also had an office in the school. St. Paul has adopted a districtwide improvement model that is similar to America's Choice, so Dayton's Bluff is no longer formally an America's Choice school, but it continues many of the same practices. Dayton's Bluff lost some faculty to promotions within the district, and Collins was concerned that it had lost key expertise. "You can institutionalize change all you want," he said, but "that is lost" with enough loss of personnel.

Because St. Paul's student population has decreased dramatically in the past few years, a nearby school closed, and Dayton's Bluff absorbed many of its students and staff for the 2006–07 school year, which Collins called "fabulous."

Speaking just before school started, Collins said, "This is a year of recommitting ourselves." He added, "It's about maintaining momentum and continuing to make decisions in the best interest of our students."

Just as this book was being completed, Minnesota published its test results for spring of 2006. It was a new test, so results cannot be compared to previous years, but budget cuts and loss of expertise had taken its toll, and it may take Dayton's Bluff a year or so to recover.

CENTENNIAL PLACE ELEMENTARY SCHOOL
ATLANTA, GEORGIA

INTRODUCTION

A few years before, The Education Trust's senior policy analyst, Daria Hall, had identified Centennial Place Elementary as a school of poverty that posted high achievement, and every year she kept an eye on its scores. She told me she thought it might be worth a visit, particularly because it had had such a long track record.

When I called the principal, I was intrigued but skeptical about her descriptions of the school's project- and theme-based curriculum. Although "projects" and "themes" sound appealing, I had found during my own children's school years that too often those are code words for spending huge amounts of time learning very little. Frankly, I shivered at the thought of all the meaningless dioramas I helped find supplies for and all the silly "themes" teachers had explained at back-to-school nights. At Centennial Place, I found neither meaningless projects nor silly themes. Instead, I found a school that had thought deeply about its curriculum and looked at data in a rigorous way to make sure that all students were learning.

• • • • •

Centennial Place Elementary School, in the heart of Atlanta, has about 520 students, more than 90 percent of whom are African American and about 60 percent of whom meet the criteria for free or reduced-price meals. Two nearby homeless shelters provide a steady stream of new children. Most people would expect such a school to perform at low levels, but at Centennial Place all but a very small handful of children have met state standards for the past few years. In fact, said principal Cynthia Kuhlman, "It's just not

CENTENNIAL PLACE ELEMENTARY SCHOOL
ATLANTA, GEORGIA

2006 Enrollment: 530 students in kindergarten through fifth grade
2006 Demographics: 91% African American
                         57% meet qualifications for free and reduced-price lunch
Locale: Urban

Grade 5 Reading, 2006
Georgia Criterion-Referenced Competency Tests (CRCT)

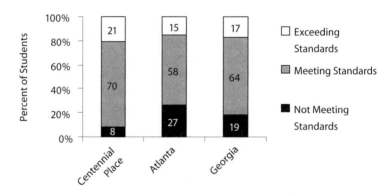

enough to meet state standards." She wants all her children to exceed standards. In 2005, almost half of her students did just that in reading, and 20 percent exceeded standards in math, meaning that Centennial Place is one of the top schools in the state. Centennial Place blows past Adequate Yearly Progress (AYP) targets—the targets set by the state in order to meet federal accountability requirements. Kuhlman hardly even thinks about AYP. "We would never be happy meeting that," she said. "AYP is not good enough for us."

Scores on state assessments—although they hint at the kind of school Centennial Place is—only begin to tell the story of the school, which is filled with art, music, Spanish instruction, and hands-on projects tied to schoolwide science themes selected by teachers.

Although Centennial Place spends some time each year helping students prepare in a concentrated way to take state and nationally normed tests, the school doesn't focus on test prep. "The best way to do well on the test is to teach the standards in an exciting way," Kuhlman said. Children learn through do-

Grade 5 Math, 2006
Georgia Criterion-Referenced Competency Tests (CRCT)

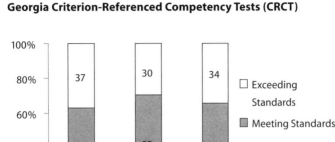

Source: The Governor's Office of Student Achievement, State of Georgia, http://reportcard2006.gaosa.org

In addition, 96 percent of fifth-grade students at Centennial Place met state standards in English language arts, 99 percent met standards in social studies, and 100 percent met standards in science.

Note: These graphs use the latest information that was available at the time of publication, which is more recent than was available when the school was visited. Previous report cards can be found at the state department of education website.

ing projects at Centennial Place. One project was to organize a "trip to Africa," where one of the classrooms was set up as an airplane, staffed by a parent who is a flight attendant. Students "traveled" to Africa, where they went on a safari, learning geography, history, and some biology. Another project was building a "tundra" out of layers of cake, ice cream, and other foodstuffs that then got eaten at a big party. Through partnerships with Georgia Institute of Technology, which is across the street, students have been able to meet with artists and musicians and go to concerts. In one memorable afternoon, school band and orchestra members met with world-renowned cellist Yo-Yo Ma, who put them to work helping him assess the acoustics of the Georgia Tech concert hall.

At Centennial Place, high test scores are not purchased with the sacrifice of creativity and imagination. But achieving such results does require teachers and administrators, along with members of the larger community, to spend a great deal of time and thought planning and focusing on each child and activity. Almost no aspect of the school's life is left unexamined.

The school building itself was built as part of the redevelopment of a devastated urban area with Hope VI federal funds, a federal housing program begun under President Ronald Reagan with the aim of redeveloping blighted public housing projects and helping residents become homeowners. It involved tearing down one of the oldest public housing projects in the country (Techwood/Clark Howell Homes, built under Franklin D. Roosevelt) and replacing it with a mixture of modest rented and owned townhomes and single-family homes, 40 percent of which are reserved for public housing clients and 20 percent for low-income residents, with the rest designated for at-market prices.

The school—a replacement for the old Fowler Elementary—and the next-door YMCA were part of the original plans for the redevelopment of the area, which is now mostly complete, although a supermarket and other retail businesses had yet to be built at the time of my visit. Near the new housing project are several small neighborhoods of small, moderately priced homes that have seen some revitalization since the redevelopment of the public housing complex. But, despite a brand-new Coca-Cola office building nearby and the presence of Georgia Institute of Technology (Georgia Tech), the neighborhood still has a desolate feel, particularly at night. No restaurants—not even fast-food restaurants—exist anywhere near the school, for example.

Two-thirds of the Centennial Place students come from the immediate neighborhood, but Atlanta allows families to transfer schools, and about one-third of the students come from outside Centennial Place's catchment area, drawn there by the school's reputation for high academic achievement. These transfers do not change the basic demographics of the school; according to the principal, the children who transfer in are just as likely to be poor as those who come from the neighborhood.

"We have the poorest of the poor—the homeless. We have the motivated poor. And the parents who choose to come here through administrative transfer are economically diverse," Kuhlman said. She added that the economic prospects of the neighborhood families at Centennial are improving, which was part of the motivation for neighborhood redevelopment. "Families where, in the past, the moms weren't working are now working."

In designing the new building, architects from Georgia Tech met with school staff and thought deeply about what kind of instruction would go on. They came up with a unique variation on the "open classroom" design, in which grade-level "pods" of classrooms are clustered around an office where each teacher has a desk. The office windows look out onto interconnected classrooms.

Teachers can observe other classrooms and can easily meet during scheduled common planning times. Although every once in a while the noise level gets a bit too high for the comfort of teachers, for the most part classroom noises do not intrude on other classrooms, despite the open flow of space. During common planning times, teachers in each grade level meet to discuss field trips or projects related to themes. For example, during the first and last nine weeks of the year, the theme was "living things," part of the focus on science that the school has adopted (other themes were earth science and physical science). Kindergartners studied farms and farm animals, first graders studied living things in the oceans, and other grade levels studied living things at increasingly greater levels of sophistication.

The school decided on a science focus because, Kuhlman said, of a "horror story that no student from Fowler [the school Centennial Place replaced] ever went to Georgia Tech." Georgia Tech, just across the street from where most of the children live, is one of the most prestigious and difficult-to-get-into institutions of higher education in Georgia and the South. "We agreed on a science theme school to prepare students for Georgia Tech—or at least college." After eight years of operation, Centennial Place now has students in high school, and Kuhlman and the teachers are crossing their fingers. "We know our kids are going to college. We hope some will go to Georgia Tech."

The curriculum at Centennial begins with state standards, which teachers study in order to closely align what they teach to what children are expected to know on state tests. The following are a couple of the science standards Georgia has established as things kindergartners and first and second graders should learn in school.

Diversity of Life
- Some animals and plants are alike in the way they look and in the things they do, and others are very different from one another.
- Plants and animals have features that help them live in different environments.
- Stories sometimes give plants and animals attributes they really do not have.

Heredity
- There is variation among individuals of one kind within a population.
- Offspring are very much, but not exactly, like their parents and like one another.

These standards leave a lot of scope for teachers' imaginations.

Teachers meet both within and across grade levels to decide exactly what each grade will do to meet those standards, and then each grade-level team meets to discuss what projects, field trips, lessons, and materials they will need to teach their lessons. Together they develop a "curriculum map" for each grade. For example, in kindergarten students are expected to sort collections of matter by physical characteristics and classify objects according to such properties as large, small, heavy, light, hot, cold, wet, or dry. By fifth grade, students are expected to group animals by observable characteristics such as body covering, number of legs, ears, presence of wings, color, and size, as well as be able to identify and describe the five major kingdoms (animals, plants, fungi, protists, and monerans) with their major characteristics. Together, teachers work on lessons that will teach all that.

"You need to create a vision across the school" is the way assistant principal Barbara Preuss put it. "If you're all going in different ways, it's going to be chaos." The coordination of instruction means that teachers can rely on their colleagues for help and advice. "If you need something, and you're all doing the same thing, you can go and ask for help," said teacher Dr. Alfred Stinson. But teachers do not complain that their time is so overly prescribed that they have no scope for their own personal twist. "Our own individual creativity will come out," noted teacher Valerie Oliver.

Right from the beginning of planning for Centennial Place, Kuhlman said, "we talked about creating a culture of achievement. As a new school you can spend too much time on, say, discipline," when what is needed is to "focus every decision on student achievement." In the beginning years, Kuhlman said, the middle school that Centennial Place feeds into did not report that it was pleased with the learning of Centennial Place graduates. So, she said, scholars from Georgia Tech came to the school, where they visited classrooms and pored over school documents. They recommended that individual profiles be developed for each child and that teachers receive additional support.

"It has really changed what we're doing," Kuhlman said. Today, Centennial Place has a bulging binder with a sheet on each child and how that child is doing. Classroom sets of the same student data are provided to each teacher, who studies them carefully to see where each student is weak and needs bolstering. Some children need help in building a larger vocabulary; others need to work on reading critically. Individual plans are drawn up for each child, but classroom plans are made as well from the data. In one fifth-grade class, for example, almost all students exceeded standards in statistics and probability, and almost all were below standards in geometry. The teacher shared the lesson she had developed on statistics and probability with her colleagues, since she had been so successful, and rethought how she was teaching geometry concepts and skills. "You start with a benchmark at the beginning of the year, and you can see how the students have progressed at the end," is the way teacher Tiffany Yarn described the data available to her.

In addition to developing the data sets on each child and each classroom, the school substantially beefed up its support of teachers. Each teacher has two individual conferences with the principal a year, one in the beginning of the year and one in January. "I give them an engraved invitation," Kuhlman said. The teachers bring their data, student work, and planned projects and lessons, and they explain how they will make sure each of their students meets state standards. "They know that not meeting standards is not acceptable," Kuhlman said. New teachers are paired with more-experienced teachers to give them support. In addition, there is monthly and yearly professional development that is specifically geared to the kinds of activities that will help students meet standards. Some of that training has been provided by Co-nect, a company that provides professional development and data services to schools. Centennial Place contracted with Co-nect in 2000, when Atlanta Public Schools superintendent Beverly L. Hall said that every city school must adopt a specific reform model. Many Atlanta schools adopted a scripted program of some kind, but Centennial chose Co-nect because it was both data-oriented and friendly to a project-based approach to learning.

In the 2004 data, the school identified an issue with its students with disabilities: Only 50 percent met state reading standards. That is a much higher percentage than in most Georgia schools, but it was a warning that Centennial Place was not ready to meet 2014's goal that all students—except those with serious cognitive disabilities—will meet state standards. "We took it to heart. We went through a period where we didn't acknowledge that our special education students weren't doing well. No Child Left Behind helped us focus," Kuhlman said.

In the 2004–05 school year, the school made sure that students with disabilities had access to all the programs and enrichment that other students had. In addition, they focused the curriculum a little more tightly. "We might have been guilty of teaching too much, but in not enough depth." In addition, the school beefed up the connections between classroom teachers and special education teachers. The result of that effort was that 87 percent of students with disabilities met or exceeded state math standards and 85 percent met state reading standards that year.

One problem that was identified early on at Centennial was communication. "When we opened the school, a constant concern was that nobody knew what was going on," Kuhlman said. "We identified communication as a concern." To address this, Centennial Place put into place several structures and procedures that have ensured not only that no one is left in the dark, but also that every staff member has opportunities for participation in decisionmaking and leadership.

First off, each grade level has a "grade chair," who meets with the principal at 7:15 every Thursday morning. The chairs explicitly work on coordinating all the schedules so that everyone knows when the field trips are, when the band concerts are, and when projects are taking place. Detailed minutes are published and distributed by e-mail, and the grade chairs also report directly back to the other teachers what was discussed and decided. That committee also works out the general thematic units that the school will work on over the course of the year.

Then there is a design team, which consists of representatives of each grade level who coordinate the curriculum with the themes. It is the design team who develop the curriculum map discussed above. In addition, a school improvement committee discusses all school operations, such as how dismissal is conducted, incentives for attendance, lunchroom behavior, homework policy, and discipline. This committee includes a teacher from every grade level, as well as a specialist teacher (such as for art or music), a parent, and a community member.

A great deal of work is done in the school improvement committee. For example, they studied the school calendar and, along with their local school committee, which includes more community members, convinced the Atlanta School Board a few years ago to allow Centennial Place to go to an all-year schedule. As a result, Centennial Place students attend in nine-week chunks, with three-week intersessions and a five-week summer break.

The yearlong schedule means that students don't have much time to fall behind during a long summer, and students who need extra help attend during the intersessions. That intersession time is used not only to catch students up, but also to propel them forward, since teachers use the time to preview future lessons.

The school improvement committee also decided that all students should wear a uniform of white or light blue shirts and dark blue slacks or skirts. "The uniform policy helps so much," said Kuhlman. She particularly appreciates that the students from the homeless shelters are quickly able to fit in with the other students, with no real differences in how they dress. The shelters work with the school to provide uniforms, and the school keeps a stash of school clothes available to students.

Another focus of the council is discipline. The school's essential philosophy on discipline is that students be given very little idle time in which to misbehave. "I link good behavior with good teaching and effective planning. There is no idle time," said Kuhlman. Students' school days are busy and filled with instruction and activity. More formally, Centennial Place implements the Consistency Management and Cooperative Discipline program, which was developed to help schools—particularly urban schools—provide a consistent, caring atmosphere in which students take responsibility for their behavior.

When a particular problem bedevils the school, sometimes it is the children who come up with solutions. For example, the school was having trouble with too many students running their hands along the walls of hallways, sometimes getting the walls dirty and sometimes dislodging artwork and other displays. The children suggested that there be a rule that they walk on the red and blue tiles in the halls, keeping them away from the temptation of touching the walls. That doesn't always work, but it works more often than not.

Assistant principal Preuss is the assigned disciplinarian of the school, and she sometimes uses afterschool detentions, but she tries to avoid suspensions from school because they disrupt instructional time. Truly serious offenses— such as a student who hits a teacher—are handled by holding a tribunal in which the student answers for his or her offense. "Discipline problems are kids who have something going on," said Preuss. That assessment is shared by school counselor Nicole Jones. "A lot of our problems come from outside school," she said. For that reason, Centennial Place works with a licensed social worker, and an Emory University psychiatrist works with families. Sometimes the issue is that the families don't get their children to school. In extreme cases, the social worker has taken families to court to compel them to send their children to school.

The standard curriculum is just the beginning of how students are kept busy at Centennial Place. In addition to regular "specials" such as physical education, music, chorus, and art, a combined grant from the state and the city has permitted Centennial Place to offer Spanish instruction to all children for a half hour a day. One of the stipulations of the grant is that the teachers remain in the classroom so that they, too, learn Spanish. The students put on plays and musicals in Spanish with scheduled performances. In addition, about 100 students participate in the band or orchestra. "It's kind of a leap of faith for us that kids are getting smarter in the music classes," Kuhlman said, citing the connections between music and such mathematical concepts as patterning and fractions. An additional science teacher works with classroom teachers on the science projects that dominate the school, and that is considered another "special."

In addition, Centennial Place also has many volunteers who have offered to help tutor, read, or otherwise work with students. Volunteers are coordinated by a full-time staff person who is paid partly by federal Title I funds and partly by Hands-On Atlanta, a citywide nonprofit organization that works with AmeriCorps, a federally sponsored volunteer agency. This coordinator recruits, trains, and coordinates volunteers. Centennial Place expects volunteers to commit to the "same time, same day, every week," said coordinator Marcia Brown. In return, the school commits that if a student is absent or on a field trip, the volunteers will be told so they don't waste their time. This kind of coordination has allowed volunteering to become a major resource for the school. Along with parent volunteers, the school has also attracted volunteers from Georgia Natural Gas, Coca-Cola, and Georgia Tech. "It's been a beautiful thing for me to see," said Brown. "The way it impacts [students] is amazing." She added that many tutors develop strong personal ties with their students that spill over on the weekends and in other ways. One tutor who taught a student to tell time bought the student a watch as a gift.

Every year, the Atlanta law firm of Holland and Knight donates the time of six attorneys, two hours a day for a week, to work on a "justice project" with fifth graders. Students who are identified by their teachers as needing some enrichment work with the attorneys to write briefs and prepare roles for cases such as "The State of Georgia v. Goldilocks," in which Goldilocks is charged with trespassing, violating curfew laws, and breaking and entering. To culminate the activity, the entire fifth grade is bused to a Fulton County courthouse where they are given a tour of the judge's chambers and where the students who have been working on the project present the case, acting as prosecutor, defense attorney, witnesses, defendant, and so forth. The rest of the students act as jury members, all presided over by the retired judge who began the project.

Having all those outsiders in a school means that there are no secrets for long. "In the beginning, someone from Coca-Cola called and said they heard an outrageous reprimand by a teacher of a child," Kuhlman said. "I asked her to come and point out the teacher and told the teacher that kind of behavior was not permitted." Some principals would not appreciate that kind of outside scrutiny, but Kuhlman is adamant that the more eyes and ears and support in the school, the better for the students.

The Georgia Tech presence exerts itself in many ways as well. The president of Georgia Tech was the graduation speaker in the spring of 2004. In addition, Georgia Tech obtained a grant at one point to bring artists who performed at the university to the school for workshops. For example, Chuck Davis, founder of the well-known African American Dance Ensemble, provided a weeklong program on African dance in which children studied the culture and the dance, made costumes, and performed. As part of that program, Georgia Tech provided 200 $2 tickets to Georgia Tech performances, allowing families and faculty members to have an inexpensive evening out. Although the grant money ran out, Kuhlman said that "the Georgia Tech folks are committed to bringing the program back."

In addition, Georgia State University orchestra performers come to Centennial Place every year to work with teachers on incorporating music with the physical sciences. At the same time, the orchestra members also mentor music majors, who then turn around and work with Centennial Place students.

Centennial Place, in other words, highly leverages its resources to benefit its children. Another resource that is in place is the next-door YMCA, which was built specifically to provide before- and afterschool care for Centennial Place students, as well as to provide high-quality preschool and recreational activities for the neighborhood. About half the students from Centennial Park go there in the afternoons, and another 20 percent go to the Boys and Girls Club nearby. Both provide places to do homework, a snack, and opportunities for physical activity. During the spring of 2005, YMCA staff members were working on a plan to have 20 members each of the Atlanta Braves and Falcons "adopt" individual students to bring to team activities for their families and to do other activities.

"We try to go for every possible resource," said Kuhlman. All of this gives the impression that Centennial Place has more official resources than other Atlanta schools. "People think we have something extra that other schools don't have," she said, "but we have the same funding every other school gets." Other than Title I funding, which most city schools receive, Centennial Place receives the same per-pupil spending as other schools—a little more than $10,000 per child per year. Per grade level, there are about 90 students, 5 classrooms, and 6 teachers, two of whom team-teach. The team-taught classrooms tend to have more children who the school has identified as needing more help and support, and those classes also tend to be a little bigger than the classes with one teacher.

The teachers are carefully chosen. Although teachers must by hired through the Atlanta Public School system, the school has the final say. A committee of faculty and community members from, for example, the YMCA and Georgia Tech participate in interviewing prospective staff, who are warned that they must be willing to undergo rigorous professional development and to collaborate with their colleagues. "We wouldn't want to hire anyone who hasn't been in our building," said assistant principal Preuss. This is because the unusual open classroom design unnerves some teachers who "want to go into their room and close the door."

But finding applicants has not been a problem. "People are seeking us out," said Preuss. She attributed that to the fact that "we allow our teachers to be very creative." This gives the school the opportunity to be very careful about hiring new teachers. "We are a little snobby about the credentials of our teachers," Kuhlman said. "We look for good teacher-education programs and good grades. Teachers need to have made good grades." Centennial Place teachers have graduated from Teachers College, Auburn, Georgia State, Howard, Fordham, the University of Michigan, and the University of Indiana. The University of Florida master's program in elementary education produces teachers who seem as if they "were educated to teach in this school," Kuhlman said, because the program has a heavy emphasis on thematic teaching.

In interviewing teacher candidates, one of the key characteristics looked for is a candidate's work ethic. "People here resent people who don't work hard. That's where the pressure comes in," Preuss said, "because teachers rely heavily on each other to get pieces of the work done." The administrators have as their job "keeping the work level reasonable," said Preuss. Kuhlman added, "We have a strong work ethic, but we also have a humaneness, a kindness." Kuhlman said that few teachers leave because of burnout. They leave because personal circumstances force them to—a spouse is transferred, or some other life change, for example. "But when they leave here, they are empowered to be leaders."

Part of her job as a principal, Kuhlman implied, is to develop leadership among her staff, in part so that the work of the school becomes systematized in such a way that it will outlive her. "Principals give the most they have to give in about five to seven years," she said. She is beginning to think about retiring, having begun in the profession as a special educator 35 years ago. All the systems in place governing school operations and school curriculum mean that Centennial Place is more than the leadership of one person.

What Centennial Place provides is an example of a school that takes seriously its mission to educate children without losing any of the richness of art, music, history, and science. When asked what the most important factor is in

Centennial Place's success, Kuhlman replied, "Our curriculum, and the fact that our children are not sitting at desks doing worksheets."

But that doesn't mean the school is complacent. "We're not satisfied with our math scores," said Preuss. "We have a high number of students who have met standards, but we need more in the 'exceed' category." In 2006, the school improvement committee was studying whether the curriculum would be improved by bringing in a more-structured approach, such as the Core Knowledge curriculum, which systematically builds content knowledge through the grades. "You've got to keep getting better," said Preuss. "We're about making sure our children are successful—whatever it takes."

POSTSCRIPT

At the end of the 2005–06 school year, Dr. Kuhlman retired, replaced by Alison Shelton, who Kuhlman said she was "really excited about." Kuhlman was certain that Shelton would take Centennial Place to new levels of achievement. And, she reported, as of the fall of 2006, one of Centennial Place's first graduates would be taking his place in the freshman class at Georgia Institute of Technology.

LAPWAI ELEMENTARY SCHOOL

LAPWAI, IDAHO

INTRODUCTION

American Indian children often get left out of national education discussions, but as a group they tend to score terribly on state tests. At Lapwai Elementary School, American Indian children were achieving at similar rates to other children in Idaho. But it was a long trip to take just to see one school. We cast around and found another promising school—Kamiah Elementary, just 50 or so miles from Lapwai, on the other side of the Nez Perce reservation. And then, following another exhaustive search for a high school to visit, Education Trust senior policy analyst Daria Hall came up with yet another interesting school, Granger High School, a little way from the Idaho border in Washington's Yakima Valley. With three schools to visit, the time and expense could be justified.

Kamiah, Idaho, was one of the more remote places I had ever visited. There are two roads to take from the small city of Lewiston to Kamiah, both 60 miles long: one follows the Snake River and one goes "over the hill." The principal advised me not to go over the hill, but my sketchy map-reading skills led me straight there, and it included 20 miles of dirt road with a very steep cliff on the right side not protected by a guardrail.

Once at Kamiah, I found a small town with a high unemployment rate following a slowdown at the lumber mill. Although most of the residents of the town are white, it is on the Nez Perce reservation and so has the inevitable casino, which sells chicken dinners at a bargain price. The new but very small Latino community helps support a Mexican restaurant. Other than that, the town consists of a few streets of houses, a supermarket, a gas station, a drive-through espresso booth, lots of tiny churches, and a fabulous, recently renovated German bakery. There's also a mastodon skeleton that a local farmer found. You can't get more small-town than Kamiah.

LAPWAI ELEMENTARY SCHOOL
LAPWAI, IDAHO

2006 Enrollment: 312 students in kindergarten through sixth grade
2006 Demographics: 84% American Indian
                        14% White
                        81% meet qualifications for free and reduced-price lunch
Locale: Rural

Grade 4 Reading, 2006
Idaho Standards Achievement Test (ISAT)

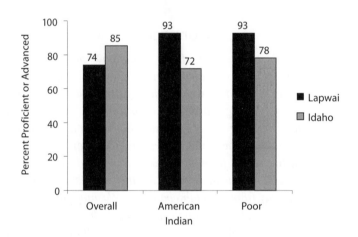

The town's three schools—elementary, middle, and high—are all on the same campus, and there I found educators absolutely dedicated to improving their students' achievement. The students, about two-thirds of whom are poor and 10 percent of whom are American Indians who live in the hills surrounding the town, had higher rates of proficiency than those in the rest of the state. As one way to fight the effects of isolation, and thanks to grants from the Idaho-based Albertson Foundation, the school was drenched with technology. It was the first place where I ever saw SMART Boards—interactive blackboards that combine laptop computers with all kinds of other technology. The school also worked hard to maintain relationships with Boise State University and, among other things, was actively engaged in the steelhead fish restoration project for the Columbia River.

Grade 4 Math, 2006
Idaho Standards Achievement Test (ISAT)

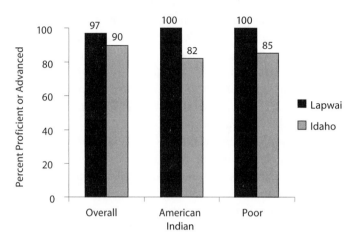

Source: Idaho Department of Education, http://www.sde.state.id.us/admin/isat/

Grade 4 Direct Math Assessment

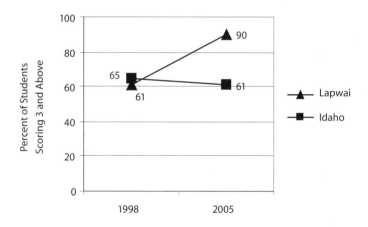

Direct Math Assessment is given in the fall of each year. Results are shown to illustrate the progress Lapwai has made.

Source: Idaho Department of Education, http://www.sde.state.id.us/ipd/dmwa/DmaDwa0405.asp

Note: These graphs use the latest information that was available at the time of publication, which is more recent than was available when the school was visited. Previous report cards can be found at the state department of education website. Enrollment and demographic information came directly from the school.

One of the teachers—an enthusiastic and dedicated professional—told me something that put the whole issue of getting highly qualified teachers in rural areas into a new light. It is widely acknowledged that it is hard to attract good teachers to rural areas. But she had a different take on the question. She had been brought up near Kamiah, and although she had wanted to leave for a more urban area after she went away to college, her husband fell in love with Kamiah and wanted to settle there. Teaching was a profession that allowed her to live in a rural area. "A lot of people want to live in rural areas but are unable to find jobs," she said. That has stuck with me as I think about the problems rural areas have in staffing their schools.

The reason there is no chapter in this book on Kamiah Elementary School is because in 2005 the rest of Idaho more or less caught up with Kamiah's proficiency rates, and the school's story was no longer as dramatic. There is another reason as well. Under Idaho's reporting rules, student groups have to number 34 before they are reported on the state's school report card. Because Kamiah is small and its American Indian population is even smaller, the proficiency rates of its American Indian children are not reported separately. So even though the school reported that its American Indian children are doing well, particularly in comparison with the other American Indian children in the state, I can't verify that using state report card data.

This is what those in the education policy world call the "n-size" issue. In this instance, n-size refers to the size a group needs to be before it is reported separately in state report cards. States vary widely in this. Maryland has the lowest n-size, reporting on groups as small as 5 (that is, if there are 5 African American children in a school, Maryland reports what percentage of them meet or exceed state standards), and Texas has the biggest—200. Most states are in the 20 to 30 range, but even that is a large enough number that, particularly in elementary schools, there are often not enough children to report separately. In an average K–5 elementary school, there might only be 50 or 60 children in a grade. Even if one-third of the school is African American or poor, there might not be enough African American children in a grade to report separately. This makes it very difficult for parents or community members to know how well that school does with all groups of children.

Leaving Kamiah—making sure to take the river road this time—I went across the Nez Perce reservation to Lapwai, where the tribal council buildings are housed and where most of the residents are American Indian, many living in tribal housing or mobile homes.

Members of Lapwai's staff told me an emotional, dramatic story of how they began their improvement process. I include that story here because it demon-

strates how much many teachers care about helping their students, but how little they often know about how to make the changes necessary and how buffeted they've been by educational fads.

• • • • •

Through the 1990s, Lapwai Elementary School was stuck. Between 70 and 80 percent of its students couldn't read or do math well enough to meet state standards, and no matter how hard the teachers worked, no matter how much they cared, nothing seemed to change those numbers, year after year. It sometimes seemed as though the students at Lapwai were doomed to perform at low levels.

Lapwai Elementary is in Lapwai, in the northern neck of Idaho not far from the Washington border. It is on the western part of the large Nez Perce reservation and is part of a complex of buildings that includes the high school, Head Start, and the tribal community center, about 12 miles from Lewiston. Although more than 80 percent of the students are American Indian, it is not a tribal school—it is a public school on tribal land. For years it mirrored the achievement levels of many schools that serve poor children and American Indian children. "We were in the pits" is the way the superintendent, Harold Ott, put it.

The teachers were keenly aware that low performance in elementary school meant that most of their students would face low performance in secondary school and very limited choices in their futures after that. But they couldn't seem to make a difference. Teri Wagner, who was then a teacher at Lapwai, said, "We were committed, we cared, but our tradition of low performance continued."

Then, in 1999, a delegation of teachers went to a conference where they heard predictions of how vital a good education would be for children, who would need ever more complex and sophisticated knowledge and skills as they entered the 21st century. Flying back home in a puddle jumper, the teachers held hands and pledged to each other that they would do whatever it took to make sure their students wouldn't be left behind by the future.

That dramatic moment was followed by years of difficult slogging—adopting a coherent curriculum, reorganizing the school day, learning to use individual student data to drive instruction, learning to work together as teachers and with the larger community, and all the time learning about the research that should underlie instruction. But all that work paid off in 2003, when roughly 80 percent of the school's 280 students met state standards.

The strongest performance is consistently turned in by the fourth grade. In 2005, for example, 100 percent of the fourth graders were considered proficient or above on the state's math standards, 94 percent on the state reading standards, and 92 percent on the language usage standards. Even those figures understate the facts, however, because in fourth-grade math, two-thirds of the students did not just meet standards but exceeded them; in fourth-grade reading, half of the students exceeded the standards. In the third, fifth, and sixth grades, the percentages of students who were proficient or above were closer to 75. Even those percentages outpaced the rest of Idaho, where fewer than half the students exceeded standards, and only about one-quarter of the state's American Indian students exceeded standards.

The staff is not yet satisfied. They worry about the approximately 20 percent of students who don't meet state standards. The teachers study those students' scores, work with them individually, and fret about what else should be done to make sure they read and do math well. Staff members are concerned that scores seem to have leveled off and occasionally have even dropped a little in the last year. But every once in a while, said Wagner, "I slap my hand on the table and say, 'We're worried about 20 percent!' We used to worry about 80 percent."

Back in the days when 80 percent of the students could not meet state standards, the school operated the way many elementary schools operate. Each teacher closed her door and taught what she could, using lots of different approaches to reading and math. Few knew what the teacher next door was doing, much less those down the hall. When teachers did get together, discipline was the key conversation. Grants would come and go, pushing in one program or another, which would be picked up and dropped with regularity. "We were teaching faddism," said superintendent Ott. "We wanted success and would try anything for a short time." But nothing seemed to work.

Then came that pivotal conference, which had showcased several whole-school reform models that promised to help schools improve. Wagner and the other teachers who had attended the conference reported to their colleagues and to principal Mike Halverson about what was available, and together they chose to adopt Success for All (SFA), a Baltimore-based program that offered extensive training in reading instruction and the use of student data. "The data screamed at us that we needed to start with reading," said Wagner.

One of the cores of SFA is a tightly managed—sometimes even scripted—reading program, where phonemes (sounds) and graphemes (letters) are taught systematically in kindergarten and first grade. It continues with vocabulary instruction that includes the systematic introduction of prefixes and suffixes and the teaching of root words. All this is done while students read a wide variety of books and write about them, often in cooperative groups, which is another hallmark of SFA. The school day was reorganized to allow for an uninterrupted 90-minute block of time for reading and writing instruction. One of the appeals SFA held for the Lapwai staff is its consistency across classrooms and grade levels, which means that each teacher knows what each student has been doing and what each class is currently doing. In addition, SFA has an emphasis on monitoring student data, so that each teacher knows exactly how each student is doing at regular intervals. This allows teachers to notice gaps in understanding that individual children or groups of children may have, which then allows the teachers to adjust their instruction. Every eight weeks, children are reshuffled into groups based on what is being taught and what their achievement levels are, which means that teachers need to know what is going on in each other's classrooms.

But getting to the point where classroom instruction is that transparent has required that teachers spend a lot of time learning new skills and learning to work together. To make that time, the school closes at 1 P.M. every Friday. The teachers initially spent their Friday afternoons mostly on professional development, learning about reading instruction and assessment, among other things. Ott said that too few educators know how to assess performance: "Nobody ever taught me how to write a test. In the old days, it was how to trick the students and make it as hard as possible. I guarantee I'll produce a bell-shaped curve like that. But when your goal is to ensure learning, you construct tests differently." Now that teachers have become sophisticated about such issues, they mostly use their common planning time to coordinate instruction, sometimes in grade-level teams and sometimes in cross-grade teams.

Once the staff felt that reading was under control, they scheduled an uninterrupted block of 60 minutes for math instruction and adopted Everyday Math, a program that focuses on making sure students understand the underlying concepts of math and master the algorithms of calculations. The fourth-grade teachers have become so adept at teaching math that every single fourth grader met state math standards in 2004.

To further ensure that all teachers are able to work together, the staff chose to adopt a single discipline model. Teachers went to Arizona to get training in what is called *positive classroom management*. The teachers came back and trained their colleagues in how to structure classrooms and instruction so that children are busy and on-task at all times, and thus less likely to cause disruptions. Years later, discipline is a minor issue at Lapwai.

First-grade teacher Sheila Hewett—herself a graduate of Lapwai Elementary—remembers that when she began teaching in 1989, "everyone was fighting." The teachers all cared about their own students, she said, but rarely felt responsibility for other students in the building. And each teacher had her own approach to reading instruction. "There was a whole-language emphasis, but no training." When the school began using "a proven curriculum with training, it opened all the doors." Among other things, she said, "It forced us to work together. All of our kids became *all* of our kids."

Principal Halverson admitted that focusing so closely on reading, math, and discipline has meant that some areas of the curriculum received less emphasis. "Social studies has taken the biggest hit," he said. That doesn't mean it isn't taught, along with science, art, and music. But it has taken a bit of a backseat. "Social studies and science instruction still depend on individual teachers," agreed Wagner. "There's less standardization, so some kids will get more and better social studies and science than others. Eventually they will be standardized."

Wagner—who by the time of my visit was no longer a classroom teacher but the curriculum coordinator for the district—gives a great deal of credit to standardization (some would call it alignment) of reading and math instruction as the driving force behind Lapwai's improvement. William Parrett, director of the Center for School Improvement and Policy Studies at Boise State University, who worked with Lapwai through the years as it underwent its improvement process, agreed that making sure that teachers aligned their curriculum to standards and were all expecting the same things from their students is one of the keys to Lapwai's success. "They didn't even have a curriculum," he said about the old days. "They had textbooks, teachers, and classrooms. That's it." Now they have a curriculum aligned to state standards and a plan for how to meet those standards.

But beyond ensuring consistent instruction to each child, the school has also worked to engage the larger community in the school improvement effort. Once a month, for example, superintendent Ott holds a "Lapwai Education Summit," which meets in the tribal council chambers. "It's an honor to be invited there," Ott said, to emphasize the importance the summit has for the tribe. During those meetings, tribal representatives, representatives from nearby colleges and universities, school staff members, and occasionally students discuss the school's strategic plan, the latest data, and, in Ott's words, "what we have done that you like and what could be done better." It is sometimes tempting for school officials to get defensive, but Ott said he is determined to face the issues squarely, without excuses. In addition, in the fall the school system holds a community dinner where students share school data with about 300 people, mostly parents.

By constantly sharing information and data, the community has learned to develop a greater stake in what happens at the school. Brenna Terry, who was appointed to the school board to fill a vacancy, sees the role of the school as crucial to helping the Nez Perce become more productive and engaged with the world outside the reservation. "I want us to reflect the real world," she said.

Ott gives the school board a lot of credit for focusing on student achievement and improving relations between the school and the community. When he first arrived, only two members of the five-member board were Nez Perce—today three are, and they are committed to raising the academic achievement of the students, he said. "This is the most educated board I've ever worked with."

In addition, the school has included the tribal council as partners in the cultural education of the students. For example, the council cosponsors events such as the "mini powwow," held in May, that all students from the district attend. Ott, whose district consists of one each of an elementary, middle, and high school, said the district has begun thinking about how to push students who have met state standards further academically. "We've done an excellent job to meet minimum standards," said Ott. "Now we are asking, 'How do we take it to the next level?'" His plan is to have students work on large academic projects that will link the school to the community, thus serving several purposes at once. By working on projects such as salmon recovery, the effects of dam removal from the Columbia River, and wolf recovery, the students will be able to engage directly in scientific research and see its importance to the larger community. "They will find the data, mine the data, analyze the data, and report to the tribe," Ott said.

As in many small, poor districts, money is a constant issue. "The state legislature said that education is a priority, but they never give more money," superintendent Ott said. Idaho teachers are among the lower-paid teachers in the country—the American Federation of Teachers ranks the state 32nd in teacher pay, for example. In addition, Lapwai has a small local tax base on which to draw, though the local tribal casino has helped provide some money in recent years. The relative lack of state and local support for education in Idaho means that Lapwai has had to rely very heavily on foundation and federal money to fund its professional development, afterschool programs, and other improvements. That federal money has come in the form of Title I (to poor students), Title II (for teacher training), Title VII (Indian education), impact aid (money in lieu of taxes paid by federal installations), a 21st Century Community Learning Center grant (which pays for afterschool programs), and a Safe Schools and Healthy Students grant (which pays for counseling and programs to prevent drug and alcohol abuse and violence). What that means is that federal funds provide more than a third of the Lapwai district's $6 million budget, a much higher percentage than in most places. "It speaks to the impoverishment [of the district] and to the underfunding of schools in Idaho," said Parrett.

Many of the improvement efforts have been funded with special grants. The initial money to adopt Success for All came from a federal Comprehensive School Reform Development grant, and the program was later supported by a three-year grant from the Idaho-based Albertson Foundation. That ran out in 2004, however, which means that the school has had to continue implementing SFA without the support of regular outside training and a dedicated SFA coordinator. Halverson and Wagner, the curriculum coordinator for the district in the 2004–05 school year, divided the responsibilities between them, but the lack of a dedicated person helping teachers implement SFA may have been a factor in why scores flattened in 2005. And with further cuts for the 2005–06 school year, Lapwai lost the curriculum coordinator position, which once again threatens to undermine the gains Lapwai has made.

"Every year is a continuing struggle," said Parrett, who wrote about Lapwai in the January 2005 issue of *School Administrator*. Parrett cites as the "elephant in the room" the fact that Lapwai has a very high mobility rate, similar to many other schools serving poor children. Among the Nez Perce is an established tradition of moving regularly between northern Idaho and Washington State—the Yakima Valley in particular—and Parrett is concerned that some children are simply not in Lapwai long enough to learn what they need to learn. Still, he is optimistic about Lapwai's chance for continued success, because the teachers and the principal are so committed to "connecting research to practice."

Lapwai has built a strong foundation of a coherent curriculum and a culture of collaboration. With all the worry about the flattening of the scores, it is unthinkable that it would ever slip back to the old days, when only 16 percent of Lapwai's third graders met state reading standards and 17 percent met state math standards. It has come too far.

POSTSCRIPT

Mike Halverson became principal of Lapwai Middle School and Teri Wagner became principal of Lapwai Elementary School during the 2005–06 school year. Wagner said that overall she was pleased with the state test scores. "Math scores are great—they went up even higher, to 87 percent proficient or advanced [of all students tested]. Reading scores went down a little. We're at about 74 percent proficient or advanced, which is down from the low 80s. The state changed its reading standards a little and I think we didn't have a tight enough alignment. It isn't that I think our kids aren't learning to read." Once again, the fourth grade posted the strongest scores in the school.

About her first year as principal, she said, "It was very hard work, and it was a great challenge. I feel good going into a second year with that behind me."

GRANGER HIGH SCHOOL
GRANGER, WASHINGTON

INTRODUCTION

One of the many criteria I used in determining whether to visit a school was whether it met Adequate Yearly Progress goals, or AYP, an artifact of No Child Left Behind. Each state is required to determine whether a school has met its targets each year, with the idea that by 2014, every school will have as its goal that 100 percent of its students will meet state standards as well as other criteria, including, in the case of high schools, increasing graduation rates.

Each state has set targets for meeting AYP from 2002 through 2014 so that, in most states, by 2006 roughly half the students were supposed to meet state standards. But the real power of No Child Left Behind is that it requires each subgroup to meet the goals of the total group in order for progress to be counted. This means, for example, that if half of all a school's students are expected to meet or exceed state standards, then half of each subgroup in the school is expected to meet state standards. The subgroups that most states report are white, African American, Latino, Asians and Pacific Islanders, American Indians, students with disabilities, and students who receive free or reduced-price meals. Some states have chosen to identify additional subgroups, such as boys and girls and, in California, Filipinos.

All the schools I visited made AYP except for Granger, which still didn't have a good enough graduation rate to make it. It had improved its graduation rate dramatically since 2001, but still too many students were dropping out. Part of the reason for making an exception of Granger was that it had proven very difficult to find a high school that met all the criteria for selection. Granger had started way down toward the bottom of the state in 2001, and regularly posted improved scores until, at least in reading, it was nearing state rates of proficiency. Simultaneously, it had reduced its dropout rate and increased its grad-

GRANGER HIGH SCHOOL
GRANGER, WASHINGTON

2006 Enrollment: 324 students in ninth through twelfth grade
2006 Demographics: 83% Latino
7% American Indian
10% White
83% meet qualifications for free and reduced-price lunch
Locale: Rural

Grade 10 Reading
Washington State Assessment of Student Learning (WASL)

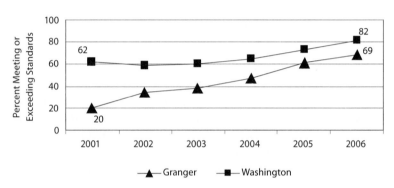

Note: In 2005, Washington State lowered its reading test's cut scores slightly, causing both Granger's and Washington's proficiency rates to be a couple of percentage points higher in 2005 and 2006 than they would have been if the cut scores had not been changed.

Grade 10 Writing
Washington State Assessment of Student Learning (WASL)

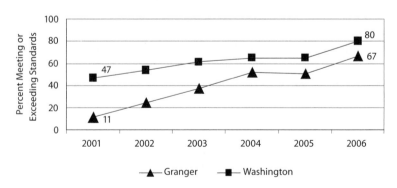

Grade 10 Math
Washington State Assessment of Student Learning (WASL)

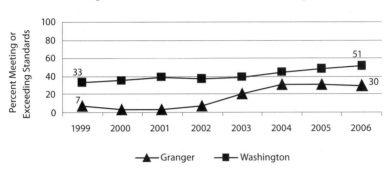

Source: Office of Superintendent of Public Instruction, Washington State, http://reportcard.ospi.
k12.wa.us/summary.aspx

Note: These graphs use the latest information that was available at the time of publication, which
is more recent than was available when the school was visited.

*uation rate. These improvements might not have been good enough to make
AYP, but they were quite significant nonetheless.*

As it turned out, the trip to Granger proved well worth it.

· · · · ·

When Richard Esparza, principal of Granger High School, shows visitors
around, he likes to show them where his students live. Although some
students—the sons and daughters of farmers and ranchers—live in the
surrounding hills of the Yakima Valley, a large agricultural area in Washington, most live in the small town of Granger. First, Esparza drives past the modest stucco bungalows that surround the school. "This is where my rich students
live," he said. Then he enters the mobile home park, with single-wide trailers
parked in fixed spots. "This is where my middle-class students live," he said.
Then he swings around into a park with small trailers pulled behind pickup
trucks. "This is where my poor kids live," he said. "People wonder how they
can live like this, but it's better than outside under a tarp."

About one-third of Granger High School's 330 or so students are the children of migrant agricultural workers, but most of the permanent families are
also agricultural workers who have settled in the Yakima Valley to pick and
sort apples and other crops. About 82 percent are Latino, 6 percent are Ameri-

can Indian, and the rest are white. Almost all the students—84 percent—are eligible for free or reduced-price meals.

As Esparza sees it, most of his students have only two choices—do agricultural work or get an education. "That's what my father told me," Esparza said. His father was an agricultural worker from Mexico. "I come from poverty and where the students come from," he said. When Esparza and his siblings complained about having to work with him in the fields, his father told them, "Then go to school." Esparza tells his students much the same thing: "This is your one chance—unless you know someone with a yacht club." Esparza said that many poor students and students of color can be likened to "academic refugees" and have been told over and over that they are incapable of success. "How many times have they been told, 'You guys are as dumb as a box of rocks'?"

Esparza grew up in a town quite similar to Granger, only 20 miles away, and he threw himself into high school both academically and athletically, winning a wrestling scholarship to Central Washington University, where he prepared to be a teacher and wrestling coach. He has returned to the area with the mission of making sure students at Granger have the same opportunities he had. To many, that mission might seem unpromising. The day he arrived to interview for the job, in 2000, he was greeted with gang-related graffiti that covered the school sign and the long, low wall that faced the school on the other side of the street. Discipline and attendance were serious problems that spilled over into the town, which had only recently begun its own program to lower the crime rate, one of the highest in the Yakima Valley. A resident of a town to the east of Granger said that years ago, police officers would escort visiting teams from the bus to the gym for basketball games.

Student achievement was dismal. Only 20 percent of the school's students met state reading standards back in 2001, 4 percent met math standards, and 10.8 percent met writing standards. Parents rarely came to the school, even for parent conferences. "I wish I had a picture from then," Esparza said. "None of the students carried backpacks. I would ask them where their homework was and they would say they didn't have any."

Today, just about all the students carry backpacks, even in the last week of school. Attendance at student conferences by parents or guardians has been 100 percent for five years running. Graffiti is rare, and discipline is much less of an issue than it was five years ago. The atmosphere of the school is pleasant, with teachers and students greeting each other and Esparza roaming the halls, encouraging the students to study, read, and plan for the future. Whether because of improvements in the school or the simultaneous improvements in policing in the town, Granger now has one of the lowest crime rates in the Yakima Valley.

Most strikingly, academic achievement has substantially improved: 61 percent of students met state reading standards in 2005 on the WASL, the Washington Assessment of Student Learning; 31 percent met math standards; and 51 percent met writing standards. Granger did not meet AYP in 2004 because its graduation rate was too low—59 percent. However, that was higher than the state graduation rate for Latino students, which was 49 percent, and its graduation rate improved in 2005 to 77 percent. Its "extended graduation rate" was 86 percent. (Extended graduation rate is calculated by Washington State to include students who take longer than four years to graduate, reflecting the fact that Washington has quite a few students who arrive in the United States during high school and need additional time.)

Although Esparza is proud of his school's improvement, he is not satisfied. "To me, 'making it' is 100 percent of our kids making it." He knows it will take a little more time, however. "I'm an idealist at heart," he said, "but a realist in mind."

The gains Granger has made can be linked to organizational and instructional changes in the school. But all the changes began with a change in expectations. Esparza expects all students to succeed and believes they can, and he expects his faculty to believe the same thing. Many didn't when he first arrived. A survey conducted by the Center for Educational Effectiveness, which provides technical support to the Granger school district, then showed that only about 50 percent of the faculty believed that Granger students were capable of meeting state standards. In May 2005, 75 percent responded on a survey that they believe their students can meet state reading standards.

Esparza began his principalship with a frontal assault on gang-related graffiti and clothing. All graffiti are removed by building maintenance employees within 24 hours. A Quonset-hut-type shelter behind the school, used for storage, was a prime target for gang graffiti, and Esparza said that every day for weeks he would drive to the hut on his way to school, take out the spray paint he kept in his car for just this purpose, and paint the door, which had been tagged during the night. "I can't have gangs announcing that they control the school," Esparza said. He said that no one has tagged it for the past two years. At the same time, the town of Granger formed a police department with eight officers and began its own war on graffiti, with young offenders sentenced to community service to wash off and paint over graffiti throughout the town. Today, a casual visitor would never even consider graffiti an issue in Granger.

Esparza also banned all gang-related clothing. When a student wore a blue bandana as part of a senior project, a requirement for graduation, Esparza became visibly upset. "It's for my presentation," the student answered. She kept it on while she read poetry and journal entries to a group of assembled students. "It's how she thinks of herself," Esparza said about her wearing the bandana— "as a gang member." But immediately after her presentation, she changed out of her bandana and baggy clothing.

Tackling graffiti and clothing was just the beginning. Esparza knew he needed to make the school more personal for the students. It is a small school, but students were being lost. Granger had a high dropout rate, for example. In the 2001–02 school year, the first year for which official numbers are available, Granger had a 9.4 percent annual dropout rate. That year, Esparza organized 50 teams of adults from the school and the community to visit the homes of all 400 students in the district—including several foster homes. (At that point, Granger High School included the seventh and eighth grades, which is why there were more families then than now. The town of Granger now has a middle school.) Visitors brought voter registration cards, a brochure welcoming the family to the school, and a prepared talk to convince families to be part of the school. To those teachers who objected that they didn't think they should be expected to do home visits, Esparza responded with the same practiced speech he has used many times since in other situations. "You are a great teacher. We have a difference in philosophy. I'd be happy to write you a recommendation."

Sometimes he loses a teacher when he gives that talk. In fact, Granger has only five teachers who were there when Esparza started. He fills vacancies by recruiting teachers from anywhere he can, including in the grocery store. "There are no applicants," he said. "I'm a recruiter." He has concentrated on bringing to the school teachers who believe their students can achieve at high levels. Some of the previous teachers left through transfers; others have retired.

Esparza found his lead teacher, Mike Nyberg, while Nyberg was substitute teaching. Nyberg first began teaching history and some math at Granger High School in 1966 as a way to stay out of the military during the Vietnam War. He retired in 1996 in order to raise his grandson, but after a couple of years he began substitute teaching at Granger. Esparza hired him as a reading coach to bring reading instruction into all the content areas, and he is now the instructional leader of the school, helping teachers develop lesson plans, teaching model lessons, mentoring new teachers, and keeping in touch with students through monitoring the lunchroom. He remembers the old days at Granger, when the school had a serious discipline problem and the attitude of the teachers was "We do the best we can with these kids," based on the assumption that "these kids" were incapable of high-level academic work. He has welcomed the introduction of standards and accountability as a needed "kick in the butt."

For his part, Esparza remembers the first two years of his principalship as being "nothing but fighting." He had to battle entrenched low expectations on the part of the faculty as well as a difficult-to-change organizational structure. Those years would have been easier, he said, "if I had had a framework to follow." But because few high schools have made the journey from low-performing to high-performing, he had little guidance he could follow in the research literature. As a result, he more or less made things up as he went along, with a constant emphasis on personalizing the school, giving the students the idea that they are capable, and keeping close track of all achievement data. Of the 330 students who were in his building in May 2005, he knew the incoming reading scores, current reading scores, state assessment scores, and last semester's grades of 300—and he was learning the last 30.

One key organizational change was to make Granger's "advisory" periods the core of how students are connected to the school. Many high schools have advisory or homeroom periods, but often little is done in them beyond assigning lockers, handing out report cards, and making announcements. At Granger, every professional staff member meets with a group of between 18 and 20 students four days a week for the last half hour of the day, keeping track of what work the student is doing and whether the student is behind. That advisory teacher is the liaison between the students, the students' teachers, the administration, and the students' parents. It is up to the advisory teacher to sign students up for classes as well as to know if a student is struggling in a particular class. Each semester the teacher meets individually with the student and the students' parents or guardians. "Teachers can't meet with 150 sets of parents," Esparza said, referring to the fact that most high school teachers have between 130 and 150 students. "But they can meet with 18." When one faculty member objected to this plan, saying that he was "not a social worker," Esparza responded with his prepared speech about being happy to write a recommendation.

The first year the advisory plan was instituted, only 20 percent of students brought their parents or guardians. "The teachers told me that was great because the previous year only 10 percent had come to conferences," Esparza said. "I said, yeah, okay, we can celebrate, but we need them all." In the last week of the 2004–05 school year, Esparza was worried because two students in the school—students in his own advisory group—had not had conferences. But they sneaked in the conferences under the deadline, marking the fifth straight year of 100 percent attendance. The conferences themselves are run by the students, who are given several topics to cover, including what they are learning, what classes they still need in order to graduate, what their grades are, what their reading levels are, what interventions (if any) are needed, and what their plans are for after high school. To prepare for the conferences, the teachers have touched base with the students' other teachers, because one of the points of the conferences is to make sure everyone—students, parents, and teachers—is on the same page with the same information.

Another example of the ethos of transparency and shared information is the line of big posters in the hallway listing every student who "owes" the school academic time and how much time is owed. The idea is that any student who has an unexcused absence must make up that time, either before school (when an English teacher is paid to be available), after school (when math and writing teachers are available), or on Saturday (when several teachers are available to work with the students). If a student is late to class by 15 minutes, that student owes .25 hours of academic time. If a student misses a day and doesn't bring in a note from a parent or guardian with a good explanation, that student owes 7.5 hours. Students may not play sports unless they are in the process of making up the time. Students who don't make up their time don't get their report cards. "Come on," Esparza said to one student, urging him to make up the time, "you're going to want to see this report card." Esparza is planning to require the same kind of system for excused absences as well as unexcused absences, because the theory is the same: students must put in the time they lose due to absences.

Granger had had a long tradition of two "senior skip days" a year. Esparza fought that by holding "senior appreciation days," essentially making a bargain with students—they come to school, and he'll provide them with a substitute for a senior skip day. In 2005, he sent the senior class to a Seattle Mariners game, a two-hour bus ride away. For sophomores, to give them a break after taking the state WASL exams, he sent them to the Fun Center, a theme park in nearby Yakima. The freshmen and juniors were sent to a movie in nearby Sunnyside (there is no movie theater in Granger) so they could do something fun as well.

Granger's unexcused absence rate went from 2.4 percent in the 2002–03 school year (the first year for which data are available from the state) to 1.6 percent in the 2004–05 school year.

In the 2004–05 school year, Granger High School instituted a "no failing" rule. Students whose grades fall below a C are required to get extra help until they bring their grades up, and again the advisory teachers are the key communication link. If a student is referred for extra help, the advisory teacher is the one who keeps parents informed. Students are given the opportunity to retake tests and quizzes until they get a C or better. Sometimes, Esparza said, students will say such things as, "I got no sleep—my dad got taken to jail last night." The answer is, "I'm sorry; study some more and we will give you the opportunity to retake the test." Esparza's goal, he said, is to "eliminate the bell curve—there's no reason for it." All his students are capable, he said. "They need to be motivated." In one semester, Granger cut the number of failing grades in half, from 278 in the first semester to 138 in the second semester.

Esparza and the teachers don't ignore the many problems facing their students. A Safe Schools/Healthy Students federal grant has provided the school with a social worker, a case manager, and a therapist who can work with students and their families. The case manager, Jerry Castilleja, is the official liaison between the high school, the middle school, and the police department, and they are in constant touch, including during evenings and weekends, when students and their families often run into trouble. Castilleja is sometimes called upon to find shelter for students whose parents are arrested, for example. He also coordinates nursing and medical services for pregnant students and new mothers (Granger has 15 students who are either pregnant or mothers).

His focus, however, is to get students back on track academically. One example he described was of a middle school student who came to school only 15 days one semester. Castilleja got in touch with the student's mother, arranged for her to have a parenting coach, and arranged for the student to get medical care. In the past, her son might have talked her into getting him a scooter, Castilleja said, but now she tells her son that first he must go to school, and then she'll see about the scooter. The student is now in school and passing, though he still struggles with academic work.

Most students arrive at Granger well below grade level, with reading scores to match. A glance at the district superintendent's report on test scores gives an idea of how far behind the students arrive in ninth grade. (The district consists of one elementary school, one middle school, and one high school.) Although about 26 percent of the fourth graders in the district meet state reading standards (compared to more than 70 percent in the state), only 21 percent of the seventh graders do (compared to more than 60 percent in the state), with 18 percent scoring at what the state calls "well below standard." These low scores were posted after Washington State changed the scoring system on the state assessments in 2003 to make it easier for students to meet state standards. Although the changes were minimal in the fourth- and tenth-grade tests (in which students could meet state standards if they answered one fewer question correctly than the previous year in those grades), they were more dramatic in the seventh-grade test. Matters are even worse for the district in math, where 72 percent of the seventh graders are well below standard.

Such low proficiency rates mean that most Granger High School students have a lot of catching up to do in a short amount of time, because they have less than two years before they take the WASL state test in 10th grade, and only four years before they must enter the post-high-school world.

Any student who is two or more years below grade level in reading is automatically enrolled in "Second Shot Reading," a program developed by a Granger teacher who has since moved away. In the program, students are given what are considered "high-motivation" stories, and teachers work with them on analyzing and writing about the stories. Some of the early stories are very short—not more than a paragraph or two—but they usually pose an ethical dilemma or present some other problem that students can discuss. The classes are very small and are staffed by a teacher and a paraprofessional to provide intense focus. The idea is for students to practice reading and writing. Many of the students stopped reading years before because they became discouraged about doing something they were not good at. "Instead of doing it more, they have stayed away from it" is how Esparza described the situation. Senior Pedro Navarrette entered Granger High School reading significantly below grade level. He didn't like to read, he said, "because I wasn't good at it." The school enrolled him in a reading program and "kept pushing me." In his senior year, he took Advanced Placement U.S. History and earned the dean's scholarship to Central Washington University, where he was planning to enroll in the fall of 2005. His complaint about Granger is that "we don't have enough AP classes."

One of the new teachers hired at Granger is Jesus Sandoval, who grew up "a couple towns down" from Granger and who teaches the Second Shot reading class. Sandoval holds a master's in teaching and has three years of experience. One of the things that helped him become a better teacher, he said, was "not fighting the WASL" but helping students learn what was required by it. To reinforce their reading practice, the library has bought $100,000 worth of high-interest books as part of the Accelerated Reader program.

In addition to that extra work on reading, every third-period class, from physical education to English, does one math problem from a previous WASL exam every Monday and Tuesday. In the beginning, lead teacher Nyberg would tape a mini lesson to be broadcast to the television in each classroom to explain the problem after the students worked on it, but he realized that "sent the wrong message." Because the state says that this math is something that every citizen should be able to do, it was disconcerting for students to think that some of their teachers couldn't do it, he said. So now each teacher does the mini math lesson after the students work the problem. Some teachers were initially apprehensive about this, particularly those who hadn't dealt with math in many years. "As the math department, we would go through the problem with them," said Tony Barcenas, the chair of the math department. "That made them more comfortable. We got to the point where they didn't need it."

Esparza and Nyberg attribute the rapid improvement—from 4 percent meeting state math standards in 2001 to 31 percent in 2004—to the fact that students received that additional math instruction every day. "One student had never taken algebra or geometry, and he still met standards," Esparza said. "I asked him how he did it, and he said, 'We do the problems every day.'"

Although the school showed significant improvement in reading in 2005, its math and writing scores stayed flat after 2004. "We were disappointed with our math and writing scores," Nyberg said. To address math, the school has put in place a plan to identify specific weaknesses of individual students and provide them with extra help during advisory periods. If, for example, a student is weak in measurement, he or she will be provided with a work packet on measurement and with tutoring during advisory periods by either a senior who is particularly good in measurement or a specially trained paraprofessional. The most common weaknesses are number sense, geometry sense, and measurement. In addition, the math staff has been strengthened by the hiring of a new math teacher, Nyberg said.

One area that is of special concern is science. Washington began reporting whether students meet state standards in science in 2004, when only 7.8 percent of Granger's students met standards. That number stayed flat in 2005. Esparza said that with a new chair of the science department, he is looking for improvement next year.

Although students have not needed to pass the WASL in order to graduate (the class of 2008 will need to), Esparza said his students have taken the test very seriously. It is an untimed test, meaning that students can take as long as they want, but most students finish in an hour and a half or two hours. At Granger, "I had students sitting there for three and four hours," he said about the 2005 test administration.

He attributed that to the pride students are taking in Granger's rising test scores. After they ever-so-slightly edged out nearby school Zillah in the writing and math scores in 2004, he said, "Now kids are really believing." (At Zillah, 63 percent of the students are white and only 36 percent qualify for free or reduced-price meals. In 2005, Zillah slightly edged out Granger in writing and continued to exceed it in the other categories.) Forty students signed up to take the PSAT in 2005, and SAT and ACT test taking has increased, both signs that students are beginning to have higher educational aspirations than they had in the past. To encourage them even further, Granger put in place an Advanced Placement U.S. History course, which is designed to replicate a college freshman survey course. The AP program is still shaky, however. Senior Pedro Navarrette, a student in the AP U.S. History class, thought he was prepared to take the nationally administered test, only to find out that he had missed the test date. He had never been told when and how to register, and the school hadn't administered it.

That is a mark of how far Granger still has to go before it provides the kinds of academic opportunities students like Navarrette want and that students in more privileged high schools are used to.

Esparza is determined to give students like Navarrette those kinds of opportunities, and he sent five teachers to AP training in the summer of 2005. It is his mission, he said, to prove that his students are capable of learning to high levels, which is why he has welcomed the accountability represented in No Child Left Behind. "I love it," he said. "It has to happen if our nation is going to be competitive." The law itself "definitely needs to be tweaked. But hold schools accountable. Don't let the schools like us off the hook."

POSTSCRIPT

In the 2006 WASL scores, Granger improved again in reading and writing, bringing almost 70 percent of students to the point of meeting state reading standards and 67 percent to state writing standards—a higher percentage than nearby Zillah—but math scores were again disappointingly flat. "The school board has heard my cries and allowed me to hire a third math teacher," Esparza said, "and maybe that will help cure these wounded kids." Even with those flat scores, however, Granger High School had met AYP requirements for 2006 because of its improved graduation rate.

In September 2006, the staff was getting ready to implement a "professional learning community" model, as advocated by educational writer and consultant Richard DuFour. "It's what we were doing before," Esparza said, "but with more structure." Esparza himself has gained quite a bit of recognition for his work in turning around a high school and has spoken around the country about the things that Granger High School has done to improve.

M. HALL STANTON ELEMENTARY SCHOOL
PHILADELPHIA, PENNSYLVANIA

INTRODUCTION

Early on in this project, I called Dr. Greg Thornton, who is the chief academic officer of the Philadelphia school system. I had known him when he was a community superintendent and then deputy superintendent in my school district, Montgomery County, Maryland, and I thought he might be intrigued by my project of finding schools of poverty that are high-achieving.

For years—decades, even—the news about Philadelphia schools had been dominated by low achievement and dangerous schools. Philly was just about as dismal as urban education got. But in 2004, under the leadership of the new superintendent, Paul Vallas, Philadelphia posted a bigger improvement in student achievement than the state of Pennsylvania. That is not to say student achievement in Philadelphia was anywhere near acceptable levels—the rates of achievement were still depressingly low. But Philadelphia had improved, and my general theory is that improvement is never an accident. So I asked Thornton if there were particular schools I should visit. He said sure, and offered to take me to a few.

As it turned out, we only got to two, and M. Hall Stanton was the one that really captured my attention. To get there from the district's office in downtown Philadelphia, we had driven through vast sections of North Philadelphia. To my shame, I hadn't realized how big and how devastated North Philadelphia is. Block after block, mile after mile of what appeared to be a bombed-out city rolled by the car window. I hadn't seen anything like it since the South Bronx in the 1970s, and I wouldn't see anything worse until New Orleans after Hurricane Katrina.

Stanton had posted scores that almost belied belief in 2004. After viewing the school, I believed the scores had been gained legitimately, but I realized that

125

M. HALL STANTON ELEMENTARY SCHOOL
PHILADELPHIA, PENNSYLVANIA

2006 Enrollment: 487 students in kindergarten through sixth grade
2006 Demographics: 99% African American
                         99% meet qualifications for free and reduced-price lunch
Locale: Urban

Grade 5 Reading
Pennsylvania System of School Assessment (PSSA)

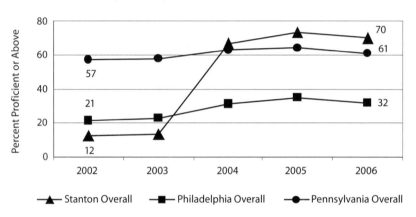

many others would be doubtful and would be likely to dismiss its 2004 scores as a fluke. For that reason I waited a year, crossing my fingers that in 2005 the scores would at least stay the same. But they took another jump up. So I headed back to Stanton for a second look.

• • • • •

Anyone looking for a dramatic turnaround of a school need look no further than M. Hall Stanton Elementary. In terms of percentage of students meeting state standards, Stanton went from being one of the most challenged schools in Philadelphia to one of the better-performing schools in Pennsylvania in just two years. When asked what made the difference, principal Barbara Adderley said, "It's no one single thing. There is no magic bullet."

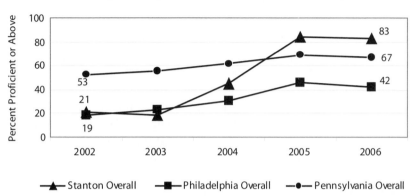

Grade 5 Math
Pennsylvania System of School Assessment (PSSA)

Source: Pennsylvania Department of Education, http://www.paayp.com/6541_default.html, and School District of Philadelphia: https://sdp-webprod.phila.k12.pa.us/school_profiles/servlet/

Note: These graphs use the latest information that was available at the time of publication, which is more recent than was available when the school was visited.

It may not be magic, but it is an effective combination of practices that are worthy of careful study by anyone interested in raising the academic achievement of children, particularly poor children and children of color.

Stanton sits in just about as difficult an urban environment as exists in America—North Philadelphia. Its neighborhood of narrow brick row houses is one where a block of houses that bravely sport pumpkins and autumn leaves at Halloween immediately gives way to many blocks scarred by burned-out and boarded-up buildings, with individual houses and even entire blocks torn down, and only piles of rubble where homes once stood. Children walking to school regularly pass crack houses. Nightly shootings are common. "This is not the worst part of Philadelphia," said the chief academic officer of the city's school system, Greg Thornton. "But it's close."

Adderley arrived at Stanton, a school of about 500 African American, mostly poor students, in the 2001–02 school year, a year when Stanton was one of 21 Philadelphia schools under a three-year restructuring process that in turn was part of a state program of supervision of the city's schools. According to teachers who were there at the time, the school was in chaos. "No one wanted to come to the top floor," where the older children were, said Christina Taylor.

Taylor was a fifth-grade teacher then, and she said her students used to beg her to allow them to eat lunch in her classroom because they were frightened to go into the halls. "We had the third- and fourth-grade gang wars," she said. "I just kept my kids with me all day." A few years before, in 1993, Stanton had been the subject of an Academy Award–winning documentary, *I Am a Promise*, which demonstrated that despite the efforts of a dedicated, hardworking, and caring principal, the students were unable to learn to high standards.

Achievement levels at Stanton were among the lowest in Philadelphia, a city where low achievement levels were and remain common. The first year Adderley was there, achievement levels didn't budge. In Adderley's second year, reading and math scores went up slightly, so that 13 percent of the students met the state reading standards and 20 percent met the math standards. The scores were still among the lowest achievement levels in the city.

In the 2003–04 school year, the scores skyrocketed: 71 percent of Stanton's students met state reading standards, and 47 percent met math standards. The growth was so dramatic, in fact, that the district retested the students to make sure there had been no mistake or chicanery. The retest confirmed that most students at Stanton were meeting state standards in reading, and many exceeded those standards. And when the 2005 test scores were released, showing that 73 percent of the students met state reading standards and 84 percent met math standards, it was clear that 2004 had not been a one-year fluke but was rather a reflection of new practices—practices that include a careful reorganization of instruction, comprehensive professional development of teachers, close examination of student data, a curriculum tightly aligned to state standards, and shrewd use of federal Title I dollars.

Success did not come overnight, but some of the changes were very sudden. One such change was the introduction of a new, citywide reading and math curriculum for the 2003–04 school year. For the first time, all elementary schools in the city were working on the same material at the same time. That meant that the children who transfer in and out of Stanton and the other city schools can be caught up quickly, and teachers can know what children are supposed to know. It also meant that teachers didn't have to create their own curriculum from scratch every day and could concentrate on teaching. Professional training of teachers provided by the district has also been tightly focused on what is in the curriculum, making the training more immediately useful to teachers.

Before, each school, and often each teacher, chose what would be taught. Chief Academic Officer Thornton called the old system in Philadelphia "a Burger King mentality—everybody got to have it their way," which made for a chaotic and unstructured learning environment for students and meant that district training was unfocused and scattershot. Even longtime teachers who lament the loss of autonomy acknowledge that children who move frequently do not get as lost with the core curriculum.

Since the introduction of the curriculum, student achievement in Philadelphia has improved. Perhaps most dramatically, the city's improvement has outpaced that of the state. For example, from spring 2004 to spring 2005, the percentage of fifth-grade students in Pennsylvania who met state math standards improved by seven percentage points, from 61 percent to 68 percent; during the same time, Philadelphia's fifth-grade students improved proficiency rates by 14 percentage points, from 31 percent to 45 percent. Reading improvements have been more modest, and Philadelphia still has a long way to go before its students are performing at the same level as students in the rest of the state—but it clearly has made a significant leap forward.

Even so, most schools in Philadelphia have not improved as much or as fast as Stanton. The credit for that must go to how the curriculum is taught and how the school is organized around achievement. The first thing a visitor notices is that despite the fact that Stanton is housed in a big, dreary, three-story school building, it is kept very clean, and the halls are as welcoming as institutional halls can be made, with a huge fish tank in the hall outside the office, a curio cabinet with Adderley's doll collection, student work posted in the hallways, and teddy bears posed on rocking chairs next to tables with lots of inviting picture books. "People in other schools tell me they can't do this because their kids would tear the stuff apart," said Thornton. "But the kids here don't do that." "The only reason things fall off our walls," bragged Taylor, "is because the tape doesn't hold." The books get disarranged because "the children are reading them," she added. Taylor, formerly a fifth-grade teacher, is currently the lead math teacher for the whole school and team leader of one of the school's three "academies."

Breaking the school into three academies—the Ruby Bridges Academy, the Bill Cosby Academy, and the Ben Carson Academy—was one of Adderley's first organizational changes. Students are randomly assigned to the academies, each of which has kindergarten through sixth grades. The only difference in their curricula is that each student is expected to know something about the namesake of his or her academy. Also, the academies may have slightly different projects. In fall 2005, the whole school adopted a travel theme, for example, and each academy studied a particular area of the world—one academy chose Africa, another the British Isles—and the hallways and classrooms of each were filled with maps, artifacts, and paintings that the students in each academy had studied and then used to explain what they had learned to students from other academies.

Adderley organized each academy to house all the grades because she wanted the older children to act as role models for the younger children rather than be kept apart, which had fostered discipline issues in the past. Also, teachers get to know the children in their academies even before they have them in their classrooms. "It becomes a family," Adderley said. In part to combat the separation that the three academies might cause, Adderley instituted a schoolwide convocation outside the building every morning at 8:25, when children, teachers, administrators, and parents and guardians say the Pledge of Allegiance, sing a song such as "Lift Every Voice," and hold a moment of silence. A closing ceremony ends the day at 3:05. The ceremonies provide "a time for the whole school to feel a sense of community," Taylor said.

Each of the classrooms for the younger children is set up similarly, with centers for science, social studies, math, reading, and writing. Teachers personalize their classrooms with colorful rugs, and student work lines the walls. Classrooms for the fifth and sixth graders are more traditionally arranged, with individual desks, sometimes in rows and sometimes in clusters, depending on the lesson.

Time is just as structured as space. Each class has a 90-minute math block in which students are given instruction, play math games, and do math activities, and a two-hour "literacy block," in which students read, write, speak, and listen to books read aloud. In the early grades, explicit phonics lessons are part of the literacy block, but after that, phonics lessons are "embedded" in the reading instruction, meaning that teachers provide mini lessons when they notice a mistake in reading.

A major part of the literacy block is guided reading, when the teacher leads the children in reading a story or article as laid out in the citywide curriculum. Then, while the teacher works with a small group of children, teaching them a skill or discussing a particular aspect of the story, the rest of the children will work their way through the centers until it is their turn to work with the teacher. For example, a class that is working on a story about Lou Gehrig will have some children working on charting baseball pitches and hits, some writing a summary and response to the story, some reading about the history of baseball, and some working on a science project. During one second-grade literacy block, children reading a picture book about a gorilla named Koko and his pet kitten were happy to discuss the ways in which they were similar to and different from Koko, one of the assignments in the writing center. "He uses sign language," said one boy. "So do I." (Quite a few of the children had begun learning sign language in the afterschool programs offered by the school, which provide enrichment and additional instruction.)

In the 2005–06 school year, the city adopted a social studies and science curriculum published by K–12 Science. Stanton began using books, hands-on science kits, pictures, and a great deal more. "Specials"—art, music, physical education, and computer classes, in addition to a weekly science lesson taught by a science teacher—are scheduled so that grade-level teachers across the academies can meet together to plan lessons.

Time is carefully husbanded. Hours and minutes are not to be wasted, as they were in the past. "Friday was movie day," Taylor said about the days before restructuring. "Now there's no time to do a movie unless it's educational." Because such a high percentage (87 percent) of students qualify for free or reduced-price lunch, all students are provided breakfast as well as lunch. Breakfast is a working meal, with students reading and working with the teacher while they eat.

Even daily classroom practice comes under time-management scrutiny. When a second-grade teacher's class consistently took more than ten minutes to gather English language arts (ELA) materials for the literacy block, his lead teacher advised him to organize the materials ahead of time in bins so that the children could get immediately to work. "The ELA bins have cut down on wasted time," said the teacher, Ted Smith.

That kind of guidance is part of a careful system of support for teachers. Each academy has a team leader who works with classroom teachers to plan lessons, look at student data, work with small groups, provide model lessons, and help plan school- and academy-wide activities. The team leaders are colleagues of the classroom teachers, not supervisors—an important distinction in Philadelphia's unionized schools. Their authority lies solely in their ability to be helpful to teachers. "The teachers trust them" is the way Adderley described her lead teachers.

The team leaders are also literacy, math, and science specialists. In many schools, math and literacy specialists are still classroom instructors. At Stanton, the lead teachers almost never do classroom instruction, except when teaching a model lesson as an example to a teacher. "[Ms. Adderley] gets really upset if we are doing classroom instruction," said Taylor about the principal. "We're supposed to teach the teachers, not the students."

During the restructuring process, Stanton had math and literacy coaches who came to the school to help guide instruction. They alternated weeks—one week of math, one of literacy. Their "all day, every day" presence, helping teachers plan, providing model lessons, and generally guiding teacher practice, Adderley said, "is something that has really supported going from correc-tive action to being just a regular school."

Additional support for teachers came from two half-day professional devel-opment programs per month, provided by the district's central office. For the first two years Adderley was at Stanton, the district sent trainers to the school to provide focused professional development in the curriculum and training in such areas as using student data to drive instruction. Now that Stanton has become one of the more successful schools in the city, the district has pulled back from its direct intervention, and it no longer requires particular training or professional development. Stanton is now in charge of designing its own professional development, and the leadership team at the school has decided to focus its attention on literacy. This reflects a need shown by the school's data, which reveal that although 16 percent of Stanton's students do not meet state math standards, 27 percent do not meet state reading standards. "We can't forget about math," Adderley said, "because then we'll slip there. But our focus has to be on literacy." Keeping focused on improvement means there is always work to be done. But Stanton has come a long way from the time when nine out of ten students couldn't meet state reading standards.

"Stanton is not an anomaly," said Philadelphia's chief academic officer, Greg Thornton. "There are other Stantons," meaning other Philadelphia schools that have shown progress despite challenging student populations. But there are also schools that rival the old, chaotic, and low-achieving Stanton. To respond to that fact, the district has designed a system of interventions whereby every school in the city is categorized along what could be called a "continuum of care." The lowest-performing schools will receive a kind of send-in-the-cav-alry approach of full-time math and literacy coaches, intense supervision, and sometimes new staff—in other words, a process similar to what Stanton un-derwent. Thirteen schools fall into that category, and Thornton is expecting that within a year or two they, too, should show similar improvement (except for one, which may be disbanded altogether). Most Philadelphia schools fall into one of the middle categories, where some coaching and dedicated profes-sional development is provided, but not with the same intensity. "When you have limited resources," Thornton said, "you have to leverage those resources." Philadelphia has only about $7,000 per student to spend a year, about $700 less than many wealthier districts in Pennsylvania. As a result, Thornton feels he must target his resources to schools with the most need.

Stanton is so far along in the process that it will be in the category of schools needing the least intervention. Thornton worries that "when you wean them away [from district support], is there a regression to the mean?" That is, if

Stanton and other schools like Stanton do not continue to get the kind of support they have had in the past, will achievement fall?

It's hard to believe, given the current staff, that Stanton will fall. The training and support it received in the past built its capacity to excel. "The restructuring process really helped," said Kathleen Shallow about the help provided to the school. "It provided materials, training, professional development." Shallow, who had taught kindergarten before Adderley arrived and is now the literacy lead teacher and an academy team leader, said that back when she was a teacher, she had had high expectations for her students, and she had had good control of the classroom, but "I had no idea what to teach. Now, everything is structured."

Taylor agreed with Shallow that the training and professional development helped focus the school on instruction. "I loved my kids. I believed I was successful. But we didn't look at the data." And, she said, "We used a lot of excuses about what happens out there [outside the school] for what happened here." What she meant was that in the past, most teachers and other school staff assumed that Stanton students couldn't reach high achievement levels because their lives were made so difficult and chaotic by poverty and discrimination.

Such assumptions are no longer tolerated. "We don't do that here," Adderley said. "Excuses for poor performance are no longer permitted." Poor performance is now a signal that instruction needs to improve in some way. "Some people didn't have high expectations for their students," Adderley said of the staff she inherited. "Most of those people are gone. They have retired or transferred." As a result, much of the teaching force at Stanton is either young or relatively new to teaching. "That's sometimes good," said Taylor, "because if you have an experienced staff, they find it hard to change." But it also means that many teachers at Stanton need considerable support—support Taylor and the rest of the leadership of the school must provide.

In addition to the district training, teachers meet in grade-level teams every day—sometimes with the team leaders—to plan lessons. Once a week, they meet with the team leaders and the principal. The once-a-week meetings are devoted to looking at student work in a focused way to see whether students are meeting standards and evaluate whether instruction needs to change. "In the past," Adderley said, "teachers looked at student work to grade it, put it up on the board, and discuss it with parents. But we never looked at it together."

At one meeting in the fall of 2005, second-grade teachers Ted Smith, Kimberly Gallagher, and Margo Pinckney met with literacy lead teacher Shallow, math literacy teacher Taylor, and principal Adderley to discuss their students' progress in writing. Smith's class was working on using rich, specific details in their writing. Smith had assigned his students to write a poem about fall and said he was looking to see if "the kids are really seeing" what they wrote about. "I see the treetops high up in the sky" was an image Smith liked in one of his student's writing. But other sentences were vague and flat. "I don't think he has a—I don't want to say clue, but he doesn't understand how to add detail," Taylor commented. Someone suggested giving students lists of descriptive words that would give students ideas about what details to add. Team leader Shallow suggested, "As you're reading, if there are descriptive words, point them out." Smith said he would try both suggestions.

Gallagher had been working on writing conventions, specifically punctuation. After the group looked at some of her students' work, with punctuation marks scattered almost indiscriminately, Gallagher concluded that they didn't understand the lesson she had taught. "I'm going to go back and reteach it," she said. Adderley suggested that the teacher write a big letter on chart paper and give kids laminated commas, periods, and question marks and have them place them in the right places as part of a group lesson.

Keeping the emphasis on teaching techniques and strategies means the discussion stays on instruction. "It's not about feeling sorry for kids," Adderley said. "It's about making sure that they understand what it is they're expected to do." She also urged the teachers to move past issues of simple comprehension and push students to think deeply and analyze what they are reading. "Who cares what color shirt Mr. Smith has," she said as an example. "What materials were used to construct Mr. Smith's shirt? Where do the materials come from? If you ask questions that are deeper and more probing, they'll learn more," she told the teachers.

To make sure students are learning what is expected, teachers administer regular assessments, including short "checkpoint" tests every two weeks and districtwide "benchmark" tests every six weeks. Any child who is falling behind is identified and is the subject of a meeting with teachers, Adderley, and the parents. The team leader will videotape a few minutes of the child within the classroom so that all team members—including the parents—have a full picture of how the child is functioning. They then agree to particular teaching strategies or interventions—for example, what reteaching will be done, what math games the student should play, what books the student should read, or whatever other intervention the team decides on—and meet again in 30 days to evaluate whether those interventions are working or whether others are needed.

The assessment wall of the meeting room is covered with Post-it notes, each note representing a child, color-coded by teacher and arranged by reading level, so that the faculty members have an instant read on the progress of all 527 children in the school, each of whom has an individual plan in place. In many schools, individual plans are done only for students identified as needing special education services—at Stanton, each student has one. Students who need special education services have more formal plans, known as Individualized Education Programs (IEPs), and Stanton has 22 such students. Although a few who cannot function in a regular classroom are in a self-contained classroom, the rest are included in the regular classrooms. Two special education teachers work in the classrooms—one in the younger grades and one in the older grades—to provide support to the students and the teachers. "As much as possible, we want special education students in regular ed classrooms," said Liz Baeringer, the head of special education services at Stanton. The special education teachers, with additional training in different methods of reading and math instruction, teach model lessons, help teachers structure their lessons, and work with struggling students—whether or not they are identified as "special ed."

By keeping the focus on high-quality, fast-paced instruction with careful attention to anyone who needs it, Adderley said that less attention needs to be paid to the discipline issues that were crippling Stanton before she came. Good instruction, she said, encourages good behavior. "We had a teacher who had poor classroom management skills," Adderley said. "She thought it was the kids, not how she planned her instructional program. But we've heard that she's having problems in her new school in the suburbs."

In addition to focusing closely on keeping the students so busy learning that they tend not to get into trouble, Stanton has a number of things to encourage students to be good school citizens. Teachers have "being good" tickets that they give children they see doing something nice for someone else, such as picking up a dropped pencil or performing some kind of good deed. Each ticket is worth 25 cents toward school supplies such as notebooks or hole punchers, and each child who receives one is entered in a drawing for a monthly lunch with the principal. In addition, each child who is on time for school is given a chance in a raffle drawing for a large prize such as a bicycle or radio.

In this way, Adderley said, Stanton promotes an atmosphere that rewards good behavior rather than simply punishing bad behavior. "I don't believe in suspension," she said, although she will suspend—on one day in October 2005, four students were suspended, a fairly high number for an elementary school. She will assign misbehaving students to community service to work with the building custodians or otherwise try to "change the behavior." Throughout

Philadelphia, all school staff members—including building service staff—have received training in behavioral management, so they are all part of the support team. Adderley still faces discipline issues, however. One day, for example, a temporary teacher needed rescuing by Adderley when her class seemed on the verge of being out of control. After leading the students in some calisthenics to get them moving, Adderley lectured them without raising her voice above normal speaking level. "I don't like what I'm hearing and in some cases I don't like what I'm seeing," she told the class before leaving. "If I speak to you again, you'll have detention." Afterward she said that it was the weak lesson, taught by a weak teacher, that led to the bad behavior. Many substitute teachers are less skilled and knowledgeable about instruction and classroom management, she said.

Other issues also crop up. For example, when a young boy was sent to the office for an unknown offense, Adderley spent many minutes trying to figure out what had happened. Stony-faced but teary-eyed, the boy refused to tell, keeping all his answers monosyllabic and barely responding. "Am I fussing at you?" she asked him in an attempt to get him to calm down. "I'm not fussing at you, I just want to know what happened." It took some time before she was able to get him calm enough to be taken back to the classroom. Out of earshot of a visitor, she finally learned that he had been too embarrassed to reveal the sexual gesture he had made to a girl. "He didn't even know what it was," Adderley said later. "He saw it on television."

Time-consuming and sometimes difficult, that kind of one-on-one discipline that has as its purpose changing behavior and has as its method establishing relationships appears to pay off. Attendance is consistently above 90 percent.

To build relationships with her students' parents, Stanton has a "community liaison" who, for example, arranges meetings with parents whose children are struggling or who are consistently absent. "I'm the link between the home and the school," community liaison Sharon Stewart said. Among other things, Stewart attends truancy court once a month to testify against parents whose children do not regularly attend. She also arranges parenting classes on Friday mornings that include nutrition information and advice on how to shop at the supermarket, how to clean up bad credit, and other practical seminars. "Many of my parents are very young," Adderley said in explanation of why such classes are necessary.

Stewart's salary is paid for out of Stanton's Title I money. Title I is the federal program that is targeted specifically to help poor children achieve at the same levels as nonpoor children, and Stanton uses the money very strategically in ways agreed to by the staff in what Adderley describes as a "collaborative process." The bulk of it goes to pay for materials, books, and supplies, but Stewart's position is paid for as part of the school's efforts to improve parental involvement, a goal of Title I. In addition, Title I funds go for afterschool and Saturday enrichment classes that are used to both help students who are falling behind and provide extras, such as sign language instruction and other enrichment, as well as for the professional development of teachers.

Out of general funds, Stanton pays for two days of the school nurse on top of the three days that the district provides. "I think it's important," Adderley said about extending the nurse's week, explaining that many of her students have asthma or other health problems that require monitoring and careful administration of medication, which the nurse can provide. The nurse also arranges for outside help for students. For example, she applied for the Eagle Eye Foundation (sponsored by the Philadelphia Eagles) to bring its bus equipped with eye examination equipment to give students eye exams and provide them glasses.

With all of its canny use of resources and its consequent successes, Stanton still faces enormous challenges. Hiring is one. In the fall of 2005, the sixth grade had two new teachers who, though they were provided with what Adderley called "the best support we had to offer," didn't last the first week. That left Stanton scrambling to fill the positions with substitutes. Just as Adderley thought she had found a good long-term substitute, he didn't show up one day, forcing the school to scatter the students throughout the school in different classes. Lead teacher Taylor, who is training to be a principal, went to the district hiring fair to find someone for sixth grade, and she said she found no one who she thought was ready to take on the challenge of teaching at Stanton. "You have to be kind of tough to teach here," Taylor said. In her opinion, the candidates were all too young and inexperienced. It was months before Adderley was satisfied that her sixth graders had good teachers, months that she said hurt the students. "They're good kids, too," she said. "They're the ones who did so well last year on the fifth-grade tests."

And as much as Stanton does to keep the emphasis on instruction, the difficulties of the children's lives outside of school intrude regularly. Students are always jittery the day after a shooting in the neighborhood, and tragedy is never far away. One day in November 2005, a student died after his aunt gave him one of her pain pills in a misguided attempt to help him through an asthma attack.

As difficult as these kinds of things are for the school community, however, none of it is allowed to stop the main job of the school: teaching and learning.

POSTSCRIPT

In December 2005, the school received new technology. Kindergarten through third-grade classrooms have been equipped with whiteboards, cameras, and laptops that allow teachers to use the Internet while teaching lessons. "This has been an invaluable tool to increase the achievement levels at Stanton," Adderley said. In addition, with the help of a grant, all teachers received laptops during the 2006–07 school year.

The 2006 data showed strong growth for the third grade, achievement that held stable for the fifth grade, but a disappointing performance for the sixth grade (only 52% of students were proficient and above in math, and 16% were proficient and above in reading). In part, this reflects that Stanton lost some of its previous year's fifth graders to charter and magnet schools, as well as receiving quite a few new students who hadn't had the benefit of the previous years of instruction. In addition, the sixth grade had substitute teachers for more than half of the school year. "It was a horrible year for them," Adderley said, adding that she was hopeful that the next year would be better, because she had hired two sixth-grade teachers she was reasonably confident would work out well. In the 2006–07 school year, Stanton began the first phase of the application program for the International Baccalaureate Primary Years Programme, and teachers received training during the summer of 2006 to prepare for that.

WEST JASPER ELEMENTARY SCHOOL
WEST JASPER, ALABAMA

INTRODUCTION

West Jasper Elementary School had been one of The Education Trust's "Dispelling the Myth" schools in 2004, and it had posted substantial and impressive gains on the state tests. When I got there, I found a school that had put in place a process of improvement that not only could be emulated by other schools, but was being emulated in a systematic, conscious way. I found this process fascinating, which is why I have chosen it as the focus of this chapter.

This is not to say that the school is where it should be yet. Third-grade student work on the walls, for example, showed none of the sophistication of the second-grade students at Lincoln Elementary in New York. But teachers at West Jasper have taken their school from being one where hardly any children could read well to one where most can; that achievement alone is worth celebrating, and their experience is worth studying.

• • • • •

On the other side of the railroad tracks from the mostly well-off schools in Jasper, Alabama, is a little elementary school where 80 percent of the children are poor. Tucked into a hilly neighborhood where many of the houses are wooden bungalows, West Jasper Elementary, which is almost evenly divided between African American and white students, was traditionally the low-performing school of Jasper City. Many still think it isn't possible for the children in West Jasper to achieve at the same level as the other children in Jasper. But West Jasper is proving them wrong—its students meet state reading and math standards at more or less the same rate as students in the rest of Jasper, and at much higher rates than those in the rest of Alabama. For exam-

WEST JASPER ELEMENTARY SCHOOL
JASPER, ALABAMA

2005 Enrollment: 313 students in pre-kindergarten through fifth grade
2005 Demographics: 53% African American
                        1% Latino
                        43% White
                        81% meet qualifications for free and reduced-price lunch
Locale: Town

Grade 4 Reading, 2006
Alabama Reading and Mathematics Test (ARMT)

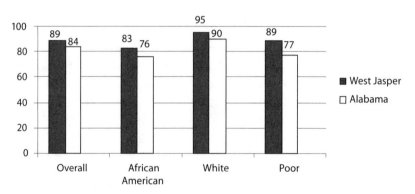

ple, 82 percent of its students—including 77 percent of its African American students and 86 percent of its poor students—meet or exceed state math standards, compared to 72 percent, 59 percent, and 61 percent, respectively, of students in Alabama. For the most part its median scores on the norm-referenced SAT 10 test are above national norms—a substantial change from the past, when students at West Jasper scored substantially below national norms.

From a school where very few children were reading in the 1990s, West Jasper has become a school where almost all the children are reading. In most places, that transformation would simply stand on its own. It would be yet another example of the possibility of making sure that all children learn, but it would not have much effect on the surrounding schools. But Alabama is doing something very unusual: It is deliberately trying to replicate in other schools the educational DNA of West Jasper and of 19 other "best-practice" schools in the state. Educators are identifying what elements have combined to improve

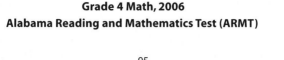

Grade 4 Math, 2006
Alabama Reading and Mathematics Test (ARMT)

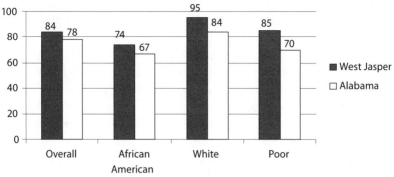

Source: Alabama Department of Education, http://www.alsde.edu/Accountability/Accountability. asp

Source for enrollment and demographic information: U.S. Department of Education, www.nces. ed.gov

Note: These graphs use the latest information that was available at the time of publication, which is more recent than was available when the school was visited. Previous report cards can be found at the state department of education website.

those schools, and then are carefully and deliberately teaching those elements of success to other principals and school leaders. In this way, Alabama is attempting to make all of its elementary schools at least as successful as West Jasper. This replication process has attracted national attention because it is a systematic and conscious attempt to change the entrenched organizational structure of schools that for generations has been built on isolation and the singular, idiosyncratic practices of individual teachers and principals. The replication process could be seen one day in February 2006, when a group of principals and reading coaches had been brought to West Jasper to observe how it operates. Joining them that day was a delegation from Massachusetts, which was planning to bring back elements of the replication process. "You can find outstanding schools in every state," said Ed Moscovitch, a Massachusetts economist. "But not many states are doing what Alabama is doing" to spread the best practices of those good schools.

The outsiders were there for West Jasper's "walk-through" and "data meeting," two key processes that have led to West Jasper's improvement. They had been brought there by Martha Barber, who works as a "principal coach" with 36 schools in that area of Alabama. Her work is organized through the Alabama Reading Initiative (ARI), which is the state initiative to improve reading instruction throughout its schools. West Jasper joined ARI in 1999, the program's second year, and by 2007 all Alabama elementary schools will be ARI schools. The stated goal of ARI, the state superintendent, and Barber is for all children in all schools to be able to read at least to state standards by third grade. Barber works most intensively with the eleven schools that were represented at the West Jasper meeting; those schools were either brand-new to the program or very low-performing. She visits the schools, comments on classroom practice, helps set up data systems, and walks principals through the process of using data to drive instruction.

In February 2006, as part of a regular series of meetings, she brought the folks from the eleven schools to West Jasper so they could see principal Eric Smith and reading coach Lynn Aaron conduct their walk-throughs and data meeting. In exchange for hosting two such visits a month, West Jasper is given a grant of $5,000 a year, which it uses to buy classroom materials. Although some schools would consider such hosting duties disruptive, Smith said that the visits are "good for our school and good for morale." Just a few years ago, he said, "Teachers felt [West Jasper] wasn't a good school to teach in" because it was such a low-status school, mostly because of the poverty of its children. "But now people are here learning from them, and they are able to go out and make presentations about their work."

A large group of almost 30 people sat in the school library that February day, watching Smith and Aaron meet with Barber to explain what they would be looking for in their walk-through. A walk-through is a systematic visit by an educator to a classroom to observe specific things. For decades, principals have evaluated teachers on the basis of more formal kinds of classroom observations, which for the most part have consisted of sitting through a whole or part of a class. Walk-throughs, in contrast, are meant to give administrators a quick snapshot of what is going on. They are not used as part of teachers' job evaluations so much as to give teachers help and guidance on things they can do to improve.

On this day, Smith, Aaron, and Barber sat at a library table pretending they were in what Barber called a "fish bowl," surrounded by the observers. Smith explained to Barber that he and Aaron had decided that today's walk-through would be focused on the third grade, because both third-grade teachers were new and the data indicated that they might need a little bit of help. The percentage of students meeting the reading standards had risen from 57 percent at the beginning of the year to 62 percent at the midyear assessment of prog-ress, and the percentage of students who were "at risk," or reading far below the goal, had dropped to 18 percent from 27 percent. "So there is progress," said Smith, "but we're going to focus on them because 38 percent of the students still don't meet standards."

The things they would be looking for, Smith told Barber, were whether students were being given ample reading practice, whether the structure of the classroom was "maximizing" instruction, whether the classrooms had li-braries, and whether student work was posted on the walls. "Part of maxi-mizing," Aaron said, is "whether instruction is challenging—especially for stu-dents who have met standards. We need to keep them challenged." Also, Aaron added, the classroom library should have a variety of books, so that students can "read at their independent level."

Once they had finished talking with Barber, Smith and Aaron led the ob-servers on their walk-through. It was a large group, so it broke into two—a principal group and a reading coach group, with the Massachusetts team split between them—so that they could separately visit the two third-grade classrooms. Both classrooms were in the middle of their 90-minute "literacy block," which is dedicated to reading and writing.

In the first classroom, 23 students were scattered throughout the classroom, three at computers, four at desks reading chapter books independently, five sprawled on the floor reading, four listening to the school's computer coach reading a story aloud, three working with a Title I paraprofessional to under-stand the vocabulary in a story, and four with the teacher, Beverly Simon. The four students with Simon worked in pairs, with one student reading aloud and the other playing "word detective," meaning that they paid attention to their partner's reading to see if every word was read correctly. All three of the adults working with students talked about the words they were reading in order to introduce new vocabulary and make sure the students understood the mean-ings of the words.

The two paraprofessionals in the room were scheduled to switch to the other classroom—they spend 45 minutes in each classroom a day. But during the walk-through the second classroom had only one adult in the room—the teacher, Kalah Morrow. Morrow was working with a small group of students while four other students worked at computers, four were reading along with a tape at a listening station, three were reading independently, and the rest were sitting at PLATO reading stations. PLATO stations are little computers that have the look and feel of video games, but they work on reading skills by giving children passages to read and then asking them to answer questions that require skills as simple as literal comprehension and as sophisticated as sequencing and inference. The school got a grant to purchase ten PLATO stations for each classroom.

During the walk-throughs, the principals and reading coaches moved quietly around the classrooms taking notes and occasionally asking students what they were working on. When they were done with the walk-throughs, everyone reconvened in the library to watch Smith, Aaron, and Barber discuss what they had observed. "They were very focused," Aaron said about the students. "They didn't look up and say hello," which Aaron said meant that the students were working hard and not distracted by the visitors.

"They were probably afraid with all of us coming in," offered Barber as an alternate explanation. But, she added approvingly, "Kids were on task, and kids were behaving. Routines are in place," noting that that was very commendable for two first-year teachers who, earlier in the year, had had some trouble establishing classroom routines. "They've come a long way," observed Aaron. "There was a lot of progress made." Smith said that what he saw was good, "but more intensity" in instruction was needed.

In terms of the specific things they had said they were looking for, the visitors said they were happy they saw small-group instruction, which allows teachers to individualize instruction to three or four students at a time. They noted that some student work was posted, though not as much as they wanted. And all three were happy with the classroom libraries, which had quite a lot of books organized by genre and reading level, so that all students would be able to find something to read independently. "I may make that something other teachers go and look at," Smith said, meaning that the libraries were so well set up that they could be used as models for other classrooms.

Barber pushed. "We need to look at the level of engagement," she said, meaning both the amount of independent reading students were doing and the instruction being given. She wasn't happy with the low level of intensity of the independent reading she saw, most of which consisted of children reading picture books.

Before beginning to plan for the data meeting, Barber turned to the audience of principals and reading coaches and asked, "What did you notice about Eric and Lynn during this meeting?" The visiting principals offered words like, "comfortable," "professional," and "respectful." One principal said, "You understand that nothing's perfect but that everything is to be worked on." Another added that it was clear that within the school, "It's not what the principal said and the reading coach said, it's what *we* expect." One reading coach asked for a list of the reading resources, such as the PLATO reading stations. Barber asked reading coach Aaron to provide such a list, but added, "It's not in the things. Things help. But when the change occurs, it's because of what the staff does." Barber, Smith, and Aaron then began going over what would happen in the subsequent data meeting.

Alabama administers several tests to elementary-grade students. One is the ARMT, or the Alabama Reading and Mathematics Test, which measures whether students have met state standards and is used for the federal No Child Left Behind accountability system. Another is the SAT 10, a nationally norm-referenced test, which Alabama has given versions of for years.

Those are the annual tests that West Jasper takes seriously. But in the interim, in the younger grades it also regularly administers "DIBELS," or Dynamic Indicators of Basic Early Literacy Skills, which are one-minute assessments developed at the University of Oregon to measure reading fluency and which have been adopted by ARI schools. The procedure is that a student reads aloud a passage selected for his or her grade level for one minute, and the teacher counts how many words are read accurately and notes any errors. The student then "retells" in his or her own words what he or she just read, to prevent both students and teachers from thinking that reading quickly without understanding is the goal.

Smith explained to the assembled principals that "DIBELS is an indicator" of how well students read and how well they will do on the ARMT and SAT 10. In third grade, 80 percent of the students had made good progress on their DIBELS, but he said, "our goal is 100 percent." Aaron added that the students' comprehension was good but that "word study" was not, and as a result, teachers, the librarian, the counselor, and other professionals in the building had been working on building students' vocabularies.

One of the observing principals asked how West Jasper coordinates its instruction to match both the ARMT and the SAT 10. "You can do both," Smith answered. "Our teachers have been teaching students the skills" they need on both tests rather than teaching to a specific test. In addition, he added, to reduce the anxiety of students, "we set up mock assessments with the same conditions" so that children will be prepared for what they will face. By providing snacks and allowing more play time when testing is done for the day, "We try to make our testing week a fun week," Smith told the group.

The third-grade teachers were then invited into the library to join Smith, Aaron, and Barber for the data meeting. Smith began with praise. "Your classroom management—exceptional," he told the two teachers. Aaron followed up with the main recommendation—the teachers need to intensify reading practice by children with books, not just on computer screens or with PLATO. The five then studied the data from the DIBELS assessments that had been given in the middle of the year. The goal had been that every child be able to read 92 words per minute fluently. This was an increase from the goal of 77 words per minute at the beginning of the year and a step from the goal of 110 words per minute at the end of the year. The mean score of all the students was 106.7, with some students way above and some way below the goal. Then the group looked at the individual data for each child. Anyone reading fewer than 70 words per minute was categorized as "at risk." Those reading between 70 and 92 were categorized as "some risk," and those reading above 92 were categorized as "low risk." The scores ranged from a painful six words a minute to a high-flying 212 words a minute.

Following a school tradition, Smith asked the teachers to "celebrate our successes and plan for students who didn't make it." A highlight of her success, Morrow said, was that one of her students had gone from reading only 23 words per minute to reading 50, a fact that all at the table applauded. "He's a special education student, and we've been keeping him in the classroom with me," Morrow said, meaning that he was spending more of his time in the regular classroom and less in the self-contained classroom for students with disabilities. But she also noted that two of her "low-risk" students had fallen a little bit, even as others had made considerable progress. Simon's "success" was a child identified with a learning disability who had gone from reading 45 words a minute to reading 95 words a minute, surpassing the goal of 92.

Later, Barber remarked that she was very happy that both teachers had chosen to highlight the successes of two students with disabilities, showing that they had taken responsibility for those children and had not thought of them as someone else's responsibility. Simon also noted that the students had made progress overall—most students had increased by 10 or more words per minute between September and January.

"What accounts for the progress?" Smith asked. "Small group instruction," responded Simon. "And we're working hard in our centers to make sure they are meeting the needs of the students." By "centers," Simon meant the activities that were set up for students to do while they were not working with the teacher during the literacy block. "Sometimes they read too fast, and they aren't understanding," Simon observed. "We've been working on self-correction," Morrow added, referring to the fact that if students noticed that they read a word wrong, they were expected to correct themselves. "We've also been working on vocabulary," she said. Both Morrow and Simon have consciously been choosing three new words a day that they use throughout the day to expand students' vocabulary.

In a little ceremony that Barber said some schools accompany with playing "Pomp and Circumstance," Morrow and Simon took a chart with every child's name Velcroed into the "at risk," "some risk," or "low risk" category, based on their scores at the beginning of the year, and moved them into new categories according to their middle-of-the year scores. Morrow and Simon were clearly happy about moving names up, and Morrow was clearly unhappy about having to move two students who had slid back slightly from low risk to some risk.

Aaron told the teachers and the assembled observers that, as they do at every data meeting, "We're going to talk about two students we're going to focus on for the next three weeks." Morrow chose to focus on Bryant, who began the year reading 71 words a minute and was reading 86 words a minute at the middle of the year—nearly but not quite meeting the goal of 92 words. As part of a "miscue analysis," Morrow listed all the mistakes he had made during his reading—he had read "hatcher" instead of *hatchery*, "encour" instead of *encouraged*, "started" instead of *starred*, and "pacif" instead of *pacific*. Aaron wrote them all down, and then the group thought about what patterns could be discerned. They agreed that Bryant had had trouble with the middles and endings of multisyllabic words, and it was decided that Morrow would encourage him to run his finger under the words as he read for a while to make sure he followed through on reading entire words. Aaron said he also needed more practice reading material he was interested in, and Morrow said that although the child had little interest in reading in general, he was very interested in sports. Smith said he would order *Junior Sports Illustrated* for her classroom.

This process was repeated for one of the students in Simon's class, and there the main advice was that in addition to general reading practice, the student spend more time reading a book while listening to it read on tape. "Is there something I can do to help you?" Aaron asked the two teachers, letting them know they could call on her for her expertise or support. "You're already great teachers," Smith told Morrow and Simon in conclusion. "But you're going to be excellent teachers."

Once the teachers had left, Barber told the assembled group that the previous week, when Smith and Aaron had met with the second-grade teachers, the data had showed so much progress that "you practically had to scrape those teachers off the ceiling." She noted that because the third grade had not made quite as much progress, the tenor of the meeting had been different—supportive and helpful, but not exultant. She asked the observers to note that Smith and Aaron had clearly studied the data before the meeting. They weren't looking at it for the first time with the teachers. "You have to know the data before the meeting, or the teachers will know you are just going through the motions." In explaining the need for the individual analysis of one student in each class, Barber said, "When we go to the doctor for an X-ray, if it's serious we then go for an MRI." The miscue analysis "is our MRI," she said. Barber said that during the next walk-through of the third-grade classrooms in a month, observers should be able to see teachers making sure more books were in the hands of the children and instruction that followed the plan laid out in the data meeting.

Then Barber asked the assembled principals and reading coaches to comment on the relationship between the administrators and the teachers as revealed in what they had seen. "The teachers didn't feel threatened," commented one. "They didn't feel that they were being judged and evaluated." One principal said he felt that "If these teachers needed something, the principal would get it for them." Barber noted that it was necessary to "build a team, and you can't do that without good relationships."

She then asked the observers to think about what they could do to "intentionally create this type of environment." One principal said, "As an administrator you have to be in the classroom and be visible." "You have to care about your people," added another. "If teachers are going through something at home, you have to show compassion." Yet another said she had realized that she needed to meet more often with her reading coach. She had been startled when Smith said he met every day with Aaron. He had joked that they met so often, in fact, that every time his wife dropped in at the school, she found Aaron in his office, which had started to become awkward. "Every day!" remarked the other principal. "My God—I'm going to try."

Barber wanted the principals and reading coaches to note a few other things from the meeting. For example, she said, the goals and strategies set for the classrooms were developed by teachers as a result of studying the data, giving a clear demonstration of what it means to be "data driven." In addition, Barber noted, the teachers never said that the kids were the problem. "They feel bad," she said about Morrow and Simon. "They feel they failed. But they never made an excuse." By this Barber means the excuses that often permeate schools where most of the children are poor—excuses saying that poor children don't bring as much background knowledge to school as middle-class children and that children of color often bring a "culture of low achievement." The common thread of these kinds of teacher excuses, she told the group, is that "learning depends on the kids and not on them." But, she countered, "God forbid a six-year-old's learning depends on him."

She told the assembled group that at the school she used to lead as principal in Birmingham—Tuggle Elementary—the students were "100 percent poor and 100 percent minority. My parents couldn't support their children. If the kids didn't learn from the teachers, they didn't learn." In the case of some children, she went on to say, "Mickey Mouse could teach them. But Johnny— little Johnny really needs a teacher." She urged the principals to begin talking to their staffs about that issue, to get their teachers to understand that prestige should accrue to teachers not because they teach the "best" kids but because they teach the children most in need of good teaching. This is aimed at the heart of a deeply entrenched sensibility of the teaching profession. Often, teachers of "gifted" classes and "honors" classes are considered to have a higher status than teachers of the "low" classes. Barber was telling the group that the status relationships need to change to better reflect the needs of the children.

Finally, she told the principals, "There's more to life than DIBELS." Although DIBELS are a useful indicator of reading skill, that is all they are, she told them. The important part of reading, she said, was to introduce children to new perspectives and new information that exceeded their own experience and have them read a wide selection of books, magazines, and other materials. "We have got to expand their horizons or we are still signing their death warrants," she told the group. In this way, Barber seamlessly linked the details of how to use data to drive instruction to her passion for improving schools, guiding principals and goading them at the same time.

"It's changing the way we teach reading" is the way Shirley Mitchell, principal of T. S. Boyd Elementary School in Dora, Alabama, said about the ARI process. In a later interview, Barber said that the principals she works with have been very receptive to new ideas. "They want to do a good job," she said. "But they need the knowledge." She argues that school reform rests on principals and other leaders. "We would not have teachers leaving the profession if there were leaders to lead them. Without the right leader, success won't last. It doesn't take superhuman leaders, it takes superhuman belief. You've got to transform your people."

Barber's work and the work of the other principal coaches in Alabama is an attempt to transform educators so that they not only have the knowledge to be good leaders but also the passion to believe that all children can and must learn. One of the Massachusetts delegation, Miffy Somers, who will be a principal coach in the Massachusetts version of the Alabama work, called it a "systematic effort to change the culture," and said that no other state had anything like it. Moscovitch, the Massachusetts economist, agreed, adding, "If you are from Alabama, it's easy to not realize how far along the state is."

But it wasn't so long ago that principals were on their own. When Eric Smith arrived at West Jasper in 1999, for example, there was very little training in place to help him be a good principal. A physical education teacher, Smith had mostly worked as an assistant principal and coach in a high school before he was sent to ARI training the summer before taking the job as West Jasper's new principal.

ARI was then in its infancy and focused entirely on reading instruction and working with data. That was certainly helpful, but Smith said he needed more help, and he systematically looked for schools with similar demographics to West Jasper's that were higher achieving. He visited those schools, interviewed the principals, and sent teams of teachers to those schools to learn how those schools operated.

Although not unheard of, that was unusual behavior for a new principal. When asked what made him think of doing that, he responded, "I'm a coach. That's what coaches do—they scout out the other teams and find out what they're doing—and steal any good ideas they find." He wishes he had had the kind of systematic training that ARI is now providing to principals—"I had to learn by trial and error," he said.

In 2000, the Alabama A+ Education Foundation, a statewide organization that works to improve schools and education in Alabama, established a "Best Practices Center" to help schools better understand and utilize effective professional development. "There really wasn't a good, comprehensive vision of what high-quality embedded reading professional development looked like" is what Cathy Gassenheimer, managing director of Alabama A+, said in explaining the purpose of the center. "Teachers and schools were still talking about summer, one-shot professional development. We developed the model of powerful conversations discussing [such topics as] what are you doing to use student achievement data to better serve students."

Alabama A+ formed a "Powerful Conversations Network" with a few schools and consciously tried to spread best practices, both through carefully designed professional development and in more informal ways. For example, at meetings of the network, they would make sure that a less-successful school with demographics similar to West Jasper's would be seated next to the representatives from West Jasper. Meetings focus on particular topics that principals identify as something they need to learn about. One recent meeting, for example, was about looking at student work, a systematic way of using papers and student assignments to improve instruction.

In more recent years, with a grant from the Wachovia Foundation, A+ has worked to make the Powerful Conversations Network an integral part of the Alabama Reading Initiative. This work supports the work of the principal coaches who are attempting to replicate the educational DNA of schools like

West Jasper. "People like Martha Barber and other principal coaches know the issues and are able to read the nuances and raise expectations while helping people understand how to run an effective data meeting," Gassenheimer said.

Barber, for her part, sees training principals as the key to running effective schools for poor children and children of color. Those children traditionally have had a greater than average chance of being taught by brand-new teachers. A very common pattern is that teachers begin their teaching careers in schools where many of the students are poor and, once they gain some experience, leave to teach in schools where the students are less needy. Many times they leave the profession altogether. It is Barber's contention that teachers would not abandon poor children or the profession as frequently if the principals in those schools were more knowledgeable and more effective. "We would not have teachers leaving the profession if there were leaders to lead them."

Aside from a couple of retirements, she said she had no teacher turnover when she was principal at Tuggle. "I had zero teacher transfers." Tuggle was one of few high-minority, high-poverty, high-achieving schools in Alabama when she was principal, but it was a very low-performing school when she arrived. "There was a teacher I wanted to transfer because she wouldn't get on board," Barber said. "I wanted to put an X on her door—her class had no books, her instruction was bad, it was a nasty place." But, Barber said, the rest of the staff wanted to keep the teacher and worked with her to improve her performance and her expertise. "Two years later I put my nephew in her class," Barber said, proof that the teacher's performance had been transformed. Barber tells that story to emphasize that the teaching force can be made more effective with good leaders who expect teachers to have high expectations of their students.

The constant refrain she has had to battle in high-minority, high-poverty schools is "Our kids are different, and we're not going to get the same results" as schools where the children are white and middle class. "I say your kids can do it," Barber said, occasionally reminding her listeners that she herself "grew up in the projects." She had to battle low expectations on the part of teachers and schools, and knows how crippling that can be.

"We can't give up on the children," Barber said.

POSTSCRIPT

As the 2006–07 school year began, Eric Smith said he was very pleased with the school's test score results for the previous year. The highest rate of proficiency was posted by the fourth grade, where 89 percent of students met state reading standards and 84 percent met math standards. In the third grade, 79 percent met state reading standards and 80 percent math, which, he said, "was pretty good for two brand-new teachers."

He said that the faculty would be mapping the math curriculum during the 2006–07 school year, one month at a time. "We're already doing it for reading, and some of the teachers will branch out and do it for social studies and science." This means that teachers will have month-by-month goals for their teaching in those subjects. In addition, he said, the school would make teaching manners and etiquette "even more of a focus" than it had been in previous years.

EAST MILLSBORO ELEMENTARY SCHOOL
EAST MILLSBORO, DELAWARE

INTRODUCTION

About a year after I had visited Frankford Elementary (chapter 2), I was speaking with its former principal, Sharon Brittingham. I mentioned casually that if she knew of any other school that I should look at, she should tell me. She suggested East Millsboro, not far from Frankford. I looked up its state report card, and its proficiency rates were as high as, if not higher than, Frankford's. It didn't have quite as many poor children and children of color as Frankford, but it still had significant numbers. Too often in integrated schools and in schools where white, middle-class children are the majority, African American, Latino, and poor children do badly, so I was intrigued by East Millsboro.

I headed back to Delaware's chicken country and found what I now refer to as Yoda to Frankford's Luke Skywalker. The principal at East Millsboro, Gary Brittingham (stunningly, no relation of Sharon Brittingham), had been Sharon Brittingham's principal-mentor and had helped her think about how to set up many of the data-tracking systems and other policies and procedures that had made Frankford so successful. I consider it a toss-up which to consider the "better" school.

• • • • •

Nothing about its external characteristics would lead one to think of East Millsboro as an academic powerhouse. It is an unassuming elementary school in rural Delaware not far from the beach resorts of Bethany and Rehoboth. Many of the school's parents work at the chicken processing plant down the road or in the burgeoning construction and service industries in the beach towns, but quite a few are unemployed. Just about half the students at

EAST MILLSBORO ELEMENTARY SCHOOL
EAST MILLSBORO, DELAWARE

2006 Enrollment: 664 students in pre-kindergarten through fifth grade

2006 Demographics: 25% African American

                            13% Latino

                            60% White

                            51% meet qualifications for free and reduced-price lunch

Locale: Rural

Grade 5 Reading
Delaware Student Testing Program (DSTP)

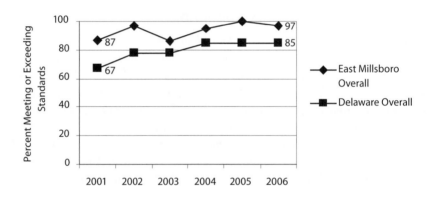

East Millsboro qualify for free or reduced-price meals. Ethnically, the school is mixed, with about 30 percent of the students African American and 10 percent Latino, many of them new immigrants from Mexico. The rest of the students are white. About 12 percent of the students from kindergarten through fifth grade are identified as having disabilities.

The building itself, which has had eleven additions in its 50 years, is a confusing, one-story cinderblock warren. At one point it held 1,200 students, but after a new school was built nearby its enrollment was cut in half. Enrollment began creeping up because of growth in the area, and the school now houses just about 700 students. Because of the relatively high rate of mobility in the area, only about half the students who finish fifth grade there began as kindergartners. A Title I school, meaning that it receives federal assistance targeted to schools with high percentages of poor children, it otherwise has the same resources as any other school in the district and state.

Grade 5 Math
Delaware Student Testing Program (DSTP)

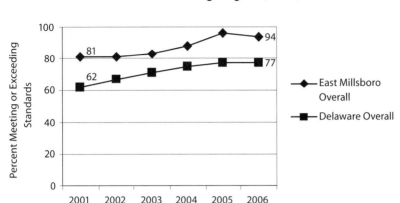

Source: Delaware Department of Education, http://profiles.doe.k12.de.us

Note: In addition, 99 percent of East Millsboro's fourth-grade students met state standards in science and 96 percent met them in social studies.

This unassuming school produces big results. Every single third and fifth grader—100 percent—met the state reading standards in 2005. In addition, 98 percent of the third graders and 96 percent of the fifth graders met state math standards, and 90 percent or more met the state writing, science, and social studies standards.

"Unachievable" is a word often tossed around in discussions of No Child Left Behind, particularly to describe its goal that just about all children—including poor children, children learning English, and children with disabilities—meet state proficiency standards by 2014. But while that debate swirls in national policy circles, the principal of East Millsboro Elementary School simply states, "It's achievable. We did it last year."

Bucking the national trend that boys are falling significantly behind girls in achievement, boys at East Millsboro score about the same as or higher than the girls, depending on the grade level and test. The test scores of fifth-grade readers who are low-income are almost indistinguishable from those who are not, and East Millsboro's low-income students outperform the rest of Delaware's students on every measure, from math and reading to writing, social studies, and science.

East Millsboro has been one of the higher-performing schools in the state for a long time. But it is only in the last few years that it has hit the stratospheric numbers that have made it, arguably, one of the best schools in the state. One of its few competitors for that title is Frankford Elementary School, just down the road. Both share a commitment to the idea that the role of teachers and schools is to make sure each child learns. As East Millsboro's Brittingham said, "If you can predict who is going to have some difficulty, we in this business should figure out some way to help that child."

The core of helping children learn at East Millsboro is instruction, and instruction begins with the school's "curriculum map." The curriculum map is a document developed by East Millsboro teachers working together in grade-level teams to map out, month by month, what they will be teaching. It is drawn in part from state standards and contains the performance indicators students must meet during the month, plus essential questions, skills, assessments, specialized vocabulary, and texts to be used to teach that unit. "Textbooks here are resources, not the curriculum," Brittingham said.

As a result of the curriculum map, even teachers new to East Millsboro have clearly laid-out guidelines for what their instruction must include. When asked whether such clear direction hindered her creativity as a teacher, fifth-grade teacher Kim Bullock, a 13-year veteran, said no. "It's impinging on what I teach when, but it doesn't impinge on how I teach it." Posted throughout classrooms are "essential questions" drawn from the curriculum map, so that students know what they are supposed to be learning: for instance, "How do I tell the difference between cumulus, cirrus, and stratus clouds?" "How can you add voice to creative writing?" and "How do I use a factor tree to find prime numbers?"

Each year, when the state test scores come in, the curriculum map is reworked to reflect where students had trouble mastering the curriculum. Teachers identify the areas of need, go to the month in which the missed content was taught, and add time or new materials or tweak the map in some other way, so that the following year their students have a greater opportunity for success. For example, said second-grade teacher Lisa Richardson, "We found we weren't doing two-digit addition until the beginning of March, and the DSTP [the state test] is March 15th. So we moved around twenty different math units, thinking about what we needed to do before DSTP and what after." Also, she added, by looking more closely at the curriculum maps, teachers identified areas of redundancy—for example, math has a unit on weights and measures, but so does science. Teachers made sure their science lessons on weights and measure incorporated all the necessary math content, thereby finding additional time for math instruction.

By breaking out the state testing data by student and classroom, teachers are also able to see who has the most success in teaching which topics. "If my kids don't do as well in percentages, I can ask the other teachers for help" is the way teacher Bullock put it. In addition to those uses of data, Brittingham gives teachers classroom lists of where students begin and end the school year in terms of their test scores. None of this data analysis is used by him to evaluate teachers—evaluations continue to be based on classroom observation. But, he said, it isn't necessary to use the data in any way that could be considered punitive; East Millsboro's teachers, he said, "want to improve—they want to get better."

The key to all this curriculum mapping, data examination, and expertise sharing is the time that is carved out of the week for teachers to spend together working as a team. By assigning paraprofessionals and other adults in the building to take over classrooms 45 minutes before school ends once every week, each grade-level team has that 45 minutes for planning, plus the following 30 minutes of the contractual day, for a total of an hour and 15 minutes. These meetings of what the school calls "professional learning communities" mean that all teachers in a grade level, plus the reading, writing, and math specialists, the ESOL (English for Speakers of Other Languages) teacher, and the special education teacher assigned to that grade level, meet to focus on instruction. One task they undertake is to compare grades with scores on the standardized tests. "You used to have 30 percent of kids not meeting standards and still getting A's and B's," said Brittingham. "If your child gets an A, you don't want your child not being able to meet the standard."

Professional learning communities also work on developing interim assessments that are given to students every few weeks to ensure that no child falls too far behind without being noticed and provided extra help. They also work to develop their own expertise by reading and discussing books—*Lincoln on Leadership* by Donald T. Phillips was one recent choice, and *Whatever It Takes: How Professional Learning Communities Respond When Kids Don't Learn* by Rebecca DuFour and colleagues was another.

The professional learning communities began a few years ago as part of the intensified focus on making sure that all students meet state standards, and when surveyed by the principal, most teachers cited them as the reason for the improvement of the test scores. "We've always been a successful school," agreed teacher Bullock. "But we've improved since the professional learning communities."

The idea for the professional learning communities grew out of district training provided to principals and assistant principals by Learning Focused

Schools, a company headed by Max Thompson that provides professional development to educators around the country. Brittingham, who has been principal at East Millsboro for 17 years, with another eight as assistant principal, has sat through a lot of professional development that was frivolous or pointless. But Learning Focused Schools, he said, brought together all the latest research in ways that are really useful and practical. He credits the district-provided training with helping push East Millsboro to its recent successes.

Additional district-provided training to teachers in math, science, and reading has meant, Brittingham said, that he hardly walks into a classroom anymore without seeing a "model lesson." Reading instruction begins in kindergarten with phonemic awareness and letter and sound recognition, and continues into first and second grade with 30 minutes a day of explicit, systematic phonics that helps students map sounds to individual letters as part of a larger reading program. Students are continually monitored to make sure none falls behind. In addition to a reading teacher, East Millsboro also has a writing teacher. Both teach model lessons and help teachers incorporate reading and writing instruction into all content areas, so that students learn, for example, how to write papers in social studies and science. The science curriculum is provided by the Smithsonian, which supplies kits that guide students through hands-on science projects. To learn how to use the kits effectively, the Smithsonian provides training to teachers.

Brittingham has hired almost all the teachers now teaching, a mixture of new and experienced teachers. When hiring, he said he looks for "personality, energy, enthusiasm, and references." The district, he said, has a good four-day orientation program that helps new teachers learn to set up their classrooms, manage discipline, and deal with parents, and the training also covers a range of other topics rarely taught in education schools. New teachers are then paired with a mentor teacher within the building, who is paid a little bit extra and helps acculturate the teacher to the way the school does things. "Twenty-five years ago, new teachers were pretty much on their own," Brittingham said, as a way of contrasting what happens today.

Co-teaching, the practice of pairing special education teachers with regular classroom teachers to teach a mixed class of students with and without disabilities, is common at East Millsboro. Classroom teachers focus more on teaching the content, and the special education teachers, with expertise in how to scaffold difficult tasks, focus on making sure the material is accessible to all students. In that way, special education training is available to any struggling student, not simply to those with identified disabilities.

Although 89 students have Individualized Education Programs (IEPs), which specify the kinds of services students with disabilities need, very few have 504 plans, which are plans required by federal disability law specifying accommodations students with disabilities need. Such 504 plans typically require teachers to write down homework assignments rather than only give assignments verbally, or permit students to tape-record lessons so they can listen to them at home, or provide extra time to complete assignments. "When I see 504 plans that students bring" when they move from other schools, Brittingham said, "I don't see the point. A lot of them just call for good teaching. We don't need a federal law for that."

In addition to keeping students with disabilities in regular classrooms, the school also works to keep its 77 students learning English in regular classrooms. Pam Warrington, the school's ESOL teacher, does pull some children out of classrooms to work on specific language skills in small groups, but more often, she said, she works to "push in" ESOL services in regular classrooms. In previous jobs, she said, she taught ESOL classes where the children were separated from other children. "They're better not to be self-contained," she said, adding that in those classes, they would have only her to learn from, instead of a class full of English speakers who model different speaking patterns and different accents. "They learn from each other" is the way Brittingham put it.

When asked what makes East Millsboro successful, several teachers quickly answered, "hard work." Many teachers are known for working long after the school day ends. But there is also a recognition that teachers' time is valuable. "[Mr. Brittingham] finds us time and shows us he values our time" is the way second-grade teacher Richardson put it.

And teachers know that their requests are taken seriously. They decide whether their classrooms should have tables and chairs or individual desks, for example, and Brittingham works to honor those preferences. Many teachers are now requesting SMART Boards or the similar whiteboards, which are electronic boards connected to laptops that serve as overhead projectors, chalkboards, and much more. "I don't know how I ever taught without a SMART Board," said Richardson, who gave as an example of how she uses it a time when her class was reading a story that mentioned an avocado. Many of the students didn't know what an avocado was, and within seconds she was able to do a search on the laptop and project a picture with a description onto the SMART Board. Eighteen classrooms now have the boards, and Brittingham is working to fill the requests for more.

Another key component of instruction is the fact that the assistant principal, Mary Bixler, can support the teachers and the instructional program because she doesn't have to spend most of her time on discipline, the way many assistant principals do. "We have fewer discipline incidents," she said. "Because the children are learning, they don't have the time to get into trouble. That means the majority of my time is spent working with staff addressing the job."

The general approach to discipline is that a good instructional program eliminates many of the problems that arise when children are bored and looking for trouble. However, Bixler said, "There's a whole component to helping shape the environment." For example, every quarter there is a student recognition ceremony to acknowledge not only good academic success and good behavior, but also "kind acts" done by a child on behalf of someone else. Teachers set up a point system, and students who earn enough points are eligible to win bicycles and other prizes that have been provided by the local Kiwanis Club.

The school counselor spends her time, Brittingham said, working as a "true counselor," by which he means helping students deal with abuse, sexual molestation, and the chaos and dysfunction that often accompany poverty. The counselor also helps the school nurse coordinate the annual Christmas project, which in 2005 provided 200 students with holiday meals and gifts, donated by local businesses and community organizations and the school's parent-teacher organization.

Teachers who have a student whose actions are interfering with other children's learning are not left on their own to handle the situation. After going through a series of steps, such as giving time-outs, teachers fill out a "staff support referral" requesting that action be taken. That spurs a meeting that includes the principal, the assistant principal, the reading specialist, the special education teacher, the classroom teacher, the counselor, and the child's parent or guardian, who together decide what action should be taken. Possibilities include contacting social services, setting the child up with tutoring, or setting the child up with a mentor who will meet with him or her regularly to eat lunch, talk, play board games, or read together. Mentors can be staff members—most staff members are mentors—or one of about 50 volunteers from outside the school, many of whom are retired. These outside volunteers receive training and a background check by the state police. "Making the right match" is crucial, according to Bixler, and a VISTA volunteer works as the mentoring coordinator. "Teachers should feel that there's somewhere to turn," Bixler said about the referral process.

Tutoring and mentoring are not only available to students who act up; any student who appears to be struggling has access to such extra help. Some one-on-one tutoring is available throughout the day ("We find every five minutes" is the way teacher Bullock put it), but the school provides other opportunities as well. For example, students who need small-group tutoring in either reading or math get off the buses first, grab their breakfast, and go immediately to tutoring while the rest of the students disembark and eat their breakfast in a more leisurely fashion. In that way, the school has carved out about 30 minutes for students to get some special attention. Throughout the year there is an afterschool math program for students who need extra help, and beginning in January the school runs one-hour tutoring sessions after school—with bus transportation provided afterward—to help prepare many of the third, fourth, and fifth graders for taking the state tests, particularly if they're nervous about them. Brittingham expected that 180 students would take part in the afterschool tutoring in 2006. "Third graders are pretty anxious," Brittingham said. "The tests carry high stakes for students—if you don't score at a certain level, you have to go to summer school, and if you don't pass there, you are retained." East Millsboro has not had a child retained for the past four years, but some students are still anxious.

To relieve the anxiety when test time comes, the school usually has some kind of "test buster program." For the spring of 2005, it was planning a talent show. But, Brittingham said, "Part of the way to eliminate stress for a test is to prepare. If you feel prepared and confident, you're not as anxious."

Brittingham can't promise that his school will hit 100 percent of students meeting standards every year. Too many uncertainties swirl around the lives of children and schools. But because of the way time and instruction are organized and the way struggling students are identified and provided help, he said, he does expect to "hit the high 90s" every year.

POSTSCRIPT

The 2006 data showed that, indeed, rates of proficiency were in "the high 90s."

CAPITOL VIEW ELEMENTARY SCHOOL
ATLANTA, GEORGIA

INTRODUCTION

The principal of Centennial Place Elementary School in Atlanta (see chapter 8) had told me that one of the schools she looked to for good ideas was Capitol View, also in Atlanta. It had demographics similar to Centennial Place's and even higher test scores, which was truly astonishing given Centennial Place's test scores.

Capitol View was the first "Core Knowledge" school I ever visited. Core Knowledge was developed by author and education professor E. D. Hirsch Jr., whose books include Cultural Literacy, The Schools We Need and Why We Don't Have Them, *and, most recently,* The Knowledge Deficit. *Hirsch argues that to be an educated person requires knowing something about a broad range of topics that educated people know about. That appears to be more circular than he makes it sound, but his point is that newspapers, magazines, books, and other text aimed at a general audience assume a background knowledge without which the text is impossible to understand. So, for example, to read an ordinary newspaper article about a Supreme Court decision—which most people would probably agree a high school graduate should be prepared to do—requires some knowledge about the role of the judiciary as well as the other branches of government, some knowledge of legal procedure, and might even require some background on the specifics of the case, such as the federal role in interstate commerce or the ways DNA can be used as evidence. Without the requisite background knowledge, readers might be able to read the individual words of an article, but they would not in any way understand its import. Similarly, the reading of many novels requires at least a cursory knowledge of Greek and Roman mythology, biblical stories, and many other cultural references.*

CAPITOL VIEW ELEMENTARY SCHOOL
ATLANTA, GEORGIA

2006 Enrollment: 252 students in kindergarten through fifth grade
2006 Demographics: 95% African American
                         88% meet qualifications for free and reduced-price lunch
Locale: Urban

Grade 5 Reading, 2006
Georgia Criterion-Referenced Competency Tests (CRCT)

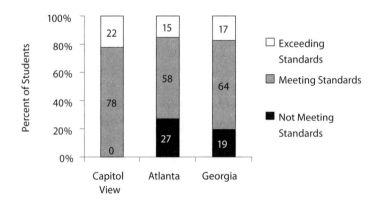

With the help of writers, editors, and scholars, Hirsch has compiled a list of things educated Americans must know in order to be considered educated citizens—that is, the core knowledge base required to participate in the political, economic, cultural, and social life of the nation. Hirsch argues that although many white, middle-class children are able to absorb at least some of that background knowledge from the conversations of their families and neighbors, children of poverty and children of color are often too isolated from those conversations to be able to count on learning from them. For all children—but particularly for children of poverty, Hirsch argues—school curricula must deliberately and systematically build background knowledge.

In this way, Hirsch has opposed a major tenet of many educators, who have argued that knowledge of content is not as important as knowledge of process. That is, many educators argue that it is more important to know how to learn rather than to learn anything specific. I encountered this argument in my children's elementary school, where the principal told parents that it wasn't impor-

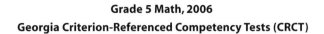

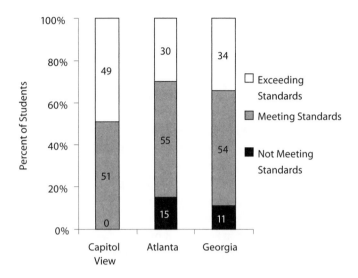

Source: The Governor's Office of Student Achievement, State of Georgia, http://reportcard2006.gaosa.org

In addition, 100 percent of Capitol View's fifth-grade students met state standards in English language arts, science, and social studies.

Note: These graphs use the latest information that was available at the time of publication, which is more recent than was available when the school was visited. Previous report cards can be found at the state department of education website.

tant for children to know where Nebraska is—what is important, she said, is for them to know how to find out where Nebraska is. The flaw in her argument, as Hirsch discusses in great detail, is that if children have to stop reading to find Nebraska every time they need that knowledge, they are less likely to continue reading, and they are less likely to understand what they are reading. In addition, a large and growing body of cognitive research has demonstrated that there is very little generalized knowledge of process that doesn't rely on knowledge of specific content. (It is beyond the scope of this book to delve into this topic, but for a fascinating description of what the research says, see How People Learn: Brain, Mind, Experience, and School, *published by the National Academy of Sciences.)*

Hirsch founded the Core Knowledge Foundation to develop grade-by-grade curricula that, if schools follow them, will provide children with the background knowledge he has identified as important. To call itself a Core Knowledge School, a school must use about 80 percent of the curriculum and must receive training and materials from the foundation.

Capitol View is identified by the foundation as one of its most dramatic success stories.

• • • • •

One thing that drives the teachers and administrators at Capitol View Elementary School to work hard is the knowledge that some people expect them to fail. "The expectation that we will fail pushes us higher" is how second-grade teacher Amanee Salahuddin put it. "There are people who say, 'They won't be able to match last year's test scores.'"

Almost all of Capitol View's 250 or so students are African American, and most are poor, with more than 80 percent meeting the requirements of the federal free or reduced-price meal program. The school sits in a neighborhood in southwest Atlanta that, although it has lately been somewhat gentrified, is still thought of by Atlantans as dominated by strip clubs and daytime prostitutes. These facts alone would be enough to explain academic failure in the eyes of many.

And yet Capitol View has been one of the top-performing schools in the state for years. In 2005, not only did 97 percent of all students meet state standards in reading and English language arts, but 58 percent exceeded them—and more than 80 percent of the fifth graders exceeded standards in reading. Math scores were a little less impressive—90 percent met standards, with 35 percent exceeding them—but with few exceptions those scores are matched in Georgia only by schools where very few students are poor.

When teachers are asked what distinguishes Capitol View from low-achieving schools, they respond, "It's the expectations." "Kids will meet the standards you expect of them," said Trennis Harvey, the school's instruction specialist and, in effect, its assistant principal. "Society in general has bought into the idea that demographics have something to do with the ability to learn," Harvey said. "If you're poor you may not have access to trips to Paris, but you can still learn. One thing that No Child Left Behind has done is to say that schools have got to teach all children. You can't take Johnny and throw him in a corner because he's not getting it. Schools have to teach Johnny, too."

"No excuses" is a common catchphrase in the school, but the school does not run on expectations alone. Principal Arlene Snowden says the school runs on "hands-on activities and engaging instruction." Its curriculum is carefully mapped to Georgia's state standards but far exceeds them in breadth and depth, in large part because of the school's Core Knowledge curriculum.

Core Knowledge, developed by author E. D. Hirsch Jr., is built around the idea of a common base of knowledge for all children. The Core Knowledge curriculum starts with Mother Goose rhymes in kindergarten and builds carefully to classic and modern literature; in history, it includes a survey from ancient Mesopotamia, Egypt, Greece, and China through to modern American history; and it covers all the major topics of science, from the structure of cells to weather systems. All students at Capitol View study French for 30 minutes a day, and the French lessons are often pegged to what the students are studying during the rest of the day.

"Most of our units are concept-based," said second-grade teacher Amanee Salahuddin. She gave as an example a problem-solving unit that she taught for six weeks. Students studied inventions that solved specific problems, learned about inventors, and invented something themselves, and in the process they had to do research and cost analyses for their new invention. "It was all integrated with science and social studies," Salahuddin said. Core Knowledge, she said, provided "plenty of resources, books, books on tape, and videos."

In stark contrast to schools that have "narrowed the curriculum" to focus on developing the skill of reading, Core Knowledge educators have broadened and deepened the curriculum to give students the background knowledge and vocabulary to read complex text. In the words of Harvey, "We teach reading through social studies and science." Reading is taught across the curriculum in several ways, from identifying antonyms and synonyms with science and social studies concepts, to reading fiction that matches the period the students are studying. "When we first started teaching reading through science and social studies four years ago," said principal Arlene Snowden, "it became really clear how excited and interested children were. They are naturally curious about the world, and this way they learn about it."

Capitol View adopted Core Knowledge in 1995 under the previous principal, Marcene Thornton, who had arrived the previous year. Snowden and Harvey, who were both hired by Thornton, estimate that it took about four years for Thornton to completely transform the school from a low-performing one to one dedicated to excellence. "It takes about that long to embed the culture," Harvey said.

Part of a school's culture has to do with developing a committed staff. Although a few of the 18 classroom teachers have remained from before Thornton's arrival, most of the staff has turned over since then. "If you're the principal of the school, you're responsible for putting in place only the staff who believe in your vision," Thornton told the *Athens Banner-Herald* early in 2006. "If you've inherited some people who don't buy into that . . . it takes time to put in place the staff you need. I didn't want anyone who didn't like my kids."

A Spelman College graduate herself, Thornton hosted many student teachers from Spelman and Morehouse colleges (the private, historically black colleges in Atlanta for women and men, respectively) and hired quite a few of their graduates. Harvey, for example, is a Morehouse graduate who first student-taught at Capitol View, and Salahuddin is a Spelman graduate. By hiring a number of Spelman and Morehouse graduates, Thornton tapped into both a long collegiate tradition of commitment to intellectual excellence in the face of difficult circumstances and a sense of service to the community.

Snowden, who had worked for years as a middle school math-science teacher, decided to come to Capitol View as instructional specialist in 1998 because, she said, she had spent years puzzled about "why children were coming to middle school not being able to read." When Thornton became principal of the Early College high school, a new high school in Atlanta, in the fall of 2005, Snowden became principal and appointed Harvey, who had taught for eight years at Capitol View, as instructional specialist and assistant principal.

In addition to having a staff dedicated to its vision, part of Capitol View's culture has to do with how decisions are made. "We do everything collaboratively," said Harvey. "Of course your leader has to make some decisions, but most decisions here are made by teams." For example, the leadership team, which consists of one teacher at each grade level, the principal, and the assistant principal, decides how to spend the school's $74,000 in Title I money. Title I is a federal program that sends money to schools with large percentages of students who meet the requirements for free or reduced-price meals. In the 2005–06 school year, the leadership team decided that science was a weak area that the school should work on. Although 93 percent of the fifth graders had met state standards, only 26 percent exceeded them, and the leadership team decided that those data meant the school needed to strengthen its science instruction. They spent some of the school's Title I money to buy science tables, stools, and materials for a newly established science lab. Now, in addition to having regular classroom science instruction, third-, fourth-, and fifth-grade students go to the science lab three times a week to do hands-on experiments and other science activities keyed to the curriculum.

Similarly, the leadership team decided to use a three-year, $150,000 federal grant from the Comprehensive School Reform program for the professional development of teachers. Such professional development included paying for teachers to visit other Core Knowledge schools and attend professional conferences.

Grade-level teams, consisting of the classroom teachers in each grade, decide what units to teach and what field trips and other enrichment activities to organize. Even hiring decisions are made collaboratively. Teaching candidates are interviewed by five or six teachers and administrators who check references, look at a portfolio of lesson plans and other materials, and ask a battery of questions designed to get at whether a teacher will fit in at Capitol View. One question asked of them, Harvey said, is how they differentiate instruction so that they can meet the needs of high-achieving students as well as those who are behind.

To make sure teachers have enough time to work collaboratively, the school's schedule is carefully built so that once a week students in each grade level go to back-to-back "specials"—physical education, music, art, science, or counseling—thus allowing the teachers at that grade level to meet for two hours with the principal and assistant principal. At those meetings, team members go over any data that have been collected that week about student achievement in order to make sure that any child who is falling behind gets help, to plan the upcoming curriculum units, and to discuss field trip schedules and other housekeeping details.

In the fourth-grade team meeting the week before spring break, discussion centered on such topics as what more could be done to prepare for the state testing that was scheduled to take place shortly after spring break and what "compelling unit" would be taught after the testing. Core Knowledge is divided into what are called *compelling units* lasting six or seven weeks, and the fourth grade agreed to teach "Around the World in 80 Days" once testing was done. The unit would encompass geography, world culture, and literature and take the fourth grade through the end of the year. Teacher Sara Johnston said that she felt uneasy with the way the unit had been organized the previous year, when a whole section was devoted to teaching about Islam. "It got uncomfortable," she said, noting that some of her students were Muslim, and their mothers had offered to come in and show the children Islamic prayers. Johnston thought it came too close to teaching religion and said that some of the other parents—Christians—had been offended. Fellow teacher Sylvia Mack agreed that religion was too touchy a subject to include in the curriculum.

Without telling the teachers how to organize the unit, Harvey offered the teachers a different way to think about it. "As an intelligent human being, you need to know that Islam exists. I am not Muslim but I know about Mohammed and the five pillars of Islam. I am not a Buddhist but I know something about Buddhism. There are parents who didn't like that we taught 'The Battle Hymn of the Republic' when we studied the Civil War, but it is part of what students need to know." He added, "There's a certain basic knowledge that every American should know to function in society." The teachers agreed to make sure that information about Islam was included in the unit, even if they changed the organization a bit so that Christian parents wouldn't have reason to feel their children were being proselytized.

This sense that schools must systematically and thoughtfully impart to children a basic knowledge of the world is part of the philosophy of Core Knowledge, and it leads directly to the idea that teachers must be curious about the world and work to expand their knowledge. "We have to keep learning," Harvey said. Such a sense is what led the school to seek out grants from Fund for Teachers, a nonprofit group in Texas, to send two fourth-grade teachers to China, two second-grade teachers to Greece, and (in the summer of 2006) two first-grade teachers to Egypt. These summer trips were specifically designed to deepen teachers' knowledge of the content areas they teach, and teachers brought back photographs and artifacts to help them expand the knowledge of their students.

Because spring break and spring testing were so imminent, some of the discussion at the grade-level team meeting centered on what more could be done to prepare students to take Georgia's standardized tests. Capitol View takes state assessments very seriously, both as an opportunity to take stock of its instruction and because third- and fourth-grade students in Atlanta are in danger of being held back if they do not pass the assessments. No students have been held back at Capitol View for some time—the few students who didn't pass in the spring were able to pass in summer school—but it is a possibility that weighs on the staff.

In addition to the danger of retention, Atlanta's superintendent, Beverly Hall, has set some exacting standards that she expects Capitol View to meet—much more exacting than the federal No Child Left Behind targets for Adequate Yearly Progress (AYP). She expects constant improvement, and unlike the way AYP is figured, she counts every student who is at Capitol View on the day of the test. In contrast, AYP only counts students who are enrolled in the school for the full academic year. Atlanta's targets are so much more difficult to meet than AYP that, Harvey said, "If you meet the system targets, you have blown AYP out of the water."

For example, Hall has said that to meet Atlanta targets, all fourth-grade children at Capitol View must meet the English language arts standards, and 24 of the 37 students must exceed them. This is a difficult target, because Georgia's English language arts assessment was set to get harder, requiring students, for example, to identify puns, idioms, similes, metaphors, and rhyme schemes of poems—not just the main idea of a paragraph. "That's all part of Core Knowledge," Snowden said, by way of saying that the harder test shouldn't pose a problem for Capitol View. For example, poetry is part of everyday instruction. Students learn Walt Whitman's "I Hear America Singing" and Langston Hughes's "I, Too, Sing America," among other poems, as part of their literacy instruction. Because the instruction at Capitol View is so comprehensive and goes far beyond state standards, the faculty did not seem to think that students would do poorly on the new test, but they were alert to the possibility that students would not do quite as well as in the past. "It will be harder to exceed standards," Harvey predicted.

Snowden asked the teachers, "Are there any of the targets that are problematic?" They shook their heads. "I don't think so," said teacher Martin Hummings. Teacher Sylvia Mack said, "My class's problem will be with the math, not reading and language arts. They are still having trouble with multistep problems."

"Really concentrate on multistep problems," Snowden advised the teachers. Hummings informed her that multistep problems would be included in the packet of work students would be expected to do over spring break.

Fourth-grade math is a concern; although Capitol View has higher rates of proficiency than the district and state, its performance in the past has not been as stellar as in reading. For that reason, fourth-grade teachers were taking some extra time in the week before spring break going over multiplication and division. Mack led a long-division contest in her class, and Hummings a multiplication and division contest in his.

The team agreed to do a quick assessment at the end of spring break to see the students' weak areas. "But it has to be quick," Snowden said. "They shouldn't be all tested out by the time the state assessment comes." Hummings suggested that perhaps the students should write down what they feel their weak areas are and what they want to work on in the last week before testing. "That's a good idea," Snowden said. "Let's have something fun on Friday," she added. "Let's have a schoolwide multiplication bee—boys against the girls."

Teacher Mack added, "Throw in some division problems, too. That will get the multiplication in."

Although the atmosphere at the team meeting was informal and conversational, a lot of business got transacted—even the social talk about vacations and diets went to building a collegial faculty that know and like each other. But scheduling the school in such a way to find that kind of time is tricky—Harvey said that a great deal of time is spent building a schedule, and the first three weeks of school require a fair amount of "tinkering" before everyone is satisfied that there is enough time for planning and collaboration.

The basic schedule of the school is that each grade spends two uninterrupted hours a day on "literacy." The early grades spend more time building the skill of reading, including decoding and fluency. The later grades spend more time building the knowledge base and vocabulary necessary to read sophisticated text. More accomplished readers in the older grades will hold "literature circles," similar to book clubs, while teachers work with less-skilled readers to get them up to speed.

In each classroom, the structure of the literacy block is similar: Teachers will introduce some new concept or skill to the whole class and then work with small groups on any areas of weakness the students have, while other students rotate through "centers" that include a vocabulary development center, a writing center, and a listening/speaking center. Students are expected to read at least 30 minutes a day on their own in school and another 30 minutes a day at home, and the school uses the Accelerated Reader program as a way to keep track of students' reading. Accelerated Reader is a commercial program that assigns a point value to books and provides short comprehension quizzes for thousands of books by computer. Each student has an Accelerated Reader point goal that they are able to reach by reading a certain number of books and by passing the associated tests. Each Friday, the school holds a celebration of students who have met or exceeded their goals, serving pizza and awarding prizes that are either bought out of grant funds or donated by outside organizations. Carter Real Estate, a local commercial real estate firm that provides mentors for each of the school's fifth graders, will sometimes donate extra tickets to Hawks or Falcons games or other Accelerated Reader prizes.

Unlike at many low-performing schools, little time at Capitol View is taken up with discipline. "When you focus on discipline," said Snowden, "that will be your focus. When kids are fully engaged, they don't pose discipline problems. We focus on rigorous, engaging, hands-on activities." For the most part, teachers seem to handle discipline problems with little trouble. A student who needs some time to regroup is sent to another teacher's class for a while. A student who really doesn't get along with a teacher will be moved to another classroom for the rest of the year. "But it's kid things," Snowden said about the discipline issues.

She said that for the most part, the students at Capitol View and their parents know how important it is to learn and get a good education. "They are very motivated," she said. And the school will accept no excuses for poor performance. She related the story of a little girl who wasn't coming to class. "I went to her house and her mother said she wasn't coming to school because she didn't have shoes. I got Tania, took her to get some shoes, socks, and some outfits, and she came to school. We don't allow any excuses."

Schools, Snowden said, "need a leader who helps look at the data." Certainly staff at Capitol View are constantly collecting data and looking at them in order to improve instruction. In addition to looking at the standard kinds of data, Snowden said, "We always try to do some action research every year." One of the experiments now going on at Capitol View is that in the upper grades, some classes are all-girl, some all-boy, and some mixed-gender. Part of the rationale for trying the separate classes, Snowden said, is that "boys don't always have a role model in how to be a gentleman, and girls don't have a role model in how to act like a lady." During the first year the data were a little bit skewed, she said, because the school hadn't counted on the fact that the male students' teacher was most passionate and knowledgeable about social studies and the female students' teacher was more excited by science. However, in general, Snowden said, the mixed-gender classes "have had better achievement."

This kind of willingness to examine data and research is a hallmark of Capitol View and is openly cultivated by Snowden, who links it to the success Capitol View has achieved. Capitol View's "fortitude to look at data and research and to implement best practices" is, she said, what has made the difference and allowed students there to be successful.

POSTSCRIPT

When the 2006 state report cards were issued, Capitol View posted 100 percent proficiency rates in reading, math, science, and social studies. This, in spite of higher standards that began to be phased in that year.

PORT CHESTER MIDDLE SCHOOL

PORT CHESTER, NEW YORK

INTRODUCTION

The middle school data were all so dismal I had just about given up on finding a middle school to visit. Then Education Trust policy analyst Shana Kennedy thought she might have found something—Port Chester Middle School in Port Chester, New York. I was a little wary at first. It certainly hadn't reached the heights of achievement that its fellow New York schools, Lincoln Elementary (chapter 6) and Elmont Memorial Junior-Senior High School (chapter 5), had, where rates of proficiency were in the 90 percents, sometimes bumping 100 percent. It still had a considerable achievement gap, particularly for its African American students, who made up a rather small proportion of the student body. But it had an impressive growth trajectory, and all groups of students, from those with limited English proficiency to those with disabilities, were performing at rates much higher—in some cases two and three times higher—than in the state of New York as a whole. Its proficiency rates more or less matched those of Westchester County as a whole—one of the wealthiest counties in the country. The data sat on my desk for a while, waiting for another middle school to trump it. None came, so I went back to New York.

Among educators, middle school is known as the hardest level. It is where the hormones start to flow—kids arrive in middle school as little kids and leave looking almost like grown-ups, and in between they hardly even know how to manage their own bodies, much less handle academic work. That, at least, is what is often said. But an assistant principal at Port Chester, Patrick Swift, had a different take on that age group that has stuck with me ever since I heard it. "This sounds terrible to say," he said, "but middle school kids are like dogs—if they trust you, they'll do anything for you." That kind of sums it up. Middle-school-age kids don't love and trust their teachers unconditionally, the way

175

PORT CHESTER MIDDLE SCHOOL
PORT CHESTER, NEW YORK

2005 Enrollment: 734 students in sixth through eighth grade
2005 Demographics: 12% African American
                          64% Latino
                          24% White
                          64% meet qualifications for free and reduced-price lunch
Locale: Urban-Suburban

Grade 8 English Language Arts, 2005
New York State Testing Program

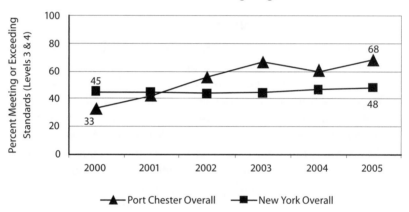

Grade 8 Math, 2005
New York State Testing Program

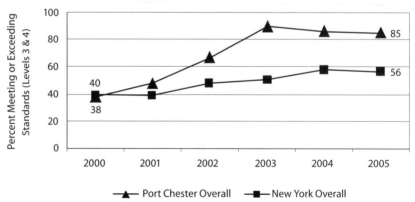

Grade 8 English Language Arts, 2005
New York State Testing Program

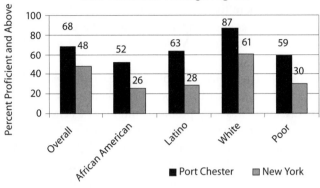

Source: New York State Education Department, http://www.emsc.nysed.gov

Note: These graphs use the latest information that was available at the time of publication, which is more recent than was available when the school was visited. Previous report cards can be found at the state department of education website.

many young children do. They need a reason to trust teachers. But if they do, they will work hard and be enthusiastic participants in school. That's what I saw at Port Chester.

• • • • •

The area that surrounds Port Chester, New York, is the part of Westchester County sardonically referred to by some as "up there in God's country," where lawns are measured in acres and houses are known by their architects. Port Chester itself has always been a blue-collar town within wealthy Westchester County, its small homes and large apartment houses occupied first by Irish and German, then Italian, and now mostly Latino immigrants.

Port Chester has its own school district with its own school tax. About 65 percent of Port Chester's students are Latino, and about the same percentage of students qualify for free or reduced-price meals. (About 20 percent of the students are white, and 12 percent are African American.) In the 2006–07 school year, Port Chester spent roughly $14,500 per student per year, which is about the average for New York State, but thousands of dollars less per student than most of its neighboring districts, which spend anywhere from $18,000 to $24,000 a student. What this means is that teachers in Port Chester could move to schools just a few miles away and make $10,000 or even $15,000 more per year in schools where the students are much wealthier and where most have college-educated parents. Why do they stay? "We're successful here," said Neil Nostro, head of Port Chester Middle School's social studies department. "And it's like family."

"Successful" and "like family" are not words teachers used to describe Port Chester Middle School in the early 1990s. Back then it was a low-performing school where discipline was a big problem, and many teachers there hoped to escape elsewhere after a few years. The story of how Port Chester Middle became a school where rates of student proficiency match those of Westchester County as a whole (exceeding it slightly in math) and teachers look forward to coming to work is one that offers important insights into some of the more difficult problems bedeviling education today, from questions about how to prepare students for state assessments without "narrowing the curriculum" to figuring out what to do about the puzzle of middle school.

Before principal Carmen Macchia arrived at Port Chester Middle School in 1992, he had moved around in education for years, teaching at both the elementary and high school levels and working as principal in an all-white public school and private international schools in Italy and Greece. When he interviewed for the job at Port Chester, Macchia said, "Members of the teacher committee asked, 'How long will *you* be around?'—because they had had a revolving door, one principal after another. I said, 'Six years.' I don't even know why I said that. It just seemed like a good amount of time." Thirteen years later, he is still at Port Chester, with no plans to leave. "This is where my heart is," Macchia said. As someone whose family had emigrated from Italy, he has a fellow feeling for his students, many of whom are first-generation immigrants from Mexico, Guatemala, and elsewhere in Latin America.

The first few years Macchia was at Port Chester, academic concerns were not at the top of his list. "It was all law and order," Macchia said, remembering that when he arrived, students went home after school with their bladders bursting because they didn't feel safe using the school bathrooms, debris littered the hallways, and students were continually sent to the office for discipline violations. Macchia concentrated on fixing those problems. "First you have to provide a safe environment," Macchia said. "We cleaned it up, we patrolled, we found out who caused the problems, and we taught the kids that telling is their duty as school citizens. That was a struggle, because kids said they didn't want to rat on other kids. But everybody needs to be safe." At the same time, he was addressing the "tense, nontrusting, skeptical" attitude of the teachers by involving them in more and more decisions.

By 1998, Macchia felt so confident that he had turned the school around that he applied for the National Blue Ribbon award from the U.S. Department of Education. The New York State Education Department gave the school a state award because of the vast improvement in the school atmosphere, but, Macchia said, the U.S. Department cited the school's low test scores as the reason why it was not worthy of the national award.

At that time, the only middle school testing program in New York State consisted of a nationally normed test, to which the school hadn't paid much attention and on which the school did not perform well. But in 1999 New York began administering its own standards-based tests, and it became crystal clear just how low Port Chester Middle School's academic achievement was. That first year of New York testing, only 33 percent of the school's students met state standards on the English language arts test, and only 38 percent met the standards on the math exam—and the numbers were much worse for poor, African American, and Latino students. For example, only 18 percent of the Latino students—who then made up a much smaller percentage of the school than they do today—met the math standards.

Looking back at the idea that they had felt confident enough about the school to apply for the National Blue Ribbon award just the year before, Port Chester's superintendent, Dr. Charles Coletti, said, "We were improving on mediocre measures." The state tests, which Coletti considered good measures, awakened the district to just how few students were learning what they should be learning. Coletti met with the faculties of each of the schools he headed (one high school, one middle school, four elementary schools).

"He told us that if we were a company he would close us down," remembered Patrick Swift, who had arrived as assistant principal at Port Chester just before the scores were released, after working at a school in the South Bronx. "When I came here I walked into fury." Coletti agreed with that assessment of the angry reaction by teachers and others. "It hurt them when I said that. It hurt *me* when I said it. I didn't like saying it." But, he added, "We always say it's okay if adults feel uncomfortable. I call it adult dissonance."

If Coletti played the adult-dissonance bad cop, Macchia played a little of the softening, we-can-do-this good cop. "He helped mediate it," assistant principal Swift said, getting the teachers to see ways in which they could improve and be successful. All the adults in the school learned to look at data carefully and to begin asking questions: Which students were doing poorly? Which were doing well? Which teachers were particularly successful in getting kids who weren't doing well elsewhere to do well? What was it that the tests were really asking students to know and be able to do? The school began a process of professional development, some of which was provided by Charlotte Danielson, who has written several books on how reorganizing schools to focus on standards and curriculum can improve student achievement. Other training was provided by Learning Focused Solutions, a private group founded by Max Thompson, which focused on aligning the curriculum with the standards.

One of the insights that emerged was that even the math, science, and social studies tests were at least in part reading tests. "A lot of times the kids could do the math—that is, the calculations," Macchia said. "They didn't understand the problem and what the problem was asking them to do. They struggled with that." But, as in many secondary schools, the math teachers and those in other content areas didn't consider reading instruction their territory. "The science and math teachers said, 'I'm a physical science teacher' or 'I'm a math teacher,'" Macchia said. "But they couldn't deny the fact that reading and writing are essential components of the assessments of those subjects."

The big change in the school occurred, Macchia said, when "we convinced all of the teachers in the school that all of the teachers are ELA [English language arts] teachers—it is in the interest of math teachers to understand that they are teachers of reading, writing, listening, and speaking." This was not an easy switch. "You have no idea" is how Macchia described the difficulties involved. He gave a lot of credit for the switch to ELA chair Michael DeVito, who worked with all of the teachers to see how students' inability to read and write hurt both their abilities to learn and to demonstrate their knowledge in the different subject areas.

Math department chair Aida Velez agreed that at first the switch was difficult. "In the beginning I said it was hard in math—now it's easy. Students are hearing the same thing in all their classes: They need to write in complete sentences. In 1999 the students couldn't write a sentence. Now they echo the question and write a nice answer. . . . The ELA is there—we can move onto other objectives." The comfort of teachers with the idea that they are, in part, teachers of writing and reading comprehension can be seen in classroom instruction, where teachers explicitly discuss such things as vocabulary—including root words, prefixes and suffixes, and synonyms and antonyms. Assistant principal Karen Walker, for example, told of a science class she observed where the teacher was teaching about different kinds of rock and connected the word *ignite* to *igneous* rock. Another example could be seen in Georgia Garay's eighth-grade math class, where she made sure that her students understood "another name for how tall [something] is: altitude or height."

Today, Macchia said, the English language arts teachers "drive the curriculum." By this he means that they have decided on 24 "key skills that are involved in reading and writing," such as "compare," "contrast," and "make inferences." Each month one skill is identified, and teachers across the curriculum are expected to incorporate the skills into their classrooms. "Classify" is an easy one for science; during that month, the science teachers taught about how to classify animals and plants. Teachers work together in teams where they work out what content they will teach in addition to those skills. Whenever possible, they develop a common theme that involves several disciplines. So, for example, when the seventh grade was studying colonial American history, they held a "Colonial Day" in which each class did something related to colonial times. The math class studied the geometry of colonial quilts; the science class made soap and candles, demonstrating the physical properties of liquids and solids; the social studies class built a model of a colonial village; and the language arts class learned colonial riddles and made silhouette cutout portraits. The day was such a success that some of the teachers, along with ten students, gave a presentation at a state-sponsored social studies convention.

Similarly, when the eighth grade studied the Holocaust, the English teachers and reading teachers incorporated literature and stories from the Holocaust. Art teacher Ida Tino, who consults regularly with the English and social studies teachers, assigned students to paint narratives in the style of American artist Jacob Lawrence about the Holocaust with clearly written labels that explained what the paintings were about. "I am an ELA teacher," she said in explanation of her efforts. By working so closely on integrating the curriculum, teachers immerse students in a particular topic for long enough to allow them to acquire new vocabulary connected with the content—something research has shown to be essential to build reading proficiency, particularly in the older grades.

Teams of teachers are at the core of the Port Chester Middle School program. Not only are the teams the place where teachers plan curriculum and instruction, they are also where teachers make sure no student is lost. "Team planning is an integral part of middle school" is the way Macchia put it. Sixth, seventh, and eighth grades have two teams each, and each team is responsible for about 120 students. They meet together every day, even though, as Macchia said, "finding the time is difficult." Administrators build the school's schedule around the team meetings so that students are at "specials" (such as art and physical education) while their core academic teachers meet. Each team is led by a lead teacher who is paid an extra stipend to coordinate the agendas and lead the meetings. Team leaders also sit in on the school leadership team meetings and are responsible for making sure information flows easily between the administration and the teachers.

Different teams have slightly different schedules, but usually three meetings a week are devoted to discussing the curriculum and planning lessons and instruction, developing assessments, and discussing assessment data; two meetings a week are devoted to discussing individual students who are struggling. Often those intervention meetings are held with one of the school counselors present, as well as the students themselves and their parents or guardians. "We try to treat [students] like adults," said Chris Halstead, a seventh-grade social studies teacher. Before laying out the problems, either academic or behavioral, the teachers will always find something encouraging or praiseworthy in the student's work. "We want him to hear the positive and the negative" is how the eighth-grade team leader, math teacher John Fazio, put it.

Sometimes the plan of action developed at those meetings involves connecting the student with outside social services, and sometimes it involves pairing the student with a mentor or a tutor within the school or with afterschool help that is provided as part of a federal 21st Century Community Learning Center grant. One option is to refer students to START (Start Today and Reach for Tomorrow), a program specifically designed to support students who are identified as at risk of failure or dropping out. START has three counselors specially trained to work with students who feel disconnected from the school. Another option is to schedule students into an "academic intervention" class during the last period of the day. Students who don't need the extra instruction are expected to read independently during that period (as part of the Sustained Silent Reading program) or to participate in a Junior Great Books seminar, but students who need extra help for a day or two—or even for the full year—go to the academic intervention classes, which are taught by teachers. "Nobody falls through the cracks," Fazio said.

Such careful scheduling is based on the idea, propounded by superintendent Coletti, that all students can reach standards if given good instruction, but some need extra time to reach them, and it is up to schools to provide that extra time. Students are identified as needing academic help from test data, from both state- and teacher-made tests. Each class takes a teacher-made monthly test that is correlated to the end-of-course exams. Monthly test data are charted and posted in the hallway for everyone to see. In this way, it is possible for students, teachers, administrators, and even the occasional visiting parent to get a quick read on whether a particular class is meeting its target. If a class is not, the principal and two assistant principals expect the teacher to provide a specific plan to reteach the content the students missed and, if necessary, to identify individual students who need additional help. If the numbers don't improve after two months, administrators develop their own plan to help the teacher deepen his or her knowledge or skill in that area. They might pair that teacher with another in the school who can help, or link the teacher to outside resources.

Having the data posted so publicly "was uncomfortable at first," superintendent Coletti said. But, he added, it was never "intended to be punitive." The point is to make decisions based on assessment, not to punish teachers. "We're not afraid of charting performance."

Examples abound of decisions made because of data. Because math and English language arts are considered so fundamental, the school sought and won from the school board two additional teachers to lower class size in those core subjects. Many teachers in the school attribute the improvement in test scores to that decision, because with no more than 18 students in each class (16 for some math classes), they are able to individualize instruction and ensure that no one falls behind unnoticed. Another decision was to "loop" between seventh and eighth grades: teachers in English, math, and social studies will teach seventh grade one year, then "loop" to teach eighth grade the following year and drop back to teach seventh grade the year after that. Looping does two things. First, it gives the seventh-grade teachers a stake in the eighth-grade test scores, on the grounds that all teachers should be fully versed in the standards across all the grade levels. "A kindergarten teacher should understand how *bat*, *rat*, and *cat* fit into the third-grade standards" is how Coletti put it. Second, it means that teachers and students develop strong bonds with each other and that teachers don't have to start at square one every year to understand where kids are and where they need to go.

As part of the effort to make sure all teachers understand the standards throughout the system, the middle school has been working with the elementary schools to study New York State's standards and to map out their curricula to make sure that they are all working toward the same ends. "It turned out," Coletti said, "that all the elementary schools were teaching contractions ad infinitum and missing other important subjects." Seventh-grade science teacher and department chair Maria Recchia was part of that process. "We remapped the entire science curriculum in line with the grammar schools," she said. In prior years, each individual teacher might have focused solely on animals or solely on earth science, depending on personal interest. Now, Recchia said, students are expected to learn about topics in earth science, physical science, and life science each year, building on the previous year's knowledge so they will not develop gaps. "Hopefully, that will serve the children well." In addition, Recchia—a career-changing teacher whose first career was as a registered nurse—said, "We're taking a more hands-on approach." In one class, she demonstrated that approach by introducing snakes and turtles to the students to let them see and feel for themselves what distinguished these creatures from other animals. As in other classes, the emphasis on vocabulary building could be seen, as when she explained that *ectotherm* and *cold-blooded animal* meant the same thing, or later when she explained what the words *geologic* and *paleontologist* meant before students read a selection on the extinction of dinosaurs. To support space science and astronomy instruction, the district built a small planetarium in the middle school, staffed by a teacher who starts with why there are different seasons and gradually moves toward discussions of atomic theory. Students from the whole district visit it.

When teachers plan a year's curriculum, they plan from January to January, not from September to June as in most schools. Seventh graders who have mastered seventh-grade material start working on the eighth-grade curriculum in January, which is when eighth-grade students begin working on ninth-grade material. State tests are given in March, and this schedule ensures that the full year of material has been taught by then, with time for extra review and practice for those students who need it. Any student who is not thought ready for the state tests is assigned to Academic Intervention Services classes and to any other help that might be appropriate. For example, by April, Georgia Garay's eighth-grade math class was learning more advanced trigonometry than was prescribed by the New York State curriculum. "I've enriched the curriculum," she said, "because they can do it."

This close attention to what is taught and what is learned is a far cry from past practice. "Years ago," said social studies chair Nostro, "you went through the book and you got to where you got to by the end of the year. If you never got past World War I, well, then, that was where you ended." Now, Nostro said, every teacher knows month by month where he or she needs to be. Nostro is nostalgic about the loss of the old freedom. "It's taken some of the fun out of teaching," he said, in part because he can't spend all the time he wants on a favorite time period. But he agrees that by pegging the curriculum to the standards, he and other teachers are ensuring that their students will not leave middle school without knowing something about recent American history, as many did in the past. Port Chester teachers speak with pride about the fact that their students perform well in social studies, even though social studies tests are not used to hold schools accountable for student progress. Eighty-one percent of Port Chester's students met the state's middle school social studies standards in 2005, in comparison to 58 percent of the students in the rest of the state.

Although teachers spend a bit of time exposing students to test formats and to the way test questions are formulated, they say they do not concentrate on "test prep." "I was talking to a colleague in another district, and he said, 'So you teach to the test,'" said assistant principal Patrick Swift. "I said no, we build the curriculum so that the students learn what they need to know to meet state standards." "It's not just for testing" is how the science department chair, Recchia, put it. "You want them to know how to interpret, compare, analyze—not for the test but to be productive members of society." The eighth-grade test does have important consequences for individual students in the Port Chester district: Students who do not meet eighth-grade standards in reading, math, and science must attend summer school, and if they don't pass muster after that, they are retained in eighth grade. Few students are held back (only three were after the 2005–06 school year), but, said Macchia, "It's an issue of quality control. We have to be able to demonstrate that they are ready for high school work."

With all this attention to teaching to the standards and providing extra help to students, Port Chester's test scores have risen dramatically. In 2005, they were not where they needed to be yet—the school was still a long way from 100 percent of students meeting state standards. But the school's improvement far outpaced that of the state, and all subgroups in the school had improved. The improvement was so great that in 2005 the school once again applied for the National Blue Ribbon award, and this time the U.S. Department of Education gave it to them.

For the most part, the improvement occurred with the existing staff. Although some teachers left during the five years that improvement was posted as part of normal attrition, the bulk of the staff had been at the school for the entire time. Coletti concludes, "We can retool," meaning that change and reform can take place in schools with the current teaching force. "Teachers are capable of change. Once they feel supported and committed, they will feel successful as well." The question for school leaders, Coletti said, is "What can we do to further support teachers?"

He estimated that it took about two years to "get everyone moving together," years filled with asking questions and getting targeted professional development focused on effective classroom practice, aligning the curriculum to the standards, and learning to work as part of teams. Coletti said it all started with the New York State assessments and the clear recognition that the adults in the schools were not performing their jobs as well as they could.

"A critical mass essentially developed," Coletti said. "Now teachers do their own policing." By that he meant in part that teachers no longer tolerate their colleagues saying negative things about the capacity of their students to learn. Where once many teachers assumed that the students of Port Chester would not perform as well as other Westchester students, and would say so openly, now most keep the focus of their discussions almost entirely on instruction and how they as professionals can help students master the required material.

One change that has occurred over the years is that most of the students with disabilities are now included in regular classes. Classes with significant numbers of students with disabilities are "co-taught" by two teachers—a content-area teacher and a teacher with special education training—a practice that brings with it conflicts over space and teaching styles. Many teachers around the country have found it too difficult to give up their own classrooms in order to co-teach, and co-teachers Laurie Morra and Jenna Broems don't deny that that issue was an obstacle at first. "You have to give up control," Broems said. "She can't be special ed and I the teacher. It has to be a team." Now that they have taught English language arts together for several years, they can almost finish each other's sentences. "It's like a marriage—you have to work together" is the way Morra put it. They also provide the kind of intense scrutiny of each other that means that if one says something that may not be clear to the students, the other can clarify and extend.

"The kids have to be the first priority," said Broems. "You have to be open enough to see that it's not about the teacher but about the learning of the kids."

Although, again, Port Chester still had some way to go in terms of getting all its students to meet the proficiency targets of the state—a little less than one-half of the students with disabilities were proficient in English language arts in 2005—it had more than four times the rate of proficiency for eighth-grade students with disabilities found across the state of New York as a whole.

As with instruction for students with disabilities, instruction for students with limited English proficiency is provided as part of classroom instruction, with two bilingual and three ESOL (English for Speakers of Other Languages) teachers going into classrooms to provide support for students who are still learning English. As a result, most of the limited-English speakers graduate from that status before they have to take the English language arts exam in English. Limited-English Spanish-speakers at Port Chester do relatively well on the state's math and science exams given in that language—72 percent and

63 percent, respectively, are proficient. This compares to 24 and 22 percent of students in New York State.

Many in the school agree that one of the keys to the improvement of Port Chester is the leadership provided by principal Macchia. "He's a unique individual. He's able to bring everybody together" is how assistant principal Swift put it. "He is passionate about every aspect of the school—he is even passionate about the guy who waters the lawn." Certainly Macchia exudes enthusiasm about what goes on in the school, from talking about establishing a "museum" in the lobby of the school with student projects on display, to picking up stray pieces of litter. But Macchia deflects any talk that he is at the center of the improvement. "We're a team," he said. "We are only as good as we all are together." Port Chester Middle School, he added, like all schools, is "a complex organization. It only works if everyone works." All important decisions made at the school, he said, are the results of collaborative effort. The teachers, he said, are the ones "in the trenches—I'm the cheerleader who facilitates."

Today, even hiring decisions are made collaboratively. Teams of teachers and administrators interview candidates, and once hired, teachers no longer drift into tenure as they do in many schools, and as they once did in Port Chester. They are closely monitored and provided support, with veteran teachers providing guidance and help. If, during their first two years, they do not demonstrate that they are able to get their students to meet state standards, they are not rehired for the third year, when tenure protections kick in. Occasionally, when the principal and teachers think that the teacher in question has unfulfilled promise, the superintendent will grant another year of probationary status, if the teacher wants to try again. "Not everyone will be an expert after three years, but are they growable?" is the question Coletti told principals to ask. And the fact that all the teachers rely on each other to help plan instruction and assess progress means that they have a huge stake in good hiring decisions.

Where once Macchia focused his efforts solely on creating a safe and orderly physical environment, today he focuses almost all his efforts on helping teachers create a challenging and rigorous academic environment, all the while using testing data as the reality check to make sure they are on the right track. In the process, he and the teachers have created a school where teachers have a lot of say in what they do day to day, and where they feel enough of a sense of success and support that they work hard and stay, year after year.

"Look at me," said math department chair Velez. "I came 17 years ago and planned to leave after four or five years to go teach somewhere easier. I'm still here."

POSTSCRIPT

During the summer of 2006, Dr. Coletti retired. Just before the 2006–07 school year started, Port Chester received its social studies and science scores from New York State. Sixty-nine percent of students met social studies standards, and 67 percent met science standards. "Social studies is aligned with our recent ELA scores," Macchia said, "but I am a little disappointed in our science score." When I asked him what his plan was to address his disappointment, he said, "We'll be looking at alignment, assessing whether there are gaps anywhere in the curriculum. Also, an item analysis of the exam will be done."

This demonstrates how the "It's Being Done" principals I visited think— when confronted with a test score disappointment, they immediately begin thinking about what can be done to improve instruction.

THE BENWOOD INITIATIVE
CHATTANOOGA, TENNESSEE

INTRODUCTION

I was beginning to feel that the outlines for what goes into improving an individual school were becoming clear. But schools exist within school districts, and most poor children and children of color attend schools in large school districts. Philadelphia's M. Hall Stanton Elementary School (chapter 11) was a vivid example of a school that had benefited from district support, but I was interested in exploring in greater detail the kinds of things that districts could do.

For some years, news had been percolating out of Chattanooga, Tennessee, about the Benwood Initiative, named for the local foundation that funded it. But the stories were confusing. Some people said that Chattanooga had redistributed teachers, moving suburban teachers into the city and city teachers into the suburbs. Others said the high-poverty urban schools in the district were paying teachers more and had in that way lured higher-quality teachers. Was this a teacher redistribution story? Was it a merit pay story? One of my colleagues at The Education Trust, Heather Peske, specializes in these kinds of questions, and she and I started referring to the conflicting stories that we had heard about Chattanooga as the "Benwood Mystery."

Questions about teacher distribution have arisen because a number of careful studies have documented that poor children and children of color are much more likely than other children to be assigned to teachers who have little experience and little expertise. In some cases, this is the result of a series of decisions, some of which no doubt seemed benign at the time they were made. For example, most teacher contracts—like many union contracts—are written to make seniority the major factor in work assignments. In a world where all schools were equal, it wouldn't pose any real problem if senior teachers were better able than junior teachers to get work assignments near where they live

THE BENWOOD SCHOOLS
HAMILTON COUNTY, TENNESSEE

2006 Enrollment: 3,320 students in eight kindergarten-through-fifth-grade
elementary schools
2006 Demographics: 82% African American
10% White
6% Latino
About 95% meet qualifications for free and reduced-price lunch
Locale: Urban

The Benwood Initiative has been focused on eight elementary schools in Chattanooga (an additional school closed because a nearby housing project was torn down): Calvin Donaldson, Clifton Hills, East Lake, East Side, Hardy, Hillcrest, Orchard Knob, and Woodmore.

Grade 3 Reading
Tennessee Comprehensive Assessment Program (TCAP)

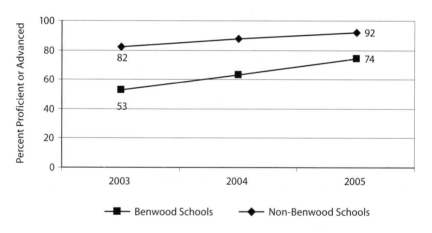

or where their best friends teach, or according to any other criteria they chose. But that isn't how it has worked out. In general, many teachers begin their careers in low-status schools (usually high-poverty schools or schools with large concentrations of students of color) and, as they gain seniority, choose to move into jobs in higher-status schools (usually wealthier and whiter schools). Conversely, ineffective and weak teachers who are eased out of functional schools often go to lower-status schools, a process that principals refer to as the "dance

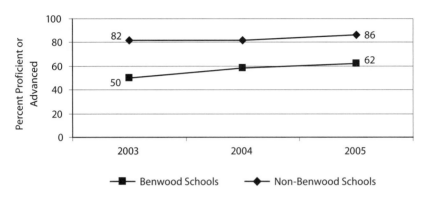

Grade 3 Math
Tennessee Comprehensive Assessment Program (TCAP)

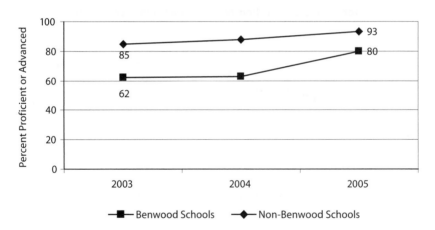

Grade 5 Reading
Tennessee Comprehensive Assessment Program (TCAP)

of the lemons" and "pass the trash." The combination has left many schools where most of the children are poor or of color with weak and either inexperienced or inexpert teaching staffs.

Talk of redistributing teachers by assigning high-quality teachers to high-poverty schools elicits howls along the lines of "Teachers can't be treated like slave labor—you can't just assign them to work where they don't want to work. They'll quit before they'll work in schools they don't want to work in."

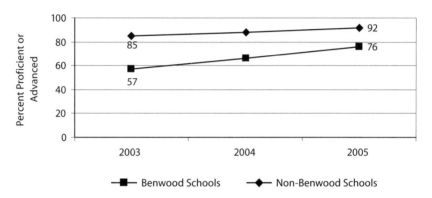

Grade 5 Math
Tennessee Comprehensive Assessment Program (TCAP)

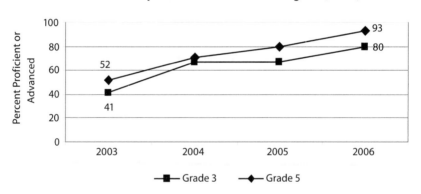

Reading, Hardy Elementary School
Tennessee Comprehensive Assessment Program (TCAP)

Source: Hamilton County Department of Education.

Note: On the Tennessee Department of Education Report Card (http://www.k-12.state.tn.us/rpt-crd06/), the Benwood schools show a slight drop for 2006 in the reading/language scores. Hamilton County Department of Education officials attribute that to the fact that the report card includes a writing score. In 2006, Tennessee increased its cut score for what was considered proficient on the writing assessments, which makes it difficult to compare results over time. When only the third-grade reading scores are considered, six of the eight Benwood schools increased their rates of proficiency from 2005 to 2006.

The other issue, merit pay, is equally controversial. Many people say that the solution to teacher distribution problems is simple: Pay more to teachers who have been identified as effective and who are willing to work in difficult schools. However, this assumes that the only or main incentive teachers respond to is money, which is a doubtful assumption. Also, the problem that many teachers have raised about merit pay is that the basis for deciding who is the most effective teacher, if left solely to a principal's discretion, is liable to be somewhat arbitrary. In the 1970s, horror stories emerged from the few places that tried merit pay of principals giving bonuses to their friends but not to the best teachers. Merit pay is an area where test scores can be useful—if eligibility for merit pay is determined by whether the test scores of a teacher's students increase substantially, the issue of arbitrary principal favoritism fades. But this solution leaves open the question of whether merit pay will attract teachers to difficult-to-staff schools. And many merit pay schemes leave out the many teachers and school staff, such as reading specialists and consulting teachers, who may also legitimately claim responsibility for increases in student achievement.

Heather and I decided to investigate the Benwood Mystery, and we found a complex, interesting story that illuminates issues of teacher distribution and merit pay but actually points to a whole different story—one that could be called "capacity development."

• • • • •

When test score data were used to publish a ranking of all Tennessee schools in 2000, Chattanooga claimed the dubious honor of having nine of its schools listed among the 20 lowest-performing elementary schools in the state. This came as something of a surprise to the city's residents. Why, many asked, does Chattanooga, instead of the larger, poorer cities of Memphis, Knoxville, or Nashville, dominate the list of Tennessee's worst schools?

That question launched what eventually became one of the more notable reform efforts in the country, a reform effort that has systematically addressed many of the obstacles faced by schools serving children of color and children of poverty. Although the rates of improvement have been uneven, all of the original "worst in the state" schools in Chattanooga have improved, some quite dramatically, and the school that was once at the absolute bottom of the state was identified in 2005 as the fastest-improving school in Tennessee.

Understanding the Chattanooga story requires some history. Chattanooga, which had seen a massive decline in its urban core, deeded its schools to the

surrounding Hamilton County in 1996, saying that its tax base could no longer pay for a school system. Although the majority of the city's population was
white, the majority of the schools' students were African American, most of
them poor, and the schools tended to be very low-achieving. Hamilton County
schools, ringing the city, mostly served white students, most of whom were
more affluent than students in the city, although some of the schools were in
rural areas with poor students. The original city schools are known locally as
"urban" schools, even though some of them are in areas that look very suburban, and the county schools are known as "suburban" schools. In many conversations in Chattanooga, *urban students* is the phrase used to describe African American students, and *suburban students* means white students.

The suburban schools tended to outperform the urban schools by huge margins. For example, in 1998, Hamilton County third graders as a whole were just
below the national median on a national norm-referenced test; their average
scores were 49 in reading and 48 in math. In contrast, at many of the Chattanooga schools, the average score was in the teens or twenties, meaning that on
average the students scored below about 80 percent of the rest of the students
in the country who took the same test. Only about 12 percent of the students
met state reading standards.

By state law, if the city ceded the schools to the county, the county could not
refuse to take them over, but the takeover was an uneasy one. A long history
of intertwining race and class tensions made the merger of the districts messy
and at times rancorous. Many Hamilton County residents and politicians ex-
pressed open dismay at the prospect of having to share their tax base with the
city schools. Many African American parents openly feared that their children
would not be educated properly by the county.

Overlying this situation was the fact that the area has a very strong and
growing system of private schools, attended by roughly one in five children
in the area. Some of the private schools are long-established, and some began
shortly after the court-ordered desegregation of schools in the 1960s, as white
families fled the newly integrated schools. It is commonly acknowledged in the
area that the strong tradition of private schooling has weakened the sense of
civic responsibility and urgency many people in business and public life have
toward improving public schools.

To manage the merger of the two school systems, Hamilton County hired
Jesse Register as superintendent in 1997. Register, who had presided over the
merger of districts in another state on two other occasions, was considered
something of a "merger specialist." The first two years of his superintendency
were dominated by questions of budgets, central office staffing, attendance

boundaries, transportation issues, and the many other details that accompany the merger of two districts with a combined total of almost 41,000 students in 80 schools. When he first arrived, he asked the state to give him student achievement data broken out by school and different demographic groups so he could see how African American kids did compared with white kids, how poor kids compared with nonpoor kids, and so forth, but such data weren't available. "I could not get it," Register remembered in an interview eight years later. Register, who had come from North Carolina, where student achievement data had been easily available, was very frustrated by not having information that would tell him how the schools and students he was in charge of were doing.

Then, in 1999, "we started getting data," he remembered. That is when Tennessee began publishing school-level test score data, and shortly thereafter was the publication of what Register called the "infamous list." He took the list of schools ranked from best to worst, with Chattanooga dominating the worst twenty in the state, to his three elementary school directors and said, according to one of those directors, "The achievement gap between the urban and suburban schools—this has to change. If I don't have the people to change it, I'll get them."

That list focused the attention of a group of civic leaders that had been brought together by the new director of a local foundation to discuss local schools. The Benwood Foundation, funded by Coca-Cola Bottling and local banks, had recently hired Corinne Allen, who had formerly run the Charlotte-Mecklenburg Public Education Foundation, a member of the Public Education Network (PEN). PEN is a national organization founded to promote public investment in public education, and one of its members is the Hamilton County–Chattanooga Public Education Foundation (PEF). A couple of months before the list came out, Allen had called together a group of about ten people, including Register, representatives of local philanthropies, and the head of the Chattanooga PEF, Dan Challener. Challener saw the list as an opportunity to begin a substantive discussion about the need to improve the education of Chattanooga's poor children and children of color.

Allen asked Challener to think about what a partnership with the school district would look like. "We had six months to respond," Challener remembered years later. Together, the PEF and the school system sat down to, in Challener's words, "figure out how you can change this within five years," so that Chattanooga would no longer dominate the list of the state's lowest-performing schools. Six months later, convinced that the PEF and the school system had a reasonable plan of action, the Benwood Foundation agreed to spend $5 million over five years, and the PEF another $2.5 million, on the nine lowest-performing elementary schools in Chattanooga, later to be dubbed the "Benwood schools." The Benwood Foundation was very specific and very bottom-line oriented. It was paying to increase the percentage of third-grade students meeting proficiency on state reading tests. If it didn't see improvement, it would stop payments. Results would be reviewed every year. The reason Benwood chose to focus on third-grade reading scores was that extensive research linked early reading scores to later school failure and high school dropout rates. The idea was that if all kids were reading well by third grade, they would have a better chance later in school.

The first attempts to talk to teachers and principals at the Benwood schools yielded important information. Challener and the Foundation's Allen went to one of the schools to tell of the kinds of reforms that they envisioned. "Bright-eyed and bushy-tailed philanthropy" was how Challener characterized their talk. "Afterward, three teachers came out to my car and told us it won't work unless you get rid of the principal and six teachers. 'Unless you can do that, buddy, keep your money,' they told us."

The teachers' admonition had raised a key issue at the Benwood schools—teacher and principal quality. When PEF analyzed the data, they found that the average level of experience of teachers at the Benwood schools was not much different from that of the suburban schools, but that the average was misleading. In reality, few teachers had an average amount of experience. Most teachers in the Benwood schools were either longtime veterans of 20 or more years or brand-new teachers with fewer than 3 years of experience. Few were the 5- to 15-year veterans that are often the backbone of a high-functioning school. The pattern that had developed was that teachers who had not been successful at other schools would land in a Benwood school. "Bad teachers had been allowed to collect in urban schools," Register said. "Bad teachers could survive there; they had created a safe culture for themselves."

At the same time, teachers who were just starting out were able to get jobs at Benwood schools, teach for a couple of years until they became experienced enough to be attractive to a suburban principal, and then switch to what was considered a more desirable school. Natalie Elder, who is now principal of Hardy Elementary, one of the Benwood schools, said, "Turnover was constant. For three years you trained [new teachers] to be effective with these kids, and then they'd leave. That would wear out the savviest principal."

The result was that overall, the teaching force in the Benwood schools was weak and ineffective. There were some good teachers in those schools, but they were outnumbered and tended to work in isolation and with little support. Principals, Register said, had the attitude that "I'm not going to be able to change the quality of teachers because I wouldn't be able to hire anyone better than what I have."

Facilities were also an issue. Most of the suburban schools were in relatively good physical shape, but most of the Benwood schools were not. Register started a building program so that in 2006 most of the Benwood schools were new, built with the same designs as the newer suburban schools. Only one, Orchard Knob, was still in its original building. Built into a hill, Orchard Knob had several levels, with lots of dark, inaccessible areas and remote bathrooms. Since it was scheduled to be replaced in the next two years, Orchard Knob also had not had ordinary maintenance, such as new paint, in some time, giving it an uncared-for air. Register said that most of the Benwood schools were in a similar condition when he first arrived.

The issue of facilities was a fairly straightforward one, however. The issues surrounding quality of instruction were what took creative and sustained effort. Even before the Benwood Initiative began, some groundwork had been laid. For 18 months, with funding by the Annenberg Foundation that had been secured by the Public Education Foundation, hundreds of teachers from the two merged districts had worked on developing a common set of academic expectations in each subject and each grade. For the first time, teachers at all of the Hamilton County–Chattanooga schools could know what students were expected to know and be able to do at each grade level, with a coherent sequence leading from kindergarten through the upper grades. In addition, Register had early on begun spending money on professional development in order to improve the skills and knowledge of teachers. "When I first arrived," Register said, "the staff development budget was zero." He ordered a review of how Title I money was used and began shifting its use from the more traditional hiring of teacher aides to providing "embedded, intense" staff development, including hiring consulting teachers and paying experienced teachers to mentor and support new teachers, most of whom, it was generally acknowledged, emerged from their college or university education programs unprepared for the job of teaching.

The district provided seven days a year of professional development, which was mostly devoted to training in the newly adopted systemwide math program, Everyday Math, and in the Balanced Literacy program adopted by the district, including DIBELS—Dynamic Indicators of Basic Early Literacy Skills—a reading assessment method that helps teachers gauge the fluency and accuracy of their students' reading. In addition, each school in the system was assigned a curriculum coordinator. However, Register said, many teachers in the suburban schools were offended by the implication that they needed more training and refused to participate in professional development. "When we first started investing in professional development," Register remembered, "the reaction in the suburban schools was, 'We know what we're doing.'"

With a common set of expectations, districtwide reading and math programs, and professional development initiatives already in place, Register appointed one of his directors, Ray Swoffard, to head the Benwood effort in a newly created position, director of urban education. Swoffard had grown up in the rural part of Hamilton County on a 60-acre farm that grew corn and sweet potatoes and raised hogs, cows, and horses. He had attended segregated three-room schools until desegregation opened the door of the local high school to him. After he had attended the newly integrated school for a while, he complained to his father that he was once again doing arithmetic; the previous year in his segregated school he had been doing algebra. His father went to the school and demanded that his son be placed in the more advanced classes available to the white students.

Having personally experienced the low expectations teachers often have for African American children, when Swoffard became principal of Woodmore Elementary, one of Chattanooga's schools serving children who were mostly poor and African American, he was determined to make a difference. Swoffard spent precious time battling to rid the school of what he considered bad teachers. Some teachers had no basic grasp of the material they were supposed to be teaching, such as those who, he said, did not know that "the word *wet* only has one syllable." In addition, some teachers were openly abusive. "One teacher punched a child in the ribs for using a magic marker instead of a pen," Swoffard said.

According to Swoffard, the school saw dramatic improvements, only to decline again when he was pulled into the central office and many of the teachers he had assembled drifted off to other schools. But as a central office administrator, in charge of several elementary schools, he developed what he later called the "Donaldson model," after Calvin Donaldson Elementary School, one of the schools he supervised. He redirected how the school used its $180,000 in federal Title I dollars, so that instead of pulling low-performing children out of the classroom to work with teacher aides, he got teachers more training and support. Some of that support came from two new positions he created: Instead of having one assistant principal, he had two lead teachers who acted as assistant principals for instruction—one in math and the other in reading. "She could teach a dog to read" is how he characterized the lead reading teacher.

With that experience in Swoffard's background, in 2001 Register gave him the task of getting 100 percent of all third graders in the Benwood schools reading on grade level by 2006. Swoffard saw the Benwood Initiative as representing a key moment. For the first time, Chattanooga had "a progressive superintendent and a once-in-a-lifetime mayor." In addition, he said, the people behind the Benwood Foundation and the PEF "believed it's not the kids" who were responsible for the low achievement levels of the Benwood schools. Years later, he remembered thinking, "This is the only chance we will ever have. If we squander this opportunity, we will never have it again."

Swoffard began by asking what the principals thought were the key barriers to improvement. When asked, the principals cited discipline, lack of parental support, poor teacher quality, and lack of staff support. He asked the same question of his fellow central office directors, who came up with a completely different list. "Defeated attitude and low expectations" were followed by the low-level skills of principals in how to analyze data, how to draw up a budget, how to hire and evaluate teachers, how to develop a plan, and in general, how to lead.

In three schools, he instituted the Donaldson model that he had used before: Convert one assistant principal into two lead teachers, and use Title I money to supplement the salaries of the lead teachers. In the other schools, additional administrators were added. This meant, in effect, that not only did the teachers have more support, but so did the principals, because they had more administrators to share the workload. Federal Title I money was focused on additional staff such as literacy teachers, and the Benwood Initiative money went to pay for the professional development of teachers and to hiring consulting teachers—master teachers identified from existing staff—who helped teachers with every aspect of classroom instruction, from physically setting up their classrooms to managing student behavior to delivering quality instruction. Some Benwood money also went for books and materials, including classroom libraries.

Because weak leadership had been identified as one of the key problems in the schools, Swoffard began developing a leadership academy for principals to build their skills. "At first I argued that you needed a different skill set to be an effective principal in an urban school. I was wrong. To be a good principal anywhere you need to understand time management, leadership, content of the curriculum." Over time, Swoffard said, he realized "You can be a not-strong leader in some schools and it won't be exposed for a while, but a poor principal in an urban school is felt immediately. I started training well-rounded principals." He and most of the principals also began what he expected to be a years-long process of battling to get rid of ineffective teachers.

One exception was East Side Elementary School, where principal Emily Baker, who had previously had a career in banking and then as a high school English teacher, had spent the previous four years systematically getting rid of teachers the old-fashioned way: by making miserable the lives of the teachers she considered weak, grade by grade, and replacing them with mostly brand-new teachers whom she felt she could train. She had been astounded by the "lack of professionalism and pride in their work" that she had encountered with the teachers she had inherited. "Who hired these people?" she remembered thinking. She had almost finished the process of driving out the weak teachers, but she still had to contend with regular teacher turnover. "Every year was a building year at a Benwood school," she said years later, still the principal at East Side.

Then Register decided to allow Swofford to reconstitute the Benwood schools. Reconstitution was an opportunity to completely overhaul the staffs at the Benwood schools, and it was legally possible because under Tennessee law the superintendent has the power to assign staff. All 300 or so teachers at the nine original Benwood schools (one has since closed because the housing project it served was torn down) were told that, although they could retain a job in the district, they would need to reapply to stay at a Benwood school. According to the school district's central office, 70 chose to transfer at that time, and another 28 of those who applied were not selected to be on the Benwood schools' staffs and were placed elsewhere in the district. Register was very direct with the principals in the suburban schools. He asked them to take "one weak teacher," with the idea being that in another setting, with more support, those teachers might be fine. "We've got to find someplace for everyone to be successful," Register said. "I feel the obligation to make them successful." He has said that many of those teachers did go on to be successful in other schools with better support. But the idea that teachers who weren't good enough for the urban schools were sent to the suburban schools still rankles some people in the county, especially some county commissioners, who have accused Register of shortchanging suburban schools in favor of urban schools.

Susan Swanson was one of the principals asked to take a teacher from a Benwood school. Now director of urban education under Ray Swofford, who has since become associate superintendent of elementary education, she was at that time a principal. She said principals never like to be given staff they haven't chosen. But Register appealed to them, saying, "A school system is only as strong as the weakest school." Swanson said, "I knew that was right and it was the right thing to do."

Six of the nine Benwood principals were similarly reassigned and sent to other schools in the county, often as assistant principals. Only two suburban teachers applied to teach at the Benwood schools, which meant that the Benwood schools for the most part had to continue to hire brand-new teachers just beginning their careers, as they always had.

Having new principals and new teachers was just a start. The group of Chattanooga leaders who were in effect the steering committee of the Benwood Initiative, including the representatives of the major philanthropies and the superintendent, wrestled with how to create the conditions that would make teachers want to stay. Then, even if the schools continued to mostly hire people at the beginning of their career, those teachers would want to stay through their most productive years. "We surveyed teachers to ask what was most important to them," Register said. "Number one was the opportunity to be successful." They wanted, Register said, "a good support system and a good principal." Swoffard put it this way: "It's tough working in these schools. The reason teachers stay in a school is a good principal."

To help get them that, the Public Education Foundation worked with the school system to develop a specific training program, and the principal leadership academy went forward. Principals and assistant principals were given a great deal of training in how to use data, how to evaluate classroom instruction, how to explain the state's standards and the district's curriculum, and how to lead staff discussions on all those topics. Often the meetings of the principals and assistant principals consisted of looking at the school system's data in new ways, simplified and clarified by the Public Education Foundation to tell the story of a school and of the students in that school. Together they learned that achievement data are not a set of meaningless numbers but, as Swanson said, "that data represent a kid's face or a group of kids' faces. That's a life, that's a future. If you look at it that way, you get courage."

One by-product of this academy was a strong bond among the principals and assistant principals, who learned that they could call on each other for advice and support. "We share information constantly" is how one principal described the communication among the Benwood schools. This is important to note, because the job of principal—particularly of high-poverty schools—is often a very lonely job. The academy also developed what Swoffard calls a "strong bench." In the instances when principals have since been replaced, they were replaced by assistant principals from that leadership team, and still others began preparing for leadership.

In addition, principals began using more collaborative forms of decision-making. They brought teachers together as team members to review test score and other data and make decisions about lesson planning, school routines, and classroom management based on the data. Teachers began sitting in on interviews with prospective teachers, thus playing a role in building the school teams. Effective teachers who were able to articulate the curriculum and explain how it fit together from year to year were given the new position of grade-level chair, similar to the department chair in secondary schools. The lead teachers and the outside consulting teachers focused on helping new teachers understand the curriculum, manage their classrooms, and improve their instruction.

In an outside evaluation of the Benwood Initiative, educational consultants Bruce Wilson and Dick Corbett, hired by the Public Education Foundation, noted that new teachers they interviewed repeatedly said how helpful the lead and consulting teachers were and how welcoming the principals and other administrators were. One was quoted as saying, "I am very happy with the support of [the administrators]. They are willing to talk to us and establish a relationship. It helps me improve and want to be a part of the school." One even said, "Many of my first-year teaching friends are really jealous of what I have."

Their words are echoed by Gerry Dowler, coordinator of the Hamilton County Education Association, who said that the success of the Benwood Initiative can be attributed to "Number 1, professional development; number 2, professional development; and number 3, professional development."

Administrators also began taking very seriously their role in evaluating teachers. This, Swoffard said, was key to not allowing the kind of weak teacher corps that had been allowed to develop in the Chattanooga schools in prior years. "The union has always said that someone gave that person tenure," Swoffard said, saying that he agreed with teachers unions that administrators are responsible for allowing bad teaching to go unchecked. That sentiment was echoed even more bluntly by director of urban education Swanson: "A lousy teacher never got tenure without a lousy principal."

Principals were now expected to observe and evaluate each teacher three times a year. An intensive assistance program was set up so that if a teacher received a poor evaluation, a team consisting of the principal, the school system's personnel director, and the central-office-based curriculum director, all of whom were obliged to observe the teacher within two weeks of the evaluation, met to discuss the strengths and weaknesses of the teacher and what extra training or support they would provide. If no improvement was noted after six

months, there would be another round. New teachers who were found unsatis-
factory were denied a third-year contract, meaning that they never earned tenure protections; in 2005, about ten untenured teachers were "not reelected" in
the Benwood schools. Tenured teachers continued to go through the process
of evaluation, again and again. Eight decided to leave rather than go through
another cycle of being found not to have improved, but others were able to improve. Swoffard told of one teacher who, he said, was "pretty bad." The team
asked her to allow them to videotape her classroom. When she watched the
tapes, he said, "She could see what they were talking about." She improved
enough so that she got off the assistance program.

Teachers and principals have one set of data available to them in Tennessee that is not available in most other places: a "value-added" measure. The
test scores of each child throughout the state are measured and plotted against
each individual child's predicted growth in test scores for each year, somewhat
like the growth chart parents of babies are given by their pediatricians. The
amount of progress a teacher produces in each child, compared to the predicted progress, is called "value added." In this way, it is possible to get an idea
of the effectiveness of a teacher or of a school, because the value-added data
account for where a child or group of children begins the year.

Chattanooga's mayor, Bob Corker, gave as one of his contributions to the
Benwood Initiative a $5,000 bonus to any classroom teacher in a Benwood
school whose students' test scores grew more than 15 percent more than the
expected growth. He also held a reception once a year at his home for the
high-performing Benwood teachers to affirm the importance their work had
for the city, and he arranged for Benwood teachers to get low-interest mort-
gages. Principals of schools whose scores increased more than 15 percent more
than the expected growth were eligible for a $10,000 bonus. By the time that
money ran out at the end of the mayor's term in 2005, 115 teachers had earned
the $5,000 bonus. In addition, Hamilton County decided to grant a $1,000 bo-
nus to any teacher in any school (including reading coaches, music teachers,
and so forth) where score growth exceeded the state average by 15 percent. By
the middle of 2006, 120 teachers, eight principals, and seven assistant principals had received the $1,000 bonuses.

One of the benefits of value-added data is that teachers who teach students
who arrive far below grade level can be given credit for growth. If the students
don't end the year meeting grade-level standards but have learned two years'
worth of material in one year, that teacher looks as good as she is. Likewise, if
a teacher has a class of students who are very high-achieving but don't improve

much during the year, the value-added data reflect that as well. Many teachers prefer such data because the teachers don't feel penalized for having students who arrive behind. However, many teachers also fear that value-added data will be used punitively, and the Tennessee state teachers union was able to negotiate as part of state law that districts would not have long-term access to the value-added data. As a result, although the state sends the data to the districts, the districts are supposed to immediately send the data on to the schools without compiling it or looking at individual teacher results.

Although principals in the Benwood schools say they don't use the value-added data as part of their formal evaluations of teachers, they do go over the data carefully with teachers to see which students demonstrated the most improvement in which area. If the students of some teachers learned more about, say, probability and statistics, principals send other teachers in to observe their lessons. Teachers ask each other for advice on how to teach that topic. If a whole school was weak in an area, principals would often find that the teachers themselves didn't understand the subject well, and they would arrange for an expert to do some focused professional development on the topic. Hardy principal Elder said that the data allow her "to look at each teacher individually. . . . Then we look at teams. The third grade was weak on number operations, so we had them model lessons [for each other] and see what the weaknesses were."

In this way, the schools used state testing data to closely monitor whether teachers knew the material they were supposed to be teaching and knew the best ways to convey the material to children. By paying close attention to the teachers whose students improved the most, they were also able to notice and use the expertise they already had in the building.

In another use of the value-added data, the local Urban League chapter agreed to fund an afterschool program in which the high-value-added teachers worked with the students who scored in the bottom quintile of reading, thus closely focusing the best teachers on the kids who needed them most. Teachers applied for these positions by showing their value-added scores.

To both improve the effectiveness of the existing staff and try to stabilize that staff, the PEF asked a second local foundation—the Osborne Foundation—to fund a program that would provide Benwood teachers a free master's degree. The PEF asked universities around the South to design a program that would be tailored to teaching in the Benwood schools and would be offered on-site in the schools. The local university, University of Tennessee–Chattanooga, successfully bid on the proposal, and the Osborne Foundation agreed to pay $1.5 million to fund it. Any Benwood teacher recommended by his or her principal after at least a year of teaching became eligible for a free two-year master's program if the teacher was willing to commit to staying at a Benwood school for four years after earning the master's. Although Hamilton County does not require its teachers to earn a master's degree, it does pay roughly $4,000 to $5,000 more to teachers with a master's degree, depending on years of experience. Although many teachers were not willing to make such a long commitment—it would keep teachers at Benwood schools for a minimum of seven years—quite a few agreed.

The University of Tennessee–Chattanooga's program emphasizes information teachers can put into practice right away, not simply abstract theoretical information. Topics include how to create classroom assessments, how to use assessment data, and literacy. Activities include "field trips" to successful schools and districts to learn about new strategies and approaches. Effective teachers serve as coaches to lead study sessions, and they also visit participating teachers in their classrooms to make sure the teachers understand how the academic work links to classroom practice. Over the years, more than 50 teachers have participated, and at two schools the majority of the teachers are now Osborne Fellows, as they are known. Osborne Fellows are considered the leaders in their schools, helping lead teachers' conversations about curriculum, standards, assessment, and data.

This strategy of developing the capacity of the teachers at the Benwood schools has been considered key to making sure that the children in these schools have high-quality teachers, rather than consistently having either brand-new or worn-out teachers. "By growing your own, you have redressed the inequities" is the way Leslie Graitcer of the PEF put it. Graitcer, who for many years headed the Bell South Foundation, has led the Osborne effort.

At a meeting of some of the alumni of the Osborne program, teachers agreed that the program had awakened them to new ways of thinking about their teaching that went far beyond what they had learned in their undergraduate programs of education. "All of my professors dealt with how to teach English—not how to teach Johnny who has no books at home," said Rachel Stephens, a teacher at Orchard Knob Elementary School, of her undergraduate experience. In the Osborne program, she said, "We got the theory on Saturday and—boom—we used it on Monday." Lindsay Starnes, a teacher at Clifton Hills Elementary School, said that she learned many new strategies to teach students the material they need to know. "When I was [a student] in fifth grade," she said, "all we did was kill and drill. My kids love doing centers and paired learning," two of the strategies that she learned about as part of the Osborne master's program. Even more important, she said, the Osborne program means that "principals see us as leaders."

Many teachers spoke of the fact that as a result of receiving their master's through the Osborne program, they are now considered master teachers who can help their principals lead their schools through the difficult questions of what changes need to take place in order to improve student achievement in their schools. In those schools where the majority of teachers are now Osborne Fellows, there is real momentum for improvement, they said.

As some of the teachers who received the $5,000 bonuses offered by the mayor and the $1,000 offered by the district, the Osborne teachers have definite opinions about whether the bonuses play an important role in attracting and retaining teachers. "It's appealing," said Kathy Robertson, a teacher at Hardy Elementary School, the school that was named the fastest-improving in the state. But, she added, "That all faded into unimportance." The general consensus was that although extra pay was always nice, it was not the reason they had stayed in Benwood schools or would stay at any school. "You've got to have an administration committed to success and willing to mold you," said Dustin Dotzler, a teacher at Hardy, a sentiment echoed by Judy Bullington of Clifton Hills, who said that the most important thing for a teacher is a supportive principal who on bad days will "let you know tomorrow will be better." They were expressing exactly what Register had discovered years before, when he found that the things teachers wanted most were "the opportunity to be successful" and a supportive principal.

Even with all these initiatives to improve the capacity and effectiveness of teachers, the school system's transfer policy remained a difficult barrier. The teachers union contract was written in such a way that as each position became vacant, it was posted for ten days, after which a principal could hire a teacher, giving preference to those teachers with seniority. This is a fairly usual contract provision and is written in order to protect the right of experienced teachers to have more choice in their teaching assignment than new teachers. The unintended consequence, however, has been to put low-status schools at an extreme disadvantage, because an end-of-the-school-year vacancy at a high-status school (in Hamilton County, this meant a high-performing suburban school) often triggers a domino effect of hiring. In general, suburban principals hired a teacher from a somewhat lower-status school, which, after posting the job for ten days, hired from a lower-status school, and so on down the line, until the lowest-status schools—in Chattanooga, the Benwood schools— would find out sometime in August that some of their teachers had been hired away. This left little time to fill vacancies, and the schools would often have to compromise on quality in order to simply fill the position (Swoffard called the people hired in these cases "Labor Day Specials"). Many years saw Benwood schools having to open with vacancies. As recently as 2002, there were 20 vacancies in the nine schools on opening day.

Register asked the Hamilton County Education Association, an affiliate of the National Education Association, to agree to a change when the contract was renegotiated that would allow all the schools to be on a relatively even plane. The union agreed, and the way the system works now is that in February each teacher in the system who wants to transfer lists five schools at which he or she would like to work. "Every principal knows who might leave and who wants to come," said Register. If an opening at one of those schools comes up, the principal is obligated to interview seven of those who bid, including the three most senior people from that list, but may hire the teacher who is the most qualified for the position available—even if it is a person who is not on the list.

This system means that the Benwood schools hire at more or less the same time as the other schools in the system and are no longer the dumping grounds for other schools. In the falls of 2004 and 2005, all of the Benwood schools were fully staffed by July. In addition, the percentage of Benwood teachers who were new to their school dropped from 31 percent in 2002 to 18 percent in 2005.

With all of these initiatives, the Benwood schools have begun attracting the kind of experienced teachers who once would have avoided them. "My first years we were lucky if ten people applied," said Elder, principal of Hardy Elementary. "This year we had maybe sixty." Barbara Walker, for example, moved to Chattanooga from Bradley County, where she had been a school librarian. Rather than look in the suburban schools, she came to Hardy. "A lot of people say, 'Why do you want to stay there?'" she said, reflecting the fact that even now the Benwood schools retain their low status among some teachers in the school system. "I love it because of the high expectations and the way the children meet them."

Hardy Elementary is one of the successes of the Benwood Initiative. In 1998, the average third-grade reading score at Hardy was in the 19th percentile, meaning that of all the students who took the nationally normed test that was given back then, the students at Hardy scored below 81 percent of them. That test is no longer given, so it is hard to demonstrate the gains exactly, but as recently as 2003 only about half of the students met state reading standards; in 2005, three-quarters of the students at Hardy met or exceeded state reading standards. These scores are still not where the rest of the state's scores are, since statewide almost 90 percent of students meet state standards annually. But the scores are close to those of the district, where 80 percent of the students met standards in 2005, and the improvement trajectory is impressive.

Principal Elder, who grew up in the neighborhood in which Hardy sits, has been there from the beginning of the Initiative, and she and her staff have instituted several structural changes, including going to a year-round calendar, a decision agreed to by both the teachers and the parents. The school has four nine-week sessions separated by intersessions. Most children take "workshops" during the intersessions—except for the longer summer intersession, when the school is closed—which focus on some hobby or interest of the teachers who teach them. Topics include basket weaving, dancing, crocheting, Pilates, acting, gardening, gymnastics, chess and other board games, and many more. Children sign up to try something that appeals to them, and then spend the balance of the day getting additional help in reading or math, depending on what teachers have identified as the child's weakness.

"We've created plans for each child," Elder said. Those plans take into account the student's test scores as well as the portfolio of work that is maintained for each child, which follows him or her on to the next school. "We are almost at a point where we have an IEP for every child."

Breakfast at Hardy starts at 7:30 in the morning—because 96 percent of the students qualify for free or reduced-price meals, every student is provided breakfast—but a voluntary "early morning math" class starts at 6:30, taught by a teacher who is paid extra, and Elder says that often 55 or 60 children show up for that.

Although Hardy is unusual in having a year-round schedule, it shares other routines with the other Benwood schools, such as devoting a two-hour uninterrupted block of time to literacy and another 90 minutes to math. Because each of the Benwood schools has similar processes, students can more easily move among them, which is fairly common as families constantly seek new housing. Unlike most of the other schools, however, Hardy has departmentalized the third, fourth, and fifth grades, meaning that some teachers teach literacy and some math. Elder did this, she said, "so that teachers can concentrate on one field."

Teachers meet as part of their grade level for 45 minutes every day—the school's schedule is built so that they meet when their students are in "specials" such as art or music—and they also meet regularly as part of cross-grade teams, both to plan programs for the school and to receive high-quality professional development. "I try to find professional development that focuses on serving these students," Elder said, adding that most of the teachers come from middle-class backgrounds and sometimes need help understanding what their mostly poor students need. "I don't want missionaries," Elder said. "I tell my teachers, 'Don't worry about whether they get love. That'll come. Worry about teaching them.'" Once a week, either Elder or a lead teacher meets with the grade-level team. "We focus on instruction," Elder said. In addition, the school's Title I committee meets regularly to decide how to spend the school's federal Title I allocation. All the grade-level teacher leaders, the guidance counselor, the administrators, and some parents meet on the committee to make sure that the Title I money goes to things that are important to school improvement.

The most important element in school improvement, Elder said, is to have "high-quality teachers who are effective." But, she added, "the key thing is to maintain and sustain them." One of the ways to maintain and sustain teachers, she said, is the full-time consulting teacher paid for by the Benwood grant, who helps new teachers organize their classrooms, goes through lesson plans and materials, models lessons, and even co-teaches some classes. The consulting teacher is not a supervisor, and so is not involved in the formal evaluation of teachers. As a result, help from her is not seen as criticism. "She helps teachers feel safe," Elder said.

Jennifer Ayers, a second-grade teacher at Hardy who had previously taught elsewhere in Chattanooga, said the key to Hardy's improvement has been both the high-quality professional development, mostly in reading instruction, and a "higher level of principal." Administrators at Hardy, she said, help keep a sense of perspective. "If something goes wrong, we laugh at it, make it better, and move on." The administrators both expect more and allow the kind of creativity that will get better results, she said. "I teach thematically," Ayers said. "Last week I taught about the Civil War, slavery, and the differences between the North and the South. I'm teaching stuff I never thought I'd teach in second grade." The atmosphere at Hardy, she said, is one of collaboration and team work. "My team level meets outside school hours, on weekends, et cetera—not because we have to, but because we want to."

Other schools in the Benwood Initiative are not as far along as Hardy in terms of putting in place all the elements that will help them improve and achieve at high levels. But those schools that were lagging had been given a new set of principals and staff. One is on its third principal. In that case, Register said, the original staff at the beginning of the Benwood Initiative was "the worst I had ever seen." He said that the first principal he appointed at the beginning of the Benwood Initiative was unwilling to make the massive changes necessary. The second made the necessary personnel changes but had built up so little goodwill that Register found the need to replace that principal as well, this time with an enthusiastic young principal who had been trained as an assistant principal in a Benwood school. By the spring of 2006, he was confident that the school was poised to make big gains in the following year.

By that time, however, he had announced that his retirement would begin in the summer of 2006, saying that he had been in the school district for almost ten years and that that was long enough. An election had brought a new majority—more supportive of the public schools—to the county commission, and he said he felt he could entrust the future of Hamilton County schools to a new superintendent. He said he was confident that the school board and the philanthropic community in Hamilton County would not permit the school system to backslide in its commitment to Chattanooga's schools. "The school board has been united and supported the work," he said. But he acknowledged that he was retiring in part because he was worn out from the hounding he had taken from a few angry school board members and county commissioners who had accused him regularly of shortchanging the suburban schools and called for him to resign.

With all that has happened in Hamilton County schools, Register said, "The urban schools are now considered the haves." Shortly after announcing his retirement, he said, "The baggage I have now is that suburban teachers ask, 'Why don't we have the same opportunities?'"

This feeling has been enhanced by the fact that the Benwood principals are now considered the leaders in the district. "These folks have become the stars," said Swanson. "They're pushing other principals to higher levels." When principals throughout the system began learning about how to institute a school improvement process, it was the Benwood principals who led the discussions and presentations. "The comments I got were 'Wow!'" said Swanson.

Register was at pains to point out that the achievement of students in non-Benwood schools went up at the same time as the achievement of students in Benwood schools. The successes of the Benwood Initiative have not come at the expense of the rest of the school system, he said. Also, high schools throughout the system were part of a comprehensive reform funded by $14 million in grants from the Carnegie Foundation and the PEF. Although a middle school reform effort, funded in part by a $2.5 million grant from the National Education Association Foundation, began as an urban school reform, it has since been expanded to the entire system. Even Register's staunchest supporters, however, said that Register did not communicate well the idea that Hamilton County's suburban schools were not shortchanged by the urban schools. And in 2005, when an Annenberg Foundation assessment of the school system recommended improving communication, Register agreed. "As I look back, I realize we made a mistake five years ago by not putting more resources into communications. In order to build stronger relationships with all of our constituents, we must place a priority on telling our story and successes to our constituents as well as do a better job of sharing information with the public."

As Register was about to leave office, he pointed to another factor that he said led to his political difficulties. "There are still people who are not concerned with issues of equity and quality for all children. Some in power still carry their prejudices."

Register's departure raised the anxiety level of those who have been involved in the Benwood Initiative. Even though there was great hope for the incoming superintendent, Dr. Jim Scales, who had previously served as deputy superintendent of the Dallas Independent School District, new superintendents have a well-known tendency to want to unravel the work of previous superintendents as they build their own legacies. "These schools are on the right path, but there's a fragility there" is the way Swoffard put it. "I would hope the commitment would be there with the new superintendent."

For its part, the Benwood Foundation announced in the summer of 2006 that it would extend the original grant for a sixth year and would put in $750,000 for the 2006–07 school year while putting together a planning committee with the PEF, the Benwood Foundation, and the school system now headed by Scales. The idea, said Allen, director of the Benwood Foundation, would be to "study how to take the Initiative to scale." Citing the fact that the most enduring criticism of the Benwood Initiative has been the fact that it has been focused solely on the urban schools, she said that she is hoping that Scales would see the opportunity to bring the same kind of systemic approach to all of Hamilton County's elementary schools. If so, she said, a further large, multimillion-dollar grant would be possible. The importance of the Benwood Initiative, Allen said, is that it "took a cadre of the most-challenged schools and produced change not only in individual schools but in a culture, to produce a belief that all kids can learn if given adequate resources."

Although it would be easy to focus attention on the additional funding provided by the Benwood, Osborne, and Public Education Foundations as being at the core of the Benwood Initiative, the PEF's Challener said that would be a mistake. The money provided an important catalyst, but what really made a difference in the Benwood schools, Challener said, was that the district helped teachers and principals learn to do their jobs more effectively.

That sounds simple, but helping teachers and principals took a complex and systematic approach, including clear guidance on what students were expected to know and be able to do at each grade level; help in assessing whether students were meeting those expectations; training in how to use achievement data to recognize problems, set goals, measure progress, and celebrate achievements; and the establishment of a structure for principals to learn to work with other principals and to help teachers work together, so that teachers and principals no longer worked in isolation but as part of functional teams that made decisions together. In addition, the district took specific steps, such as providing good facilities, working with the teachers union to stabilize the staff, and making sure teachers had the opportunity to advance and improve through a master's degree program, to make the Benwood schools—which have as high a concentration of poverty as any schools in the country—places where teachers and principals feel successful and want to work.

And almost everyone in the process says that the outside role played by the Chattanooga PEF was central. Calling itself a "critical friend," the PEF brought a coherence and focus to the work by providing careful analyses of the data and making sure that attention didn't wander from the initial goal. "Everything that was done was focused on the goal set in 2001 to get every third grader reading at or above grade level" is the way Challener put it. "We made sure this wasn't random acts of kindness."

POSTSCRIPT

State report card data hadn't been posted by publication, but the unofficial reading scores provided by the district confirm that, although the Benwood schools still had not met the goal of 100 percent of third graders reading on grade level, they had shown progress.

CONCLUSION
WHAT CAN WE LEARN?

Although all of the schools profiled in this book have large concentrations of students of color, students of poverty, or both, they are very different in just about all other ways. They are big and small; integrated and racially isolated; high-tech and low-tech; urban, rural, and suburban. Some require uniforms, some do not. Some follow traditional school calendars, some follow year-round calendars. Some are in big districts, some in small ones. Some have adopted prepackaged school improvement designs, some have developed their own model of improvement. Some have beautiful facilities, some are in buildings that should have been torn down years ago. Some have successfully engaged their parents and communities, some have not.

Those are the characteristics that many say make the difference in school quality. And yet, despite those differences, all of these schools either have very high rates of proficiency or impressive trajectories of improvement. So the question arises: Is there something deeper that these schools share? Is there something more than uniforms and school size and computers that makes the difference?

I have become convinced that there is no one single factor that is at the core of a successful school. That is, there is no one structure, or one curriculum, or one set of policies and procedures that, if every school in the country were to adopt it, would transform them into high-achieving schools. Schools are complex organisms that can't be changed that easily. Over and over, the teachers and principals in these schools told me, "There is no magic bullet."

But there are some characteristics that they all share, and while I was pondering how to try to convey them, I had an experience that brought into stark relief some of the things I wanted to highlight. I visited a "crummy poor-kid school." I use this term to describe the typical school that serves children of poverty—chaotic, dismal, and low-achieving, though often with pockets of he-

213

roic teaching off in isolated classrooms. I had been to crummy schools before beginning this project, but for two years the only schools I visited were good or rapidly improving schools that were very different in many ways. To bring them together in one descriptive formula seemed a daunting task. Then I went to this aforementioned crummy school.

I should admit that I hadn't expected to go to a crummy school. On paper, this school looked like another success story: It posted very high proficiency rates on state tests in a state with high standards. The students were all African American and almost all poor, mostly living in a nearby housing project. I was looking forward to another "beating the odds" story.

As I walked up to the school building early in the morning, I joined a mother and her two young children, the older one a boy in kindergarten. Hopping with enthusiasm, he was clearly looking forward to the day, and his mother said he was like that every day. "He wakes me up every morning. He won't let me be late," she said, laughing. This seemed very promising, and I was excited.

That was the last promising moment. The hallways were filled with children gathering for the start of school, but they were milling in a purposeless way and few looked as if they had anything to look forward to. The adults seemed to lack energy, and when they weren't ignoring the kids, they were yelling at them to get into line. When I got to the office it was locked. When I asked an adult where the principal was, she said, "She's not here yet," as though it were normal for the principal not to be there at the beginning of school. When the principal did show up, she was surprised I was there, even though I had called and e-mailed several times in the previous weeks to confirm my visit.

The principal showed me around the school. In many classrooms, she opened the door onto quickly dampened noise. The teachers and substitute teachers (there were several substitutes that day) looked up with relief. Quite a few said things like, "Oh, I'm glad you're here—the kids are really acting up." On those occasions, the principal yelled at the disruptive students in front of their teachers, classmates, and me, a stranger taking notes. "What did you promise me?" she shouted at a young boy who looked absolutely miserable being humiliated in public. "You sat in that office and promised me and your mother something. What was it?" She yelled at teachers and even a parent in the same way. At no time did the principal say she wanted to introduce me to a teacher or a student or see classroom teaching being done. In fact, there was very little classroom instruction visible. The two exceptions were a kindergarten teacher who was enthusiastically leading her students in a song they were preparing for an end-of-the-year ceremony and a class where a poet had come in as part of a foundation grant to introduce older children to poetry. Finally, the principal stated the obvious: "Once the state tests are done we don't do a lot of instruction—we're doing field trips and getting ready for the end of the year." The state tests are given in March and April, months before school lets out. What little she did say about instruction made it clear that it was focused almost entirely on what would appear on the state test, such as teaching students the specific words that the state tests use and teaching them to take notes on reading passages.

Some students had been left behind from a field trip that day, either because they hadn't gotten their permission forms in on time or because they were being punished for poor behavior. They had been given an assignment to write about what job they would like in the future. Although the students were in seventh grade, none of their essays was longer than a paragraph, and none included many salient details. Two of the most ambitious of the students said that they would like to run a laundry and a hair-braiding-and-nail salon. The principal gave the students a lecture about how they should think about other possibilities, such as running a shaved ice booth or selling cold water on a hot day.

At one point on the tour, the principal announced to a teacher, in front of her class, that she had good news—the teacher would be teaching a science class the following year, and only to the "high" kids. The teacher gave a little victory whoop. It was a K–7 school, and the principal told me that she organized the school to strictly segregate the older students from the younger ones—older students were not permitted to use the same bathrooms or be in the same room as the little kids, because she didn't want any possibility of the older kids intimidating or harassing the younger ones.

From all I had seen—the atmosphere of distrust, disrespect, and barely controlled chaos; little interest in instruction; and extremely low ambitions for the kids (a water stand!)—I concluded that the high scores the school posted had not been attained in a legitimate way. That conclusion was strengthened when the principal told me, as part of a long conversation, that teachers administering state tests were "under strict accountability to not allow students to turn in half-filled-out answer sheets—and they can't have any wild answers either." Though I tried to keep my face as deadpan as possible, I think the principal knew she had made a self-damaging admission: There are no legitimate ways to keep students from giving "wild answers" on a state test. I could barely wait to escape, and I caught an early flight home, depressed by what I had seen. Except in the poetry class taught by an enthusiastic outsider, I hadn't seen any older kids who looked anything but angry and belligerent, and I feared for the little kindergartner who still eagerly hopped to school. Months later my suspicions about the lack of learning going on at that school were confirmed. The principal had said she had some concerns because the testing protocols had been changed, and those changes must have made concealment more difficult—fewer than 10 percent of the students had met state standards.

Seeing that school helped crystallize in my mind what I wanted to say about what I had learned about schools that are getting the job done in terms of teaching all their children to learn to high levels. I am calling them, for want of a better term, "It's Being Done" schools to distinguish them from run-of-the-mill schools and the all-too-common crummy poor-kid schools.

WHAT "IT'S BEING DONE" SCHOOLS DO THAT IS DIFFERENT

They teach their students. This seems like a flip thing to say, but it is at the heart of high performance and improvement. In "It's Being Done" schools, educators think deeply about what their students need to learn and how to make sure they learn it—"not for the test," as teacher Maria Recchia at Port Chester Middle School said, "but to be productive members of society." Teachers and principals in these schools are acutely aware that their students are reliant on them for their academic learning, and they take that responsibility seriously. They begin with their state's standards, but in most cases they are not limited by them. Teachers in these schools teach increasingly complex and sophisticated material, aiming their students to exceed standards—which helps ensure that they meet them. "We push our kids to excel," said teacher Alicia Calabrese at Elmont Memorial Junior-Senior High School in New York. "When you believe they can do that, they rise to the challenge."

Teachers don't stop teaching just because the state tests have been given for the year. And they use the verb "to teach" properly. That is, they do not say what many teachers around the country say: "I taught it, but the kids didn't get it." Although common, this formulation actually makes no sense. If I were to say "I taught my child to ride a bike," you would expect that my child could ride a bike. She might be a bit shaky, but she should be able to pedal and balance at the same time. If she can't do that, you would expect me to say something like, "I *tried* to teach my child to ride a bike." I won't say that no one in any of the "It's Being Done" schools ever uses the verb "teach" improperly, but for the most part, if teachers say that they taught something, that means their students have learned it.

They don't teach to the state tests. All the schools make sure their students know what their state's tests look like in terms of the format, and they try to ensure that their students aren't surprised by the material or the kinds of questions asked. Some of them make a big deal of state testing day with pep rallies, and some do a bit of "test prep" in the form of giving practice tests. But none of them spends a huge amount of time teaching their students what will be on the state tests or teaching them how to "bubble in" a scoring sheet. They teach a rich, coherent curriculum tied to state standards. They don't teach the test, particularly in those states where the tests are low-level reading and math tests. In the states where the tests are a bit more sophisticated and high-level, such as the Massachusetts MCAS and the New York Regents, the schools might spend more time teaching directly to what will be tested, but that is because those tests are more closely tied to a set of high standards.

They have high expectations for their students. They assume that their students are able to meet high standards and believe their job is to help their students get there. Liz Mullins at Oakland Heights Elementary School in Arkansas says that teachers tell students, "It's our job to get you all to the train station." They do not assume that their students are so crippled by poverty and discrimination that they will never be able to meet high standards. "It's not about feeling sorry for kids," says Barbara Adderley, principal of Stanton Elementary, in an economically devastated part of North Philadelphia. "It's about making sure that they understand what it is they're expected to do." They talk with their students about going to college or into high-level technical training. This is true for all the levels of schooling—elementary, middle, and high.

They know what the stakes are. They know that if their students don't get a good education, they face the probability of a lifetime of poverty and dependence. "We have got to expand [our students'] horizons or we are still signing their death warrants," principal coach Martha Barber tells principals she works with in Alabama. And many of them are quite open about sharing this understanding with students. "This is your one chance," principal Richard Esparza tells his students at Granger High School in rural Washington.

They embrace and use all the data they can get their hands on. They want to know how their students are doing, and they know that classroom observation by teachers, though important, is fragmentary and doesn't allow overall patterns to be observed. State test data, district data, classroom test data, and any formative assessment data they can get their hands on are all eagerly studied. When they are lucky, they are able to use their district or state's data systems to give them the tools they need to analyze the data. But if the district doesn't provide the data in the form they need, they come up with their own ways of charting and displaying data, because they consider it so important. They know, as Susan Swanson, director of urban education of Hamilton County, Tennessee, said, "that data represent a kid's face or a group of kids' faces. That's a life, that's a future."

They use data to focus on individual students, not just groups of students. Each of these schools has found ways to pay attention to every student. Stanton has its "assessment wall," Granger has its advisory system, and Elmont has its "hidden curriculum," but they have all found ways to ensure that, as Port Chester's John Fazio said, "Nobody falls through the cracks."

They constantly reexamine what they do. Tradition is never invoked as the only reason why something is done, the way it is in crummy schools. If the data show that the way they teach reading isn't getting all kids learning to read, teachers research and incorporate new methods of reading instruction. And that same willingness to examine what's not working and make changes extends to every area of school life. The discomfort this causes teachers cannot be underestimated. "Change is hard, change is feeling uncomfortable," said Sheri Shirley, principal of Oakland Heights Elementary School. It can be very difficult for teachers to change long-established patterns or to diverge from what they learned in their university teaching programs, but that is the logical consequence of putting student achievement ahead of everything else. "The kids have to be the first priority," said Jenna Broems, a teacher at Port Chester Middle School in New York. "You have to be open enough to see that it's not about the teacher but about the learning of the kids."

They embrace accountability. They know they have an obligation not only to their students but to their communities to demonstrate that they are doing the job that has been entrusted to them—to educate future citizens. And, in a kind of extension of that obligation, they are competitive in a way that many educators have traditionally not been, at least outside of sports. If another school nearby outperforms them, they are the first ones to try and figure out what that school did and try to incorporate that new information into their own practice, so they can beat that school the next year. "I'm a coach," says Alabama's West Jasper Elementary School principal Eric Smith. "That's what coaches do—they scout out the other teams and find out what they're doing—and steal any good ideas they find." And most are quite open about sharing the data with the students themselves, explicitly teaching students that poor performance on an assessment simply means that the students and teachers need to work harder and more effectively, not that the students are in some way deficient and incapable of learning.

They make decisions on what is good for kids, not what is good for adults. To those outside the field of education, this might seem a puzzling characteristic. Outsiders might assume that decisions are made to benefit students in most schools. But it is less common than one would think. Take, for example, the way most high school schedules are built. Typically, department chairmen will ask the teachers which classes they want to teach and when. Often the senior members of the departments (or the chairmen's friends) are able to request that their prep time (time spent preparing lesson plans and grading papers) be scheduled during first or last period so that their late arrival or early departure won't be noticed as easily. Or they ask to teach the "high" kids who need less concentrated teaching expertise and often pose fewer discipline problems, even when that means that the "low" kids will be taught by new and inexperienced staff. In "It's Being Done" schools, student needs, not adult needs, drive decisionmaking. "Every time we have a decision to make," said John Capozzi, principal of New York's Elmont Memorial Junior-Senior High School, "we think about what will be the best for the students, not the adults." When decisions are made consistently and backed up with solid reasons and compelling data, good teachers embrace this kind of decisionmaking. "It was difficult at first," said one teacher, who was the union shop steward in her school. "But we could all see that the decisions being made helped the kids."

They use school time wisely. They establish classroom and school routines to ensure that endless amounts of time are not spent going to the bathroom, getting out and putting away books and materials, and going from one activity or class to another. School time is time for instruction, and instruction is treated as something almost sacred. Most of the schools establish uninterrupted blocks of time for instruction so that classes aren't disrupted by bus announcements or by students being pulled out for speech therapy or counseling. Using time wisely doesn't mean, by the way, that the kids don't ever have fun or move around or have recess. But it does mean that students are engaged in productive activities just about all the time.

They leverage as many resources from the community as possible. They organize outside mentors and volunteers, ask local organizations and companies for specific help, link with outside social service agencies, and welcome outside scrutiny as a way of helping them see themselves more clearly. This is in direct contrast to many crummy schools, where outsiders are viewed with suspicion and are often explicitly kept out on the grounds that they would be "disruptive." It should be acknowledged that the schools profiled in this book have wildly different opportunities available to them. Rural schools don't have universities like Georgia Tech or sports teams like the Philadelphia Eagles to help provide support. But they still have local colleges that can help train teachers and direct research projects, retired neighbors who can read to children, and service organizations like the American Legion and the Kiwanis Club that can donate money for school clothing. The point is that the schools leverage whatever is available for the benefit of their students.

They expand the time students—particularly struggling students—have in school. Different schools do this in different ways. Some have before- and afterschool classes during the school year, as well as summer school. Some have year-round calendars with intensive tutoring done during the intersessions for children who haven't yet learned what they need to learn. Some use their federal Title I funds to pay for the extra time; some get grants from other sources, such as from the federal 21st Century Community Learning Center program or from local foundations or organizations. But they all figure out ways to get their children more time for instruction, and they do so with the same kinds of resources (often involving federal funds) that are available to most schools of poverty and within the parameters of the teachers union contracts. Many also see that extra time as an opportunity for enrichment for students, and they offer all kinds of interesting classes, such as music, drama, and sign language.

They do not spend a lot of time disciplining students, in the sense of punishing them. They do spend time disciplining children in the original sense of the word: leading them (think of the word *disciple*). They teach students how to act by noticing and encouraging kindness and consideration, and they teach kids how to have good social and professional relationships by explicitly teaching them how to disagree with someone without getting upset and fighting. They often have formal programs—with names like "Stop and Think" and "Responsive Discipline"—so that the whole school shares a common vocabulary around, for example, what kinds of things students need to do if they lose their temper. But their main method of discipline is to aim for high-quality instruction every moment, on the theory that busy and actively engaged students do not have time to misbehave and get into trouble. "When you focus on discipline, that will be your focus" is the way Arlene Snowden, principal of Capitol View Elementary in Atlanta, put it. "When kids are fully engaged, they don't pose discipline problems. We focus on rigorous, engaging, hands-on activities." Teachers aren't left high and dry, though, in those instances when behavior issues are deeper than boredom-induced mischief. "It's Being Done" schools have additional interventions that they use when needed, such as pairing disruptive students and their families with mentors or with outside social services. Knowing that they will have issues that arise, these schools have systems in place so that they are not caught without a plan.

They establish an atmosphere of respect. Students are treated with respect, teachers are treated with respect, and parents are treated with respect. For the most part, this starts with the principal or, in some cases, with the district superintendent. Because adults don't bully and browbeat each other, teachers don't bully and browbeat their students, the way they do in many crummy schools, poor and nonpoor.

They like kids. This characteristic seems almost too simple to include in a list, but the fact is that in too many schools—and not just crummy poor-kid schools—the dominant emotion among teachers and administrators seems to be a kind of contempt for students—and their parents—that can only grow out of dislike. At "It's Being Done" schools, students are brought into conversations, student work is highlighted and proudly displayed, and older students are explicitly taught to be the role models for younger students. Teachers tell affectionate stories about their students and boast about the work their students have done. Principals know many of the students by name, and often something about them. The struggles that students have outside school only increase the regard teachers and principals have for what they are able to achieve in school. "I respect them so much," a teacher told me about her students, after telling me about the heavy responsibilities many of them had in caring for younger brothers and sisters. Such respect never translates into expecting less from students, just into appreciating the effort that they must put in to achieve.

They make sure that the kids who struggle the most have the best instruction. They don't ignore their advanced students; in fact, they often spend a great deal of time worrying about them and making sure they have interesting things to read and do. But these schools all act on the belief that the child who is struggling needs the most concentrated teaching expertise, whereas the children who are not struggling are able to work more independently. The schools differ in how they group students for instruction. Some insist on heterogeneous instruction, meaning that they teach groups of children with different levels of expertise, and some insist on homogeneous instruction, in which students are grouped by their levels of knowledge and skill. But the most consistent pattern I found was that teachers would teach a lesson to the whole class and then divide the class into different groups, providing extra help to those who need it while other students were engaged in other activities, often involving reading and writing.

Principals are a constant presence. Although, like all principals, they are called out for meetings to the central office or other places, the expectation of everyone in "It's Being Done" schools is that for the most part, the principals are in the building and walking the halls, conferring with teachers, looking at student work, and interacting with students, teachers, and parents. They do not hide in their offices. Many of them explicitly say that they do their paperwork when children are not in the building. Depending on how big the school is, some principals even stop in on every class at the beginning of the day. One such is Eric Smith at West Jasper Elementary School, who goes to every class to say, cheerfully, "Good morning, scholars!" It is the principals' version of the medical practice of "doing rounds." They are gauging the pulse of their buildings. And when they quietly slip in to observe instruction, teachers and students hardly even notice, because the principals are not hostile intruders but nearly constant presences.

Although the principals are important leaders, they are not the only leaders. Teachers and other administrators, and sometimes parents and community members as well, sit on committees that make important decisions for the school, decisions such as hiring, curriculum, school policies and procedures, Title I spending, and much more. Trennis Harvey, assistant principal of Capitol View Elementary, said, "Of course your leader has to make some decisions, but most decisions here are made by teams." The academic term for this is *distributed leadership*. In most cases, this is part of an explicit practice to institutionalize improvement so that it is not reliant on a single individual. The principals in "It's Being Done" schools are well aware of the fact that many schools have improved only to fall back again when their principals left. These principals are consciously trying to build the kinds of enduring structures that will outlast them.

They pay careful attention to the quality of the teaching staff. In many of the schools, teachers and sometimes parents sit in with administrators on interviews with potential new teachers. Sometimes the interview panel asks potential teachers to teach a lesson so they can gauge the quality of instruction the teacher offers. Often the schools will test out teachers before hiring them by allowing them to student teach, substitute teach, or teach summer school. Principals and other administrators regularly sit in on classes to evaluate and recommend improvements. "I taught . . . for four years and thought I was a pretty good teacher, but until I came here I had never taught a lesson," said Elmont teacher Wendy Tague about the help she received from administrators and fellow teachers. And teachers do not just drift into having tenure protections—they must demonstrate their knowledge and skill and take recommended steps to improve before they get that third- or fourth-year contract that guarantees them tenure protections under most union contracts.

They provide teachers with the time to meet to plan and work collaboratively. Either the principal or an assistant principal spends a great deal of time building a schedule so that children have coherent instructional days and teachers have time to work together. The most common strategy in elementary and middle school is to schedule an entire grade to have "specials" (usually art, music, physical education, or sometimes science) at the same time so the teachers can meet. And those teacher meetings are carefully structured, often by the principal in early days, but later by the teachers themselves. Teachers review data, go over student work, develop lesson plans, and map curriculum. These are working meetings, not gripe sessions, and even though initially they require a great deal of effort, eventually they lighten the workload of teachers by allowing them to share responsibility for instruction.

They provide teachers time to observe each other. In crummy schools, teachers will hardly know what another teacher across the hall is doing, much less the teacher on the other side of the building. Good teachers learn to close their doors and keep their heads down so they won't be noticed and interfered with. But in "It's Being Done" schools, teachers are encouraged to seek out and observe colleagues who have perfected a particular lesson or are trying something new and want feedback about whether it is clear and coherent. This helps all teachers become better teachers. Gary Brittingham, principal of East Millsboro Elementary School in Delaware, says that he "rarely walk[s] into a classroom without seeing a model lesson" anymore. At the elementary level, providing such time takes careful planning and sometimes requires principals and assistant principals to take over teaching responsibilities. At the secondary level, it often involves teachers using their planning time to observe their colleagues.

They think seriously about professional development. The general theory among the schools is that if students are weak in a particular area, that means the teachers need to learn more about it. Teachers and administrators seek out the best sources of information and training they can find so that the teachers become better teachers. "I was not as good a teacher with four other principals" is what 75-year-old fourth-grade teacher Mary Anderson says at Lincoln Elementary School in New York. It should be noted that the emphasis on the quality of professional development is what distinguishes the "It's Being Done" schools, because just about all teachers have been subjected to professional development in some form or another. Nearly every veteran teacher in the country has a professional development horror story to tell about sessions that wasted time and money and did nothing to deepen teachers' content knowledge, understanding, or pedagogical skill. The professional development session that stands out in my mind as emblematic of all the waste-of-time sessions teachers have had to endure is the one in which I saw a big ball of yarn tossed from teacher to teacher, with about half an hour taken up to demonstrate that people and topics are woven together in an elaborate web. That kind of professional development isn't typical in "It's Being Done" schools.

They assume that they will have to train new teachers more or less from scratch and carefully acculturate all newly hired teachers. They know that new teachers often don't know the first thing about classroom management, standards, curriculum, assessment, reading instruction, or even how to physically set up a classroom. To noneducators this might seem remarkable, because most teachers enter the profession with degrees in education. But teachers and principals in the "It's Being Done" schools widely agree that for the most part, university education programs do not even begin to prepare teachers for teaching. In many cases, schools assign consulting teachers or new-teacher mentors to help induct new teachers into the profession. But they also must carefully retrain experienced teachers who have come from other schools where they may not have been exposed to effective instruction. Principals in "It's Being

Done" schools talk about liking to have a mixture of veteran experience and new enthusiasm, but they know that they have to work hard to make sure enthusiastic newcomers are channeled into being productive professionals.

They have high-quality, dedicated, and competent office and building staff who feel themselves part of the educational mission of the school. This isn't something that is highlighted in any of the previous chapters of this book, but in thinking about all the schools I visited, it stands out as one feature they share. The reason this is important is that it means the principals and assistant principals are able to focus on the core of their job—academics—and don't have to spend huge amounts of time on the logistics of running a building. In crummy schools, visitors' first impressions often consist of buildings that are dirty and offices that are dominated by barely civil school secretaries who seem to spend a lot of time on personal phone calls. This phenomenon stems at least in part from the fact that, in too many places, schools are seen as jobs programs, not as places where important work demands competence from everyone in the building. A new superintendent of my acquaintance found that when he arrived in his poor rural district, seven of his eight principals were first cousins, and many of the teachers, teacher aides, building service workers, and secretaries were related to each other. He says his district is on the "friends and family plan." Being related doesn't mean that none of them were competent—in fact, the superintendent said he was surprised how many of them were—but it does mean that competence might not always be the deciding factor in who gets hired.

They are nice places to work. This was the biggest surprise. After all, these schools are achieving at higher levels and improving at faster rates than many in the education world think is possible. It would be reasonable to wonder if the teachers and principals are nearing nervous breakdown level. But, overwhelmingly, that's not what I found. Mind you, the schools are not easy places to work. "We work really hard," is the most common thing teachers in these schools say. "It's Being Done" schools have high and constantly rising expectations for teachers, who are expected to learn more every year, to constantly improve their skills and knowledge, and to work collaboratively with their fellow teachers. They also have students whose lives outside of school sometimes break their teachers' hearts. But because their work is organized in a way that allows teachers to be successful and take leadership roles, and because the atmosphere in these schools is one of respect, they are nice places to work.

Another quality comes through as well. These schools have the kind of camaraderie that comes from teams of people facing difficult challenges together, not unlike the camaraderie that is built in military units, sports teams, theatrical groups, and any other group that goes through an arduous process to achieve a common goal. As a result, they do not have the kind of turnover that many schools with similar demographics have. When people leave, for the most part it is because they retire, or their spouse is transferred, or they are promoted to new positions of leadership, not because they are fleeing to teach in easier schools. Those schools with the longest and best track records have built a reputation of being good places to work and have little trouble filling vacancies. Elmont High School in New York is the extreme example here, with 350 applicants for every opening—but this fact points out that many teachers want to work with children of poverty and children of color if they can work in an environment where they will be helped to be better teachers. In other words, the huge attrition rates of new teachers in crummy poor-kid schools don't mean that teachers do not want to work in schools with large populations of poor children and children of color, but that they do not want to work where they have to succeed or fail totally on their own.

To sum up: The adults in "It's Being Done" schools expect their students to learn, and they work hard to master the skills and knowledge necessary to teach those students. After visiting all the schools profiled in this book, I began to feel as if the folks in these schools can be likened to the Wright brothers, who proved once and for all that manned flight was possible. Once Orville and Wilbur demonstrated how to answer the challenges of drag and gravity, getting from their experimental plane in Kitty Hawk to the Boeing 747 was no longer a theoretical challenge but an engineering one. In the same way, the schools profiled here demonstrate that the job of educating kids to high levels—even kids traditionally considered "hard to teach"—is theoretically possible. The challenges these schools have overcome include the ideas that poverty and discrimination are insuperable barriers to academic achievement; that today's kids are so damaged by television, video games, and hip-hop music that they are impervious to books and scholarship; that good, qualified teachers simply won't work in difficult circumstances; and that existing teachers and principals are incapable of improvement. The theoretical arguments pile on, seemingly insurmountable.

Except that in the case of the schools profiled here, they are proved wrong. When you overcome drag and gravity with enough thrust and lift, you get flight; when you overcome poverty and discrimination with enough thoughtful instruction, careful organization, and what can only be recognized as the kind of pigheaded optimism displayed by the Wright brothers, you get learning. The schools profiled here are not perfect, any more than the Wright brothers' plane was perfect. But they have tackled the theoretical challenges one by one and proved that those challenges can be conquered.

I'll end with the words of former University Park Campus School English teacher James McDermott, who laid down a challenge to his fellow educators. "We know what works in education. The research is prolific," he said. "Amazingly, then, the question today is not about what works, but about why we do not implement what we know works in all schools for all kids."

ABOUT THE AUTHOR

Karin Chenoweth is a longtime education writer. Before working on this book, she wrote a weekly column on schools and education for the *Washington Post*, and was previously a senior writer and executive editor for *Black Issues in Higher Education* (now *Diverse*). As a freelance writer, Chenoweth has written for such publications as *Education Week, American Teacher, American Educator, School Library Journal*, and the *Washington Post Magazine*. In addition, she has been an active parent volunteer throughout her children's public schooling in Montgomery County, Maryland.

INDEX